GREAT ADVENTURES IN NURSING

GREAT
ADVENTURES
IN
NURSING

EDITED BY

HELEN WRIGHT

AND

SAMUEL RAPPORT

HARPER & BROTHERS, NEW YORK

GREAT ADVENTURES IN NURSING
Copyright © 1960 by Helen Wright and Samuel Rapport

Library of Congress catalog card number: 60-5785

The following selections are reprinted with the kind permission of the publishers and the copyright owners:

ADVENTURES OF A NURSE'S AIDE by Enid Day, copyright 1951 by Whiteside, Inc., reprinted by permission of Whiteside, Inc.

BIRTH OF A NURSE by Dora E. Birchard, reprinted from THE TRAINED NURSE AND HOSPITAL REVIEW, February, 1935, and reprinted by their permission. Copyright, 1935, TRAINED NURSE AND HOSPITAL REVIEW.

YOUNG WOMAN IN WHITE by Quentin Reynolds from The Reader's Digest. Reprinted from Woman's Life. Copyright 1956 by The Reader's Digest Association, Inc. Reprinted by permission of the author and The Reader's Digest.

OLD BATTLE-AX—Anonymous. Reprinted from The Saturday Evening Post, April 1933. Copyright, 1933, The Curtis Publishing Company.

DAMIEN THE LEPER by John Farrow, copyright, 1937, Sheed and Ward, Inc., New York, and reprinted by their permission.

IN THE AUSTRALIAN BUSH. Reprinted by permission of Dodd, Mead & Company from AND THEY SHALL WALK by Sister Elizabeth Kenny in collaboration with Martha Ostenso. Copyright 1943 by Dodd, Mead & Company, Inc.

HOSPITAL OF THE QUEEN'S HEART by Princess Ileana. Copyright, 1954, by Princess Ileana of Romania. Reprinted by permission of Rinehart & Company, Inc., New York, Publishers.

NURSES ON HORSEBACK by Ernest Poole. Copyright, 1932, by Ernest Poole. Reprinted by permission of Margaret Ann Poole.

Contents

ADVENTURES IN WAR

Introduction

HAVE YOU EVER thought of nursing as a career? Would you like to know more about those wonderful women in caps and uniforms? Or would you simply enjoy reading about the thrilling adventures which nurses have had in times of war and disaster and in faraway places? If so, you will find much of what you are looking for in the pages that follow.

Most of you have been in a hospital at least once, not counting the time when you were born. If so, you have been impressed by the ordered bustle and starched efficiency with which nurses go about their work. You have watched someone you know being attended to or have peeped into the diet kitchens. You have wondered about all the things in a hospital which only the staff members are allowed to see—the X-ray rooms, the administrative offices, the holy of holies—the operating room.

And of course you have wondered what the hospital nurses are like, what they think about, and how they act, on duty and off. This book tells the story.

After our short prologue, we take you into this strange and fascinating world in our section "Hospital Adventures." Our selections show you how young girls have started their careers in nursing and why they feel that, despite the hard work and demanding requirements, no other career will suit them. You will see them in the operating room and by the bedside. You will watch them getting along with their ever-present companions, the doctors. You will feel the tingling drama of an emergency, which makes a hospital one of the most exciting places on earth.

But some of the greatest nurses have worked not in starched uniforms along shining corridors, but in steaming jungles and mountainous forests and frozen seacoasts; or in the tenements of great cities where dirt and disease have been rampant. In our section called "From the Jungle to the Slum," you will read about the dangers they have faced and the difficulties they have overcome. Many of you have heard of Father Damien, the priest who gave his life to nurse those degraded outcasts, the lepers, who until recent years were considered no better than the dead. Perhaps you have heard of Sister Kenny, who got her first nursing training in the Australian bush; of the frontier nurses in the Kentucky mountains who can reach their patients only on horseback; of the equally famous Grenfell nursing missions, which minister to the sick in barren Labrador; or of Lillian Wald, who founded the Visiting Nurse Service in the poverty-stricken slums of New York City. Here you will read about them and others—glamorous figures who have dedicated their lives to humanity.

Some of the greatest nursing adventures have taken place during wars. Indeed, as you will see, the whole profession of modern nursing had its beginnings in time of war. In our section entitled "Adventures in War," you will read of the experiences of Florence Nightingale, the greatest nurse, during the Crimean War, of how she brought order out of utter chaos and misery and of how the whole world honored her for her achievements. You will read also how Jean Henry Dunant, a Swiss gentleman in white, had the idea for the Red Cross on the battlefield; and how Mother Bickerdyke succored thousands of wounded men during our own Civil War. You will read about Nurse Edith Cavell, who gave her life for her country; and you will see nurses fulfilling their duties on land, on sea, and in the air during wars in which your own parents may have served.

Our story is one of strength, of heroism, sometimes of great sacrifice. It is inspiring in its picture of devoted people who have dedicated their lives to aiding the sick.

PROLOGUE

To the Nurse

BY VICTOR ROBINSON

YOU WERE A SLAVE IN HOMER'S TIME, and washing the feet of a wandering beggar who sat in the hall of Odysseus, you were the first to recognize the returned master by his scars when his own wife doubted. . . . In the harbor of Corinth, on the Saronic Gulf, where stood the pagan temple to Aphrodite, you were a Christian deaconess visiting the afflicted. . . . You were a cloistered nun in the Hôtel-Dieu of Paris, walking for centuries through endless corridors, serving countless patients for Christ's sake. . . . You were a king's daughter, and were married to a king by Anselm in Westminster Abbey, but you put a hair shirt on your queenly body and lovingly kissed the feet of lepers and dried their wounds with your hair and built a hospital for their comfort. . . . You were a Béguine of Flanders, and became known for your skillful ways with the sick. . . . You were a Daughter of St. Camillus, perishing with your Order when you went to the final plague in Barcelona. . . . You were a sister of Charity of Vincent de Paul, all France was your hospital, and then your white cornettes were seen abroad. . . . You were a pauper in London town, heavy and filthy and drunken, and in the absence of other employment you became an asylum nurse, but as you could not read, you asked the lunatics to decipher the labels on the medicine bottles. . . . In the lost abyss of Scutari you were the Lady-with-the-Lamp, and with the background of a vast cemetery for statistics your pity and your passion created Modern Nursing. . . . You were a modern girl, and you became a trained nurse for humanity's sake. . . . In the zero hour of democracy, you

3

landed with the American troops, and giving sulpha drugs and plasma under fire, you died on the beachhead of Anzio. . . . You were a graduate of Lincoln Hospital, for your skin was colored, and in the European Theater of Operations you cared tenderly for German prisoners of war. . . . You were a Hadassah nurse in Palestine, and refugee Jews from Poland and families of Arabs from the desert came to you for relief. . . . You served at Bataan, where you had little to give the soldiers except a smile, and when the Japanese bombers blew your hospital to pieces you escaped by clipper to Australia. . . . Now the war is over, and peace has come again, but Mother Earth, sick and hungry and tired, awaits your healing hands. . . .

The Florence Nightingale Pledge

~>>«<~

At the time of their graduation, all nurses take the following pledge, which is something like the Hippocratic Oath taken by doctors when they graduate from medical school. It is an ethical code, a promise to live by the highest standards of the nursing profession. It was written by Lystra Gretter and first used in 1893. Fittingly, it was named in honor of Florence Nightingale, the mother of modern nursing, about whom you will read later on in this book.

I SOLEMNLY PLEDGE MYSELF before God, and in the presence of this assembly, to pass my life in purity and to practice my profession faithfully. I will abstain from whatever is deleterious and mischievous, and will not take or knowingly administer any harmful drug. I will do all in my power to maintain and elevate the standard of my profession, and will hold in confidence all personal matters committed to my keeping and all family affairs coming to my knowledge in the practice of my calling. With loyalty will I aid the physician in his work, and as a "missioner of health" I will dedicate myself to devoted service to human welfare.

HOSPITAL ADVENTURES

Adventures of a Nurse's Aide

BY ENID DAY

->»«<-

During times of war there are never enough nurses
to go around. Many are needed to take care of
wounded soldiers; but people at home also are
taken ill and must be cared for in hospitals. During
World War II many young women volunteered
as nurse's aides, to take the place of regular nurses
who had been called away to the battlefields. In
that way they got their first taste of what hospitals were like. It was a strange, fascinating, sometimes hilarious, but always exciting world.

NURSING IS A NOBLE PROFESSION. I had heard this truism long
before I took my seat at the end of the third row in the Volunteer Nurses' Aide night class. I was even more convinced as
the class progressed and I managed to find my own pulse at
the first go-round.

Then came respiration and temperature. I had a little trouble with the thermometer. But after many minutes, and as
many efforts, I finally turned the slender glass tube at the
right angle and was as pleased as Punch to find that the high
fever I imagined I had was probably just the warm glow from
the halo I was wearing, for the mercury held a steady finger
on 98.6.

I could hardly wait for the next class to begin. Promptly at
6 P.M. I put on my halo and hurried to the little Nurses'
Aide building on West Peachtree Street to be thoroughly in-

structed on the admission and kind treatment of patients and
the mitering of bed sheets. It had never occurred to me that
I would be the guardian angel of a patient's confidence, much
less his dentures. But when it came to the stomach pump (pardon—the gastric lavage) I began to wonder if my own confidence wasn't going to need a bit of boosting, and I felt my
tummy do a flip-flop as the nursing instructor said, "The patient may be given sips of water or cracked ice before swal-
lowing the tube."

I gulped a few times, and Eunice smiled a friendly little
smile that made the corners of her mouth as curly as her hair.
She reached over and patted my hand as it gripped the note-
book on my lap.

"It's all right," she whispered. "You can look now. She's
not going to swallow it." I opened my eyes and smiled back
weakly. It was *so* good to have her as a partner. We took each
other's respiration and temperature and counted each other's
pulse. We made adjoining beds, and if I failed to do a good
job of mitering a corner, or of tightly drawing a rubber sheet,
Eunice came to the rescue before the instructor inspected. I
was grateful, for it was plain to see I wasn't the domestic type.

Then came the night when we learned how to bathe the
patient and Eunice bathed me and I bathed Eunice, and two
by two the class joined the order of the thoroughly washed.
We all felt a bit shy and silly, but we soon got accustomed to
playing patient as well as nurse.

It was a red-letter evening when at long last we received
our blue pinafores and white shirts with the beautiful red,
white, and blue emblem proudly displayed on the left sleeve
and fastened our Red Cross pins at the center of the
bib. Then we pinned on our name plates, our watches, and
slipped our surgical scissors into the opening between the two

buttons at the back of the belt. At long last we were honest-to-goodness Nurse's Aides, ready and eager to fulfill the objectives of the corps, to observe all hospital ethics, never to gossip with or about the patients of the hospital, to accept criticism, and to treat patients with sympathetic understanding.

I looked at the girls who had spent many long hours in this, my class, evening after evening, each with the same high purpose of giving personal service—perhaps sacrifice—to nurse the sick and the dying, and I knew our hearts were beating in unison as we were assigned to the various hospitals of Atlanta, Georgia. Duty would begin at seven on Sunday morning. And this was only Thursday! I wondered how I could ever wait so long, or how the patients would exist until my arrival at Piedmont Hospital at seven—three days hence.

On Duty at Last

Eunice, my bath mate, and I had been assigned to the same hospital. We had agreed to meet at six-thirty Sunday morning in front of the state capitol and go together to Piedmont. She was standing on the corner waiting for me when I arrived, and we both looked at our watches. In perfect unison they told us it was six-fifteen.

"I'm a little early," Eunice apologized, "but I didn't want to keep you waiting."

"That's why I came early, too," I said.

We smiled slyly, for each knew the other lied. We had come early because we could not bear the thought of being late. Besides, we had both been up and dressed since 5 A.M.

"You look so pretty in your uniform," I said.

"You look pretty, too," Eunice replied as she gave me a side-long glance and smoothed the skirt of her pinafore into place. "Are you scared?" she asked.

"Oh, no!" I fibbed. "I'm just tense and excited."

"You don't look tense," she flattered. "Won't it be wonderful when we have our caps?"

"Oh, we'll have those in no time! Why, fifty hours will go faster than a rabbit in a briar patch," I said.

"Well, I'm never going to leave after just three hours on duty, are you?"

"No, I should say not!" I agreed. "Let's stay all day. Don't you think three hours is a ridiculously short time to be on duty?" I loved the way the last two words felt on the end of my tongue. *Duty* is a powerful word. It made serving without remuneration seem far more worth-while than being paid for a job.

"What floor are you assigned to?" Eunice asked.

"I'm on the third floor today, how about you?"

"I'm on the third floor, too, goody." She laughed. Then she shook her head slowly. "Enid, I'm worried."

"I'm a little worried, too. But tell me what you're worried about first."

We were nearing the hospital as she confessed, "Well, you remember when we had our lesson on false tee—"

"Dentures," I corrected.

"Dentures, I mean. Well, you remember how we were warned to be so careful with them when we washed them because they're slick and so hard to hold on to, and we can't let anything happen to them because patients can't replace false tee—I mean dentures—just like that?" She snapped her fingers.

"Yeah."

"Well, I'll bet every patient I have today will have false tee—dentures, and if they do I'll just die, I know I'll *just die!*"

Five times in the first hour after we went on duty I met Eunice in the hall on our way to the utility room. Each time her trembling hands grasped a set of dentures.

My first patient was a girl in the women's ward. She had

been severely injured in an automobile accident and was in a cast from the armpits down. It was my duty to give her morning care, which meant putting her on the bedpan, helping her brush her teeth, and giving her a bath and clean linen.

"Good morning!" I greeted her as I carefully pulled the curtains to screen off her bed from the rest of the patients in the ward. "I'm to give you your morning care."

She was a pretty girl, and her eyes twinkled as she said, "You poor thing! You're new, aren't you?"

I was a little taken aback, for I'd tried so hard to be casual.

"Yes, I'm new. This is my first day on duty. Do you mind?"

"Goodness, no!" She laughed. "It's just that I'm such a hard job to handle. I'm in a cast all the way down and I'm pretty heavy. But I'll help you all I can."

"Oh, I'm pretty strong even if I'm not very big," I laughed back. "Ill fix your bath water right away."

"Would you mind bringing me a bedpan first?" she asked kindly.

"Oh, of course! I forgot the bedpan came first." I walked to the utility room and I didn't forget that all bedpans must be warmed before slipping them under the patient.

By ten o'clock I was practically dead, but I smiled cheerily at Eunice as we met in the hall on the way to the diet kitchen to fill the water pitchers with ice.

"Are you tired?" I asked hopefully.

"Not a bit!" She sighed, and filled the second pitcher with crushed ice.

"I'm not either. My back just hurts a little," I added.

"Mine does, too. And they must have given me a size too small in my shoes." She stood on one foot. "But isn't it a wonderful feeling?"

"And on Sunday, too," I said inanely as I picked up my pitchers and started for the door. "See you later!"

The floor nurse spoke to me as I passed the office door on the way to the ward at the end of the hall.

"Miss Day, when you've finished with those two pitchers, will you please see about the patient in 307?"

"I'll be glad to," I said as I glanced down the hall and saw the white light glowing above the door of 307. "Ah, this is getting somewhere," I thought, and wondered who 307 could be and what 307 could want.

I put the two pitchers beside the beds in the ward and almost ran back up the hall. Gently I pushed open the door of 307 and caught the sound of a heave as I glanced at the bed and saw a frail little old woman with snow-white hair. Grabbing the emesis basin from the stand at the side of the bed, I quickly slipped it beneath her chin—and none too soon.

"My tee—" she gasped between heaves as the basin all but overflowed, and I realized that her dentures had gone into the pan along with her breakfast.

"I'll take care of your teeth," I said softly as I brushed back a wisp of hair from her forehead. "Can you wait until I get another pan?" She nodded ever so slightly, then suddenly opened her eyes.

"My teef! Don't frow away my teef!" she begged as she leaned her chin against the second pan and let go.

I bathed her face with a wet cloth and asked, "Do you feel better now?"

"No," she said in a voice barely audible. "I'm going to die."

Suddenly I was afraid—afraid with a kind of fear I'd never before known.

What was it the instructor had said about confidence?

"You'll feel better after a moment," I soothed, and straightened the sheet. "I'll be back right away."

I picked up the two emesis basins and walked quickly to the utility room. As I fished for the dentures, I knew what Eunice had meant.

"Is the patient in 307 really going to die?" I asked the floor nurse as I made out a report for the chart.

"Why do you ask that, Miss Day?" She looked up quite calmly.

"She says she is," I replied.

"She's very ill. But don't let what the patients say upset you. Would you mind staying with her for a while?" Without waiting for me to reply, she added, "I know it's a hard thing to ask on your first day, but we're so short of nurses, and I think you're doing a good job. We hope to get a special nurse for her today."

"Oh, God, please don't let her die before the special nurse comes!" I prayed as I walked back down the hall and opened the door of 307.

At three o'clock the special nurse arrived.

I found Eunice and told her I was ready to go. She practically fell on my neck, and we went to the office and signed out. Eight hours! Our caps were only forty-two more away! In the car she told me all about the patients she'd had.

As I stopped to let her out at the corner she said, "You haven't told me a thing about you!"

I opened my mouth to speak, and sobbed instead. After a while I managed to tell her, "One of my first patients is going to die!" All the way home I cried and cried.

A week later my little patient in 307 left the hospital, as chipper as a cricket.

A Rose by Any Other Name—

Ether always has nauseated me. One whiff, and I beat it for an open window. So when the floor nurse asked me to prepare an anesthetic bed and receive a patient who would shortly be brought from the operating room, I'm sure I turned paler than the patient.

Mentally I checked the necessary articles:

(1) Clean linen.
(2) One rubber ether sheet.
(3) One extra linen drawsheet.
(4) One bath blanket.
(5) Two face towels.
(6) Three hot-water bottles. (In case they're needed.)
(7) Two emesis basins.
(8) Three safety pins. (Now what are they for?)
(9) Cellulose wipes or tissues. (To mop saliva from patient's chin.)
(10) Pad and pencil. (For recording the patient's T.P.R.)
(11) Two tongue depressors, one wrapped with bandage. (In case the patient swallows his tongue.)
(12) One paper bag. (Oh, yes, that's where the safety pins are needed. To pin the bag handy-like to the bed. The bag is to hold the used tissues.)
(13) One rubber pillowcase.

I hoped I'd have the bed ready long before the poor patient arrived from the operating room. Well, at least long enough to allow me to be elsewhere and very busy at something important, like arranging flowers in the utility room, or filling the ice pitchers again. I tried to imagine that I was arranging flowers as I drew the rubber sheet tightly across the mattress and tucked it under. I imagined it so hard I could almost smell them, as I turned the linens back to the required eight-inch cuff and folded them over the foot of the bed, I made believe I was counting roses as I put them in a vase.

"Patients are sometimes very touchy about their flowers," the instructor had said. "They even count them sometimes, and if a patient is the fussy type you'd better not come back from the utility room with one missing, no matter if there were six dozen in the box."

There! The bed was finished, its clean, fresh pillow standing as stiff at the head of the bed as an admiral.

Once more I ran my hand over the surface to be sure that no crease or wrinkle could be felt.

I pulled down the windows and adjusted the shades and surveyed the room. As my eyes turned toward the door, the stretcher came through it and I caught the sickening, sweetish smell of ether fumes. Too late to run, I took my place on the opposite side of the bed while the orderly and surgically swathed nurse lifted the patient onto my nice smooth sheet. Gently I lifted the covers fold by fold to the patient's chin.

"Note her pulse and respiration," the nurse instructed. "The doctor will be down in a moment." Then she was gone.

I clenched my teeth as I slipped my hand beneath the covers and felt for the patient's wrist. Billows of ether fumes rose to greet me. My teeth clenched tighter still and I bit my tongue. I wanted to bolt from the room—for just one breath of cold, fresh air. Then I seemed to hear a voice far, far away, the voice of the Nurse's Aide instructor.

"Never leave a patient who is unconscious from an anesthetic. Always stand by until the doctor or nurse relieves you."

I wished the patient would get up and let me lie down. My knees began to bend and I was afraid I'd fall across my unconscious charge, so I sank to the floor like a deflated balloon and put my head between my knees, just as the doctor followed the floor nurse into the room.

"The smell of ether makes you feel faint, doesn't it?" the nurse asked later after the ammonia had brought me around.

My embarrassment was matched only by the fear that I would be dismissed, as I replied, "Yes, a little."

"Then you'll soon get over that," she said. "It took me a long time to get used to the smell of ether. Now, it's like cologne. I love it."

Thereafter, when supplies were needed from the sterilizing room I was sent for them. The sterilizing room was on the far end of the building and though one could wend her way through the halls and enter from the opposite side, one could also take a short cut through the operating room. I was told to take the short cut. In this way it was assumed that I would gradually get accustomed to the smell of ether fumes.

On my first trip I walked calmly to the operating room, pushed open the door, and stepped inside. I felt the door close behind me, and I stood for a moment with my back to it, surveying the long distance to the door at the opposite end of the hall. Then my feet took wing. The swish of my starched pinafore could have been heard all the way to the office as I sprinted to the sterilizing room with the speed of an Olympic runner, powered by uranium.

I saw no one. I heard no one. But I am dead sure someone must have heard and seen me. As I entered the chart room after returning the long way around, the jolly conversation between my floor nurse and an interne stopped suddenly.

"Try holding your breath next time," the interne said jokingly as he patted me on the shoulder.

"I'm afraid there won't be any next time," I replied sadly.

"Oh, yes, there will! You see, you forgot to bring the surgical dressings!"

I looked down at my empty hands, and headed once again toward the door marked: OPERATING ROOM.

It was two weeks before I could walk, not run, to the sterilizing room by way of the ether route. Now, I think

I could drink the stuff and never even feel woozy. But it still doesn't smell like cologne.

It smells like ether.

Emergency Call for Nurse Day!

My cap was still hours away when the superintendent of nurses telephoned one night and asked that I be released from duty on the third floor to report immediately to the fifth, which was the maternity floor.

Nurse's Aides, sans caps, are allowed on the fifth floor only when they deliver flowers to the new mothers, so I climbed the stairs wondering why they hadn't told me to stop by the front office first and pick up the flowers, for the elevator had stopped running an hour ago. "Well, at least I'll get to see the babies through the window," I thought, and felt cheered.

"Miss Day," the superintendent greeted me as I reached the top step, "you will do duty in the nursery."

"But I'm only an Aide, and I don't even have my cap," I protested apologetically, thinking perhaps she'd called for a student nurse with the same name as mine.

"This is an emergency," she said. "I'll take full responsibility. We are in a difficult situation tonight. Even I am serving in the delivery room. We cannot leave the nursery unguarded. Do you know how to change a diaper?" The sentences came with staccato rapidity.

"Oh, yes, I can do that," I said, "But—"

"There is no other nurse available," she interrupted. "Come with me." I followed her into the nursery. Every tiny crib held a sleeping new-born and the air was sweet with the smell of babies.

The superintendent continued into the warming room just off the main nursery, and I followed at her heels like a puppy. The warming room is where fresh babies are kept for a few hours, after they are brought from the delivery room.

"Here are the supplies." She spoke quickly, indicating stacks of freshly sterilized diapers and tiny, soft gowns and pink and blue blankets. I looked at three small cribs arranged in a row against the wall of the warming room and saw the wee faces. All I could see was their faces. Even their heads were carefully covered with soft, warm baby blankets. The superintendent's eyes followed my admiring glance.

"These three have just arrived," she said with a smile as she touched the blanket of each. "Don't move them under any condition. They will need no changing under any circumstance." Then reaching into one corner of a crib she brought forth a little rubber hand syringe.

"Do you know what this is?" she asked.

"It's a rubber syringe," I said.

"Do you know what it's for and how to use it?"

"Tell me," I asked, "I have only a slight idea."

"This is to be used in case a baby strangles from phlegm. If one of the new arrivals begins to strangle or turn blue, you will press the air from the syringe and gently insert the tube into the side of the baby's mouth and even more gently release the bulb. The air will draw the mucus from the baby's throat. Be careful that you do this gently. I have seen inexperienced student nurses draw blood," she said—and was gone.

I looked at the small bits of humanity snuggled in their blankets. They certainly looked sufficiently in the pink not to give me any trouble.

I walked back into the nursery and peeked at my thirty sleeping charges. Suddenly from the corner crib a wail went up and I stepped over to see if what I thought had happened had happened. Yes, it had.

"Well, you darling little pink cherub," I said half-aloud, "if a clean didy is what you're crying for I can do that much for you."

I reached to pick up the baby and found it so soft that I automatically withdrew my hands, but the wails brought them back, and I rolled the tiny infant in a blanket and started to the warming room, cooing to the baby as I went.

Hardly had I placed it on the changing pad and unfastened the first safety pin before bedlam broke loose in every crib and, with one accord, as though my tiny charge had been the signal giver, each little mite was calling for a change.

"Shush, babies, I'll get to you in a minute!" I called back softly, and unfastened the other pin. As I reached with sterile forceps for a sterile pad with which to cleanse the dampened tender skin, my ears caught a faint sound. It was just a thin mewing noise from somewhere behind me and I glanced over my shoulder at the three fresh babes. The first two were pink as an angel's cheek, but the third was blue—dark blue.

Quickly I rolled my bare-bottomed charge into his blanket and carried him to his nursery crib. Then, dashing to the door, I glanced down the darkened hall as I breathed a prayer that somewhere in that long expanse between the nursery and the delivery room I would see the white uniform of a nurse. But the hall was as empty as the pit of my stomach. I raced back through the nursery and into the warming room, where the small noise continued and the new-born infant had turned an even darker shade of blue. Reaching into the sanitary towel near the corner of the crib, my hand sought and found the carefully protected rubber syringe. I pressed the bulb flat in my palm to force out the air. My knees began to tremble and my hand shook as I gently inserted the tube into the corner of the tiny mouth.

"Oh, God!" I prayed, "please let a nurse come! Please, let me be so gentle that I don't scratch his little throat."

Gradually I began to relax my hand and ease my tight hold on the rubber bulb. A sucking noise rose from the crib as the syringe drew the mucus from the baby's throat, and I saw the blue color of its face begin to disappear and a normal pink gradually take its place. "Thank God! Oh, thank you, God," I breathed through dry lips, and felt like David writing a Psalm. But my hands were like ice as I patted the blanket.

"Oh, my darling little baby, bless you, bless you!" I cried as tears of relief filled my eyes and ran down and splashed on the blue blanket. "You're all right! I didn't scratch you, so you didn't spit up any blood!"

The half-changed infant I had replaced in his crib was yelling like crazy, but not until I felt sure the strangling baby was all right did I leave the warming room. Then, with tears still streaming, I answered the call of the Prince of Wails! As I lifted the blanketed bundle in my arms from every crib came a howl for attention.

An hour later the superintendent walked into the nursery. Without a glance in my direction she examined the infants in their cribs. All was quiet. All were dry.

"You must have had experience with babies," she said; "you've done a splendid job."

With chattering teeth I told her what had happened and added, "The nearest I ever want to get to the nursery again is on the other side of the plate-glass window!"

And that's where I was for a few minutes every night after I went off duty on some other floor. On the outside looking in—at the new arrivals!

My Cap—Symbol of Rank and Service

To a Nurse's Aide, getting your cap is the thrill that comes once in a lifetime. It's like graduating from high school. There's nothing else like it in all the world. It's happiness and sadness, and humbleness and pride, all rolled into one breathless moment.

There's a ceremony that goes with it, a ceremony all for you.

Of course the other girls who've made the grade and served their required number of hospital hours are there, too. But you aren't conscious of that, any more than they're conscious that you are there.

I met Eunice in front of the Medical Center just before the ceremony began, and she looked me up and down while I looked her down and up to be sure there wasn't a wrinkle in an inch of pinafore.

"You look out-of-this-heavenly-universe wonderful!" she exclaimed.

"And so do you! I've never seen you look so pretty." We didn't say any more. We just turned and walked through the doorway.

There were a great many people there, including some of the most prominent doctors, as well as superintendents of nurses, from the hospitals; and officials of the Red Cross chapter.

I could feel my knees trembling as the class lined up in front of the distinguished guests and took its seats on the platform. Eunice must have noticed it, too, for she leaned over and whispered, "You look a little shaky, and I know I am, but just think! When we walk out of that door again we'll be wearing our *caps!* Be sure to tell me if mine's on straight. I'd just *die* if it wasn't."

I couldn't answer because one of the superintendents of nurses had begun to speak, so I just nodded and pressed my knees together real hard so the skirt of my starched pinafore wouldn't shake.

"The uniform with the joint emblem of the American Red Cross and Office of Civilian Defense is to be worn only on duty," the speaker said. "Caps are never worn on the street. Again, remember your cap is a symbol, and not only a symbol of your service. When you are wearing it, it tells all who see you that you are on duty. You have earned the right to wear a Volunteer Red Cross Nurse's Aide cap. Honor it. Wear it with pride. And always remember that the girl beneath it has a heritage to protect, a heritage that has been handed down from one generation of nurses to another—Registered Nurses. They welcome you as Aides and they are proud to have you share the job of cherishing and protecting the heritage of the nursing profession."

Then it happened all of a sudden. I heard my name called and stepped up to receive my cap. I have no idea what was said, all I knew was that the little blue-and-white cap resting so lightly on the top of my noggin was the most becoming hat I would ever own.

On the way back to my place on the platform I passed Eunice on an adjoining cloud.

Then it was over. Everybody was shaking hands and the Aides were hugging each other and telling each other how good they looked in their new caps.

I looked at Eunice, who had wanted to be sure her cap was on straight, and saw it hanging coyly over one ear. Somehow in the final burst of enthusiasm I'd hugged her all too hard.

Operation Successful—the Patient Lived

And there was the time I stepped off the elevator on the men's floor and heard one of the nation's most noted orthopedic surgeons say, "Here's one now. Perhaps she'll do."

He was talking to the surgical nurse, but he was looking at me. I had no idea what he thought I might do, but Nurse's Aides fear neither God nor man. We are so flattered when someone even imagines we can do something besides tote a bedpan and take a patient's T. P. R. that we'll attempt anything we're asked to do. And, fortunately, knowing our own limitations, we follow instructions with such exact care that we usually do at least a passable job.

"I'll be glad to do anything I can, Doctor," I said quickly. The nurse nodded in my direction and left. The tall, handsome surgeon smiled, and spoke softly.

"I believe you've been on night duty on this floor for some time, haven't you?" he asked.

"Oh, yes, Doctor, for several weeks," I replied.

"Then you remember Mr. Hensley who was here a week ago?"

"The Mr. Hensley whose arm was in a cast?" I asked.

"That's the one. The bones had been crushed in the machinery of a defense plant and I had hoped we might save his arm. Today, when he returned to the hospital for examination, we discovered that immediate amputation would be necessary. Unfortunately, it was impossible to inform the patient of this condition, since he was under an anesthetic, so he is not yet aware that his arm has been removed."

"Ohhhhhh, poor thing!" I said softly, in keeping with the doctor's tone. I didn't know whom I felt sorrier for, the doctor or Mr. Hensley, for the eminent surgeon looked as crushed in spirit as the patient's arm.

"That's why I'm glad you came along, Miss Day. Someone must be with our patient constantly and it may not be possible to get a private nurse before morning, though we are trying. Since a Registered Nurse is not available it will be better to have with him someone he will recognize when he comes out of the anesthetic. Do you think you can do emergency duty for a few hours?"

"I'll do the best I can, Doctor."

"The nurse will tell you what to do," he said, and walked toward 410. I fell in step behind him. As we passed the chart room I wondered what the floor nurse would think of my "private duty" for a patient whose right arm had just been amputated.

The office was empty and I was beginning to worry a little by the time we reached the door of 410. "Maybe I shouldn't have been so cocky, maybe I'd better go find the floor nurse and tell her about it," I thought to myself, and wondered where she was. But the floor nurse was there folding a sheet over the unconscious man on the bed as we entered. I rather hoped she'd send me off on some errand like fetching flowers from the front office or seeing if the patients wanted anything. But she looked at me with what I like to imagine was a relieved expression as I stood half hidden by the doctor.

"Miss Day," she spoke my name, and that was all.

I stepped over to the bed and watched while the interne inserted a needle in the patient's left arm as it lay strapped to a thin, flat board, and my eyes followed the little rubber tube to the bottle of fluid the nurse attached to the stand high above the bed.

"We are trying to locate a nurse. In the meantime, you will stay with this patient. He must not be allowed to move. His life may depend upon your keeping him absolutely quiet. Watch this needle. Hold his arm if he moves it. And under no circumstances should he move his right shoulder. When the fluid is almost out, please signal. If the patient begins to come out of the anesthetic, speak to him at *once*. Perhaps he'll recognize you and that will make it easier, but don't touch that bandage and don't rub his shoulder."

I wondered whom she thought it would be easier for— the patient or me. I certainly wouldn't rub his shoulder, and to touch the bandage was beyond all imagination!

The surgeon had walked out of the room while the nurse talked and I glanced at the open door. "I won't be afraid if they just leave the door open," I thought. But they didn't. The floor nurse and the interne watched the patient for a few seconds and then left, closing the door behind them.

The room was hot, but there was no smell of ether, and I wondered what kind of anesthetic they had used. I hoped it would last until a real nurse could be brought in. I'd sat with a lot of operation patients, but this was different.

I looked at the bandaged stump. It looked so short and stubby. Then I tried not to look at it, but I couldn't help it. I kept watching it, and wondered what they had done with the rest of his arm after they'd cut it off. I half closed my eyes and tried hard to think of something else. Good, clean country lawns and bed blankets hanging on a clothesline, waving in the fresh wind to make them sunny and sweet. Suddenly I knew why the blankets were waving so plainly in my mind. The patient's left hand was moving. White as the sheet it was, and moving slowly. Up and down the fingers went on the little board at the side of the bed. I put my hand on the patient's fingers and felt them relax beneath mine.

For a long time I stood without moving, watching the fluid flow drop by drop from the glass container into the tube, and wondered how long it would be before I could push the light button and signal the nurse.

I glanced down at my watch. Only five minutes had passed since the door had been closed—five minutes that seemed like five hours.

Minutes on end went marching off the face of the clock but I didn't dare look at my watch again. Then the man made a noise in his throat and swallowed, and I wondered if he were going to be sick. Then his head turned restlessly from side to side and I put my hand on his forehead, praying he wouldn't move again. For a minute he lay quiet and then I saw his eyes begin to open slowly and he looked at me, and tried to lift his hand.

"Mr. Hensley," I said, "please don't move your hand. Just lie quietly for a little while and the nurse will come and take the strap off your arm." He kept looking at me.

"I'm Miss Day," I said, and smiled. "You remember me. I took care of you in the ward."

"Yes, I know." He spoke in a voice little more than a whisper. Then he said, "Please scratch my hand." I touched the hand that was strapped to the board and glanced at the liquid in the glass jar. It had gone down about half an inch.

"Not that hand," he said. "The other one."

"What will I do?" I thought. "There isn't any other hand!"

Suddenly the man screamed, "My arm, my arm! I can't stand the pain in my arm!" He tried to lift himself, and I put my hand on his chest and talked to him.

"Please lie quietly, Mr. Hensley," I begged. "I know it's hard, but you know I wouldn't ask you to unless the doctor had said you had to be quiet. So please try to stand it until the fluid is out of the jar and then the nurse will come and do something to relieve the pain."

"Who are you?" he asked, and closed his eyes.

"I'm Miss Day. You knew me a little while ago. Don't you remember, I took care of you when you were in the ward."

He opened his eyes again and I knew he hadn't understood a word for he screamed with pain and begged me to rub his hand. I saw the stump of his arm move and before I could reach the light button to signal the floor nurse the patient lifted his head from the pillow and he gazed at the bandaged stump. I was too horrified to speak or move.

"Oh, God, don't let him realize what's happened," I prayed under my breath. "Please let him go to sleep again! Let him think it's just a bandage!"

Finally I heard myself lying, "Your arm is bandaged, and I can't get to your hand to rub it. Please try to stand the pain a little longer and it will go away in a minute." His head fell back on the pillow and rolled from side to side. Then he was quiet.

Minutes later my eyes sought the glass jar. Only an inch of liquid remained, and I pressed the signal button.

"Has he come to yet?" the floor nurse asked as she stood by the bed.

"Yes, he's conscious for a moment or two every now and then. He tried to move several times, and he looked at his arm once. He keeps begging me to scratch his hand. I told him it was bandaged. Has the nurse come yet?" I added as she unstrapped his left hand from the board and withdrew the needle from his arm.

"Not yet. We haven't located one, but we're still trying. Just do your best to keep him quiet."

"He's been screaming with pain. Isn't there anything that can be done?"

"The doctor doesn't want him to have a hypodermic unless it's absolutely necessary. The anesthetic, you know." I didn't know, but I said nothing. "If he keeps screaming it's because he's somewhat delirious from the anesthetic, but with the door closed it will not disturb the other patients. Just keep him from moving. You may give him a small puff of a cigarette," she added, and was gone.

How calm she is, I thought, and yet every gesture and every word and every glance at the patient had belied the crisp, professional tone and manner.

"She's sorry for me, too," I said to myself. "I can't let her down, and I certainly won't let my patient down."

The patient slept for a few minutes and then he opened his eyes again, and as though he had picked up the same train of thought where he'd left it a few minutes before, he turned his head to the right and gazed at the bandaged shoulder and the stump that had been his arm. He stared at it with unbelieving eyes, and I stared at him, not daring to speak. Then he screamed.

"My arm! What's happened to my arm? Oh, God, they've cut off my arm!" His screams became louder and his delirium became worse, and I begged and pleaded and prayed all in one breath. As long as he felt the weight of my hand on his chest, he remained still, but his screams continued.

With one hand I held his good left arm with which he constantly sought to touch the bandaged stump, and with my other hand I pressed gently against his chest. When I released either hand to reach for the signal light, he would try to raise himself on the bed so I dared not lift my hands again. For minutes on end I held him until I thought my own body would break in two. Finally his delirium ceased and he became rational. His eyes looked into my face and I saw the man's chin quiver like a child's. He lay still for a moment before he spoke.

"Forgive me," he said, and closed his eyes as tears ran from the corner of the lids and soaked into the pillow. I wanted to sob. It's horrible to hear a man scream with pain, even in delirium. It's worse to see a rational man cry.

"Mr. Hensley"—I spoke softly, and was surprised at the steadiness of my voice—"the anesthetic is wearing off now, and you can understand what I'm saying. I know how terrible it is for you, but I've been trying awfully hard to keep you quiet as the doctor said, but my back hurts so badly I have to change my position. If you'll just promise that you won't move at all until I can get around on the other side of the bed, I'll give you a cigarette."

"I'll try," he said. "A cigarette would taste so good!"

I reluctantly released my hold on his arm and waited for a fraction of a second before starting around the end of the bed. I was terrified that he would reach his hand toward the bandaged stump but I didn't want him to think I didn't trust him. My back felt as though it would never be straight again.

His eyes followed me as I reached the other side of the bed and he looked at my empty hands. Of course there were no cigarettes on the bedside table. I looked at the dresser. The top was bare of everything except the fresh white towel that served as a scarf. I thought of my own handbag and the package of cigarettes tucked inside, and remembered that I hadn't put it in its accustomed place in the office, but had brought it into the room with me for I hadn't gone by the office at all, but had come directly into this room. I dashed to the dresser and pulled open a drawer. Thank heaven! My handbag was there!

I opened it quickly and took a cigarette out of the package and struck a match. After the first drag I took the cigarette from my dry lips and held it to the patient's mouth and watched while he took a deep draw.

"Oh, that's so good!" he breathed as the smoke left his mouth.

I put the cigarette out, but my patient lay quiet and closed his eyes. After a moment he looked at me again.

"The pain's coming back," he said. "Couldn't I have just one more?"

"Mr. Hensley, I may be doing something I shouldn't. But if you'll try to stay quiet in spite of the pain and not go out of your head again, I'll give you another one."

"If I can just smoke, maybe I can stand it," he said. I struck the match and lit another cigarette and held it to his lips.

"Please, just one more!" he begged after a little while. I reached for the package of cigarettes again, but before I could pick up the match I saw him bite his lower lip from pain and suddenly the delirium returned. Throwing the cigarette on the floor, I held the man on the bed with one arm

and reached for the signal light. His screams must have penetrated the door and reached the office, for almost immediately
the floor nurse entered followed by an interne.

As they took over, I released my hold on the man and stood
aside, no longer able to hold back the sob in my throat. The
interne pressed the needle quickly into the man's arm and
after a moment the medicine began to take effect. Gradually
his screams subsided and the patient lay unconscious on the
bed. I put my hands over my face.

"I have a confession to make," I cried. "I may have done
wrong but I gave him more than just a little puff. I gave him
several. It kept him quiet for a long time. But if it hurt him,
I think I'll die."

The floor nurse put her arm around me.

"If you were in doubt, you should have asked permission.
But the cigarettes didn't hurt him. I had no idea he had waked
up until we walked through the hall and heard him scream
just as the light came on over the door."

But I couldn't stop crying even when the interne said,
"Keeping the patient from moving about was the important
thing. You did a fine job and you're a good Aide. That, too,
was what the doctor ordered."

The Children's Ward

The children's ward is on the fourth floor, too. Piedmont
is a funny old hospital, but everybody in the state of Georgia
loves it. Hardly a grownup from Rabun Gap to Tybee Light
can think back to the days of his childhood without recalling
some vague memory of the long, winding corridors and a visit
to Mama as she lay in the white hospital bed at Piedmont.

The older graduate nurses, regardless of the place where
they may have taken their training, like to do duty at Piedmont, for they like the friendly feeling of the place. Someday a

brand-new hospital will replace it, but the very name "Piedmont" will always bring tender memories to the minds of thousands of Georgians who have been snatched from the valley of the shadow by the warmth and spirit that are a vital part of the training of Piedmont doctors and nurses.

It was inadequacy of space that placed the children's ward in a group of rooms at one end of the floor occupied in the main by male patients. So fourth-floor student nurses and Aides also took the children's ward under their blue pinafored wings.

Children in wards are wonderful patients. They bolster each other. Their courage is inspiring, and at times very touching, for, though they may whine and cry with pain in private rooms when nurse or loving hands from the home attempt to soothe them, in the ward they grit their little air-cooled teeth and put up a brave front before an audience of their own age or younger. Sometimes the younger they are the more courage they display.

The beds are nearly always filled in the children's ward. Some of the beds are cribs, and others are regular size, but they seem always to be occupied. I remember how it was during the war with so many daddies overseas and so many hero worshipers at home trying to do what Daddy was doing. If he were in the air corps, his son was the victim of a toy plane crash. If Daddy were a paratrooper, his son was brought to the hospital after a jump from the porch roof. If he were in the Navy or the infantry most anything might have happened, but his son, too, was brought in with a wound that required hospitalization.

And the girls! Well, the girls were just brought in. Maybe it was tonsils, maybe it was a bone infection, maybe it was a broken arm or leg, or a bad cut from a fall, but they were constantly being brought in by frantic mothers, or neighbors, or uncles, or aunts, so the turnover was appalling in the children's ward. And a lot of them got penicillin. It was new then. The mothers were consoled by it. But the kids didn't like it. In fact, they hated it, and no one could blame them, for the injection hurt. And it hurt the nurse to have to give it.

The mothers were usually right there at night before visiting hours were over. Many of them worked, and night was the only time they could come.

I remember one precious little girl about four years old who was to receive her second penicillin shot at seven o'clock. She hadn't forgotten the first one.

I was taking T. P. R.'s in the children's ward at six-thirty and had just put a thermometer into Judith's mouth when the student nurse came in.

"I hope Judith's mother will be here by seven," she said. "That's the time for her next shot."

The four-year-old opened her mouth to say something, and the thermometer fell out.

"Whoops!" I said, recovering the little glass tube. "You can't have your temperature taken and talk at the same time, honey! Come on now, under the tongue again."

"I want my mama!" Judith said, and her chin began to tremble.

"Don't you worry, darling!" I consoled, and patted her hand and felt for her pulse. "Mommy will be here in a few minutes. I'll bet she's stepping off the bus in front of the hospital right this very minute!" It was the wrong thing to say but I'd said it anyway, and it kept the thermometer where it belonged. Besides, I believed it, too.

I finished the round of little patients and carried the tray of thermometers to the chart room. The student nurse looked up from the desk.

"It's nearly seven and her mother isn't here yet. She's never been late before."

"What are you worried about?" I asked. "Maybe she's just late getting off from work, or maybe the bus is off schedule."

"But she knows Judy is due for another shot at seven, and she promised the child she'd be here."

"Oh, she'll probably make it. The kids don't understand, though, if they're not right here at the same time every night. It kind of breaks your heart to see them watching the door every time anyone comes into the ward, and to see how disappointed they are when it's only you or me."

"Well, I just don't know what I'll do if she doesn't come!" The student nurse sighed.

"Oh, don't worry about it. You're as bad as Judy. But she's a very brave child and maybe she won't cry at all."

"Well, I just wish I could change places with you at seven o'clock!" she replied, and sighed again.

"For heaven's sake, why?" I laughed.

"You don't know Judy!" she replied. "But you will, because if her mother doesn't come you'll have to hold her while I give her the penicillin."

"Hold her? You mean *hold* her? Hold her *down?*" The student nurse nodded. "But I thought you meant her mother just promised to hold her on her lap! Oh, I couldn't! I just couldn't hold her *down!*" I was horrified at the thought.

"Well, this is one time you'll have to. I can't run the risk of breaking a needle off in her leg. She fought like a wildcat before."

"Couldn't you get somebody else to do it? An interne or another nurse?" I asked.

"And where would I get another nurse with you and me the only ones on duty on this whole floor? And I wouldn't dare ask an interne. Besides, all he'd do would be to tell me to tell you to hold her."

We both looked at the clock.

"Five more minutes," she said. "Guess I'd better get it."

I answered a signal light in the men's ward. "Might as well take a bottle on the way," I thought. But the man wanted intake instead of output, so I filled the water pitcher with crushed ice.

I met the student nurse on the way back to the chart room.

"Come on," she said. "We'll just have to do it."

Judith saw the hypodermic in the nurse's hand as we entered, and began to cry. I walked over to the bed and put my arm around the tiny patient.

"Look, darling," I began, "you're a big, brave little girl, and I love you. Your mommy is on her way to see you right now, but the doctor wants you to have your medicine at seven, so let's be real good and when Mommy comes we can surprise her and tell her we've already had our shot. Don't you think that would be nice?"

"No!" Judy said emphatically.

"Oh, come now! You're just fooling! Think how proud Mommy will be of her little girl!" I cajoled, and sat on the edge of the bed.

"No!" The finality of the child's voice was like a sudden push in my direction.

"She's got to have it. We just don't dare wait any longer," the student nurse whispered. Judy's big eyes were swimming with tears.

"Go 'way! I want my mommy!" she wailed.

"Judy," I said, and tried to be very professional. "You want to get all well and go home and play with your dolls and all the little girls who live close to you, so please be a good girl. We want you to get well fast, and maybe if you'll just let the nice nurse give you your medicine, you'll be well before you know it."

"No!"

I glanced around and saw the other children watching. Some were sitting up in their beds for a better look, and even the smallest patient in the ward had rolled to the edge of his crib and was peeking between the bars for a better look at the drama being unfolded before their big, wide eyes.

"Judy," I whispered in her ear, "all the other children are watching. They don't think you're a very good little sport to act like this. They think you're afraid." She looked up at me, ashamed, and snuggled her head against my shoulder. "But I know you're not afraid, so let's just show them what a brave little girl you are. I'll pretend I'm your mommy and I'll hold you in my lap just like your very own mommy would, and it'll be over in just a minute." She put her arms around my neck and I lifted her off the bed and carried her to a chair in the far corner of the room. "Now put your arms around my neck real tight," I spoke softly, "and hang on, and I'll hold you real tight, too."

I rolled her on her side in my lap in a big bear hug and the student nurse quickly unbuttoned the little pajamas and I flinched as I saw the needle go into the bare bottom. Judy knew the children were still watching and she didn't make a sound except a tiny catch in her throat. But I felt one small arm come free from my neck and four little fingers touched my cheek. Four little fingernails dug their way through my skin and clawed their way downward. It felt like the whole side of my face was gone, but I didn't make a sound either. I was too busy wondering how deeply her nails had gashed my face to say anything. Besides, the children were still watching. You can't inject penicillin quickly.

"There now!" the student nurse said, and patted Judy's little bare behind as she held a cotton pad over the spot where the needle had gone in. "It's all over, and Judy's a great big brave girl!" She rebuttoned the pajamas, and the smile she was about to give me froze as she looked at my bloody cheek. "Good Lord! What happened to *you!*" she exclaimed.

"Nothing," I replied, and tried to hide my face from the children as I carried Judy back to her bed. But as I tucked the cover over her, Judy looked at my face and saw what she'd done.

"I'm sowwy," she said as her face wrinkled into a cry.

"That's all right, angel," I said; "you couldn't help it." I put my hand over my wound as I turned to leave so the other children couldn't see it, but they were all peacefully asleep. The show was over and the curtain of night was down.

"Good night, my sweet!" I said over my shoulder to Judy. "Sleep tight!" Judy looked at me with a we-share-a-secret smile.

"You're a big bwave girl, too," she said.

Oh, yes! Judy's mother was just stepping out of the elevator as I walked down the hall. She'd had bad news from overseas. Her husband had been wounded in battle, and she'd been delayed in trying to get further news from the Red Cross.

But she was a big brave girl, too.

There's a New Patient in 301

Well, here I am, back on the third floor again. And to think I once wished the patients would get up and let me lie down!

Eunice has just left after giving me my evening care. Eunice, you remember, was my bath mate when we were in Nurse's Aide class. She's improved a lot since then. She left some skin on this time.

It all happened one night just as I was going off duty on the fifth floor. I'd felt a little woozy all that day, and maybe the day before. I can't seem to remember just how long my head had been swimming a little and my tummy had been doing an occasional back flop, for it was a very busy time at the hospital and the shortage of nurses was growing more serious all the time. All of us were tired. It seemed the only thing we were not running short of was babies. We had a bumper crop of those.

But, anyway, I decided to answer just one more light before I went off duty because I hated to leave the night nurse with so many things to do. But when I was walking back up the hall after answering the light, suddenly everything went black. The next thing I knew I was tucked into bed and I felt a prick in my finger and heard the interne say, "The blood test will tell us whether or not it's appendicitis, but I feel sure it is."

After that he gave me a shot in the arm to ease the pain in my tummy and I went to sleep.

First thing I knew after that, Eunice was standing over me talking a redheaded blue streak.

". . . awful! Just awful! Imagine walking into 301 and finding *you* in the very bed where my very *first* patient was on my very *first* day on *duty*. But I'm sure *glad* they put you on my floor. Just suppose they'd put you in bed in the *maternity* ward and then found they couldn't *move* you or anything? What would people *think?*" Eunice had a way of underscoring her words with emphasis as though a line were actually drawn under the ones she considered most important.

I recognized the emphasis before I actually understood what she was saying, turned my head with my half-shut eyes searching vaguely in the fog that seemed to fill the room. Gradually her face began to take shape.

"Wouldn't you like something *cold* to *drink?*" She chattered on. "I'm serving drinks to the *patients* and you're a *patient* if ever I *saw* one. What would you like? Fruit juice, orange or grapefruit, grape juice or Coca-Cola?"

I would have been glad to have just a little cold water. My tongue felt like a good-sized slice of the Sahara Desert and I looked at the tray of glasses. They all looked alike.

"Anything, just so it's wet and cold and sour," I said.

Eunice picked up a glass, slipped an arm under my head, and watched as I gulped down the liquid, crushed ice and all.

"I guess I'll *have* to be *going*," she said reluctantly as she put the empty glass back on the tray, "though I'd *like* to stay right *here*. In fact, I think it's almost my *duty* because after *all* we started out as *partners*. We were *practically* each other's very first *patients*, even if it was just make-*believe*. Gee! *Imagine* having you as a *real* patient! It's *more* than I can *stand!*" With that, Eunice drifted off into the fog again, and I drifted off to sleep.

The next time I was aware of anything at all, I felt somewhat as Alice in Wonderland must have felt when she heard the White Rabbit. A voice was piercing my eardrum with the sharpness of a hatpin and I would have sworn that it was coming from the far left-hand corner of the ceiling.

"I don't think it's blood, Doctor, but it certainly does look like it," the voice said.

"Nonsense," a deep masculine voice replied in a low tone, "it couldn't be!" Then, after a moment, "This is just a simple appendectomy."

I drifted off again only to be roused once more by the piercing voice coming from the far corner of the ceiling.

"Did you have anything to drink after I left you? Miss Day, did you have anything to drink? Anything to drink . . . to drink . . . to drin . . ."

Post-anesthesia sharpens the senses, and my ears roared from the seeming loudness of the voices that reverberated through the room. One word kept bouncing from the ceiling to the floor and striking my eardrum again and again. "Drink? Oh, yes, drink!" I said to myself, and tried to speak, but no sound came, so I just nodded ever so slightly.

"What did you have?" the voice asked. "Was it Coca-Cola?" I tried to shake my head, but it was too much effort. "Was it grape juice?" the voice kept prodding with the same sharp note. "Did you drink some grape juice after we left you?"

Grape juice . . . Eunice . . . wet . . . cold . . . I tried to nod.

"Thank heaven! Doctor, it's grape juice!"

"Don' want it," I said weakly, thinking Eunice was offering me another glass.

"Well, you certainly haven't got it," the nurse replied as she withdrew the emesis basin from beneath my chin and replaced it with another, just in the nick of time.

"She'll be all right now," I heard the doctor say.

A moment later I felt myself being lifted high in the air and I opened my eyes. A circle of lights above blinded me and I closed my eyes again. The next time I opened them, I was back in the fog of my third-floor room, and Eunice's voice was coming in on the beam.

"Honey, I *wouldn't* have done it for a *million, billion* dollars if I'd known. I had no *idea!* Why didn't you *tell* me they were going to rush you *right* up to the *operating* room and take out your *appendix?* My goodness, if I'd had any *idea*, you *know* I wouldn't have given you *grape juice*. I'd have given you *orange juice*. They *couldn't* have mistaken *that* for blood! So *please* don't hold it against me! I've asked especially to look after you. I told them you were my very *first* patient. Well, not *really* my patient. But when I saw them bringing you from the *operating* room, I was *sure* you were going to be my *last* one! You looked *dead!*"

I opened my eyes and looked at Eunice.

"Am I that sick?" I asked weakly.

"Oh, *no*, you aren't really *sick* at all! You just had your *appendix* out. But when I heard them talking about the way you'd *vomited* and how they thought it was *blood*, and I told them that it was me who had given you the grape juice, I just *knew* I'd be fired that *minute!*"

Well, Eunice wasn't fired. She gives me my evening care and pops in every few minutes to see if I want anything. But she always takes the grape juice off the tray before she serves refreshment to the patient in 301.

This morning the doctor told me that I could go home tomorrow. But it will be a month before I can be on duty again. "Geeminy! I wonder how they'll *ever* get along in the nursery without me for *one whole month!* My goodness! How we *do* need nurses!"

Birth of a Nurse

BY DORA E. BIRCHARD

→»«←

The life of a nurse is not by any means all work and
devotion to duty. Like the rest of us, nurses like
parties, dancing, and good times. Sometimes, alas,
the good times run into conflict with the work that
has to be done. Here is the story of one such conflict,
and of what one young student nurse learned from it.

INKY GAVE HER MIRROR one last intense look, patted her shining
hair, smooth in its unaccustomed waves, pursed her definitely
red mouth into a self-conscious smile.

"Oh, but I do look slick!" she thought, and instantly wondered—and worried. Would she have lots of dances? Would
she meet somebody really gorgeous? Some nice man with a
long, low roadster and a good line of chatter? Oh, she hoped
she would! The other girls had boy friends to take them out on
their hours off duty. There hadn't been anyone for Inky so
far. As a probationer she hadn't had much opportunity to
meet people. But now she was a Junior nurse, and for the first
time was invited to go on a party, one of the periodical forays
into the world of men and music which were permitted the
junior and senior nurses.

This time it was to be a Valentine's dance at the beach, at
the Rainbow Ballroom on the pier. Inky had never been there,
but Eleanor said it was divine.

Inky was eighteen, and today, for the first time in her life,

43

she had had her corn-silk hair set at a *salon de beauté*. Before she went into training she had been Ingeborg Dalstrom, and there had been no time for patience for such nonsense as beauty shops in the busy life of the dairy farm in the Santa Clara Valley.

But now she was Inky, and learning to be a nurse, and living in the city, and going to a party. Besides, her shining gold hair and equally shining coral fingertips, she had on her first long evening dress, with hardly anything in the back, and a wrap to match. Eleanor Winter, her roommate, had helped her shop for it over on Hollywood Boulevard, and it hadn't cost so much, either. Eleanor sure knew how to shop. Life was really too perfect!

"Come on, everybody, the cars are here!" "Oh, Inky! You look grand!" "That's a darling dress, honey. Where'd you get it?" "Come on, let's go!"

The gaiety bubbled and billowed along the corridor of the Nurses' Home, frothed out of the opening doors and down the stairs, rainbow-colored butterflies, each emerging from her chrysalis of starched uniform and professional dignity.

Inky was last. She floated down the wide stairway, which for her was marble, carpeted with crimson, instead of the old, familiar, and sanitary linoleum-covered stairs of the Nurses' Home.

She had almost reached the outer door, and the chattering group on the sidewalk, when a firm voice called her back to earth.

"Miss Dalstrom."

"Yes, Miss Perkins. I'm just leaving."

"Wait just a minute. Dr. Rhinehart just called in. Stay there a minute."

Inky's heart sank into her new gold sandals, but she waited, mute, ignoring the calls from outside.

The voice of Miss Perkins, on phone duty that night, came again, crisply: "Miss Dalstrom, Dr. Rhinehart is bringing a patient in with a fractured skull to do a trephine. Emergency. You are to go over and set up the surgery. Now."

"Yes, Miss Perkins." Inky's voice was small and bleak.

Numbly she climbed the stairs, plain linoleum again. Blindly she went to her room, slipped out of her new dress, hung it carefully on its hanger. Then the dam broke. Tears came in floods and torrents, and seemed to splash on the floor all around her. Gold sandals flew in every direction. Inky's carefully coifed head beat against the pillow as she flung herself face down on the bed, sobbing in great loud gulps.

Suddenly she sat up, slapped the moisture from her eyes with the backs of her hands, and spoke sharply to herself:

"You're a dumb cluck, Ingeborg Dalstrom. You got yourself into this. Nobody else. They all said you were too flighty to stick with it. Like a puddle of quicksilver, Mother used to say. About that steady. But no! You couldn't listen. You had to be a nurse. Well, you did it, and now you've got to take what comes along with it. And like it! So snap out of this!"

She washed the redness from her eyes, dressed in her uniform, and looked in the mirror, hard and straight this time.

"You're not Inky. You're Miss Dalstrom, junior nurse in the surgery."

She hurried out and across the street to the hospital. Once in the surgery, she worked quickly and well, and had everything ready by the time the senior nurse arrived to "scrub up." Dr. Rhinehart appeared. The patient was wheeled in on the narrow, rubber-tired cart, and carefully placed in position. The interne and the anesthetist were in the anteroom, putting on their green gowns and gauze masks. Inky tied the tapes in back for each one. Soon the big clean room was only a smooth, sea-green background for the great white light in the center which drew the eyes inexorably to the table directly beneath and to the inert figure swathed in white.

Inky listened, fascinated, to the brief discussion of the case history among the doctors. The patient was a young girl of fourteen, who had fallen from her horse two days ago, striking her head. This was the third injury of this kind the child had suffered. Six years before she had slid down a shed roof, gone over the edge, and struck her head on a stone coping below, causing concussion and a scalp wound, but no fracture had been found in the X-rays. Four years later she had tumbled off a bicycle and again the blow fell on her head. Just one of those children who seem to attract disaster. The second accident did not appear to be serious at the time but had left her rather peculiar mentally. And now this third blow on the same spot had caused a definite insanity, and the best brain surgeon in the city was going to operate and try to relieve the pressure on her brain.

Inky was utterly lost in interest and amazement at what followed. She had seen ordinary trephine operations before, and had marveled at the skill that could replace a part of the skull with a little plate of silver. But this was beyond anything she had ever dreamed of. For four hours she watched, and worked when she was needed, oblivious of any world outside this one of soft green walls and shining glass doors, of glistening instruments and silent, green-robed figures moving quickly to supply in advance every need of the sure hands beneath the light. Hands working to bring life and sanity to a young girl who had not yet begun to live.

She saw, without repugnance, the fringe of hemostats placed around the scalp laid back, baring the bony structure. She watched the surgeon saw an area four inches in diameter, out of the skull and try, without success, to lift it off. She heard him say to the interne: "Held fast to the dura mater, do you

see? Old adhesions from the previous injuries." She saw him
cut it back gradually, as you'd take the peel from an orange.
Then, when it was free, he scraped the fibrous material from
the undersurface and rubbed it smooth. Then came the biggest
surprise to Inky, for she had not had time before to wonder
why the girl's leg had been propped up and exposed from the
beginning. A swift incision there, and a bit of the protecting
tissue of a muscle was removed, laid over the raw spot on the
brain, sewed all around with black silk thread to the edge of
the sound dura mater. Then the polished skull section was
replaced, and the scalp stitched back in position.

The clock on the wall had made four complete cycles by
the time it was over and the passive form on the table wheeled
away. Life or death? Or a living death of mental darkness?
Time alone now held the answer.

Ingeborg Dalstrom let herself into her room quietly. She
was a little dazed to see Eleanor sitting up in bed waiting for
her.

"Oh, Inky! What a crime you couldn't go! Was it a party!
Oh, honey, we had a perfectly marvelous time! I was simply
sick to think that you missed it. What happened, anyway? I
heard Perkins call you back."

Inky brushed her hand over her hot little face. Sometimes
Eleanor seemed really too childish.

"I guess you wouldn't know, Eleanor. It was all right."

She slipped out of her clothes and into her nightie and slid
in between the cool sheets. How explain to Eleanor this feeling
she had never had before? This new knowledge of what really
mattered? "If that girl up there only gets well, that's all I
care," she thought—and then, "To think I helped!" She hugged
this new knowledge close. "To think I'll always be helping. . . ."

Young Woman in White

BY QUENTIN REYNOLDS

->>><<<-

"I think I have the best job in the world," says one
nurse in a great New York City hospital. What
makes her think so? Perhaps the best way to find out
is to follow her through a typical day of duty. That
is what Quentin Reynolds has done in the adventure
which follows.

LOUISE JAISSLE, NURSE IN CHARGE of semi-private ward No. 1
of Lenox Hill Hospital in New York City, helped slide the
unconscious patient into bed and then took the chart from the
interne. It told her that the patient had just undergone a
five and one-half hour gastrectomy, an operation involving
removal of three-fourths of the stomach.

The surgeon had done his part, and now it was the patient's
physical resources and the precise carrying out of a hundred
medical details by the nurse which would tell the story of the
next twenty-four hours.

The patient was still under deep anesthesia. A Levine tube
to his stomach projected from one nostril. Nurse Jaissle inserted the end of the tube into a bottle that had a suction
apparatus. This would keep gas from accumulating in the
stomach. The operating-room nurse who had accompanied the
patient handed Miss Jaissle a bottle of whole blood from which
blood was seeping into a tube and through the needle inserted
into the large vein on the patient's left forearm. Miss Jaissle

hooked this bottle to an upright pole beside the bed.

"Blood pressure is 110 over 70," the anesthetist said. "When he starts reacting"—the hospital term for regaining consciousness—"watch his pulse and respiration. When the patient fully reacts, have him take deep breaths and cough."

Now Louise Jaissle, a tall, dark-haired twenty-year-old girl just finishing her three years of nursing education, was alone with her patient. She ran a practiced eye over the surgeon's orders on the chart. Some of them were in the traditional Latin abbreviations. Her quick mind absorbed the instructions:

"Check blood pressure every fifteen minutes. Inspect dressing ever thirty minutes. Inject 100 mgm Demerol Q 3-4 hrs PRN." The last order told her to administer 100 milligrams of Demerol every three to four hours when necessary to relieve pain. The chart also instructed her to administer two cubic centimeters of Combiotic (an antibiotic to combat possible infection) every ten hours, and to catheterize the patient every eight hours. The patient was not to be fed by mouth, and infusions with vitamins were to start in twenty-four hours.

During the crucial period when the patient was emerging from the anesthetic Nurse Jaissle kept her vigil, watching closely for danger signals. When the patient had absorbed the blood in the bottle, she irrigated the tube with sterile salt water to clear away possible clots and attached it to a bottle of dextrose and water. She looked at the dressings covering the huge incision and checked pulse and blood pressure. At intervals she ran her hand over her patient's abdomen, searching for any distention or hardness that would tell her of intestinal complications.

As the patient's conscious mind began to fight through the haze of anesthesia, he heard a soft, comforting voice. "Take it easy now. It's all over and you're going to get well." The patient relaxed into the half-world of semi-consciousness.

Nurse Jaissle listened closely to his shallow, labored breathing. She didn't like the sound of it. Again she took pulse, temperature, blood pressure. His blood pressure was now down to 90 over 50. His lips and fingernails had a bluish tinge, and his skin was beginning to get clammy—danger signals hoisted by nature. Her first thought was of hemorrhage, although the dressing showed no signs of seepage. She elevated the foot of the bed to stimulate the flow of oxygen-carrying blood to the brain. Then she hurried to the nurses' station, a room near the ward, and said into a telephone: "Dr. Walter Ryan, Stat!" ("Stat" in hospital lingo means "immediately.")

Within five seconds every loud-speaker in the big hospital was calling, "Dr. Ryan!" Another five seconds and the resident physician was on the phone, listening to Miss Jaissle's report. "The patient may be going into shock," she said.

"I'll be right there," Dr. Ryan said. "Tell the blood bank to send down 500 cc. of blood immediately and have another 500 on call."

At the patient's bedside Dr. Ryan inspected the abdominal incision for signs of blood. Meanwhile, Nurse Jaissle substituted a bottle of blood for the one that had been feeding the patient dextrose and water intravenously. If the patient did not respond soon it might mean there was a serious internal hemorrhage, and he would have to be rushed to the operating room and the abdomen reopened. But within three minutes Nurse Jaissle could see improvement. Dr. Ryan took the blood pressure. "That's better—110 over 70," he said. "Keep a close watch and call me if it drops."

During the next four hours the other seventeen patients in the ward were being cared for by Miss Jaissle's two assistants. However, she gave three patients intramuscular injections of Flo-Cillin (an antibiotic) and renewed infusions of dextrose and saline to others not yet ready to take nourishment by mouth. She was away only briefly from her postoperative patient's bedside.

He was fully reacted now, and he shook his head when she asked if he were in pain. She urged him to move his legs, to make the blood circulate properly and prevent embolism. "Take a few deep breaths," she said quietly, "then let me hear you cough." This is a routine precaution against congestion gathering in the lungs and attendant possibility of pneumonia.

The exertion of coughing brought on pain, and Nurse Jaissle injected 100 milligrams of Demerol. She found the blood pressure satifactory. Next she wrote on the chart all developments and the medication she had administered.

The patient pointed to the tube in his nostril and made a wry face. "It's a nuisance," she said with a laugh, "but don't worry—you'll be up and taking a walk in a couple of days." He smiled. Soon he fell into a deep sleep.

Nurse Jaissle felt a small sense of triumph. This man was not just a "case" to her, though she knew nothing about him except his name.

Three years before, when she and the fifty-six other members of her class had been welcomed as freshmen at Lenox Hill, Mrs. Almeda B. MacCambridge, director of the School for Nursing, had expressed a philosophy which had made a deep impression upon her: "A nurse must give her patient support and understanding. The responsiveness of a nurse comes more from her personality than from her formal education, and there may be some among you who will not be able to meet this requirement." She had been right: thirteen members of that class had since dropped out, some for this reason.

Nurse Jaissle smiled as she recalled the way one of her instructors had put it: "It is the patient who requires attention, not only an arm or a leg. You nurses are not merely bolt fasteners on a medical assembly line."

She glanced again at the sleeping man and hurried to look at the charts of two new patients just admitted. One was due for a hernia operation; he could have the regular hospital meal. The second was to have an X ray of the gall bladder the next morning; his supper would be a "low-fat diet"—a piece of lean meat, a baked potato, and a pot of tea. But the patient had no appetite; he felt nauseated and was in pain. On the interne's orders Miss Jaissle administered 50 milligrams of Dramamine for the nausea and injected one sixth of a grain of morphine to dull the pain.

She knew that nausea and pain were signs of nervousness so she sat down and chatted with him. They discovered that they both came from the Bronx. "So now you've got to keep an eye on me," the man said.

"I will," she said with a warm smile. "I can't let a neighbor down!"

By ten-thirty that night all her charges had been given their medication and were ready for sleep. When the surgeon stopped in to take a look at his postoperative patient he studied the chart, took the pulse, ran experienced hands over the abdomen, and nodded with satisfaction. "Miss Jaissle has been taking good care of you," he said to the patient. "You have nothing to worry about."

Louise Jaissle felt a warm glow. Surgeons usually are chary of praise, taking the competence of nurses for granted, but because praise comes seldom it is the more appreciated.

The ward was quiet. Barbara Zdenek, a seventeen-year-old first-year student nurse, brought all the charts to the desk. Miss Jaissle's next-to-final task was to check each chart carefully; if there were special orders she would point them out to her relief.

A few minutes before midnight Nurse Jo Werner came to the floor. She would be on duty until eight in the morning.

At Lenox Hill and most other first-rate hospitals nurses work a forty-hour week unless an emergency cancels all schedules.

Nurse Jaissle briefed Nurse Werner on the condition of the postoperative case and the other patients. Then she unlocked the narcotics cabinet, and they went over its contents. Every grain of morphine, every bit of codeine, Demerol, Seconal, Nembutal, and papaverine used during the day has to be checked against the book in which are recorded drugs used during the past eight hours. When they were through Nurse Werner said, "You look a little beat. Busy day?"

"Just routine, Jo," Nurse Jaissle said. "See you tomorrow."

Hospitals used to regard nurses pretty much as domestic servants, paid them and worked them accordingly, and gave them virtually no responsibility beyond that of bathing and feeding patients and changing bed linen. It was less than twenty years ago that an editor wrote, "The idea that nurses must eat has never penetrated the public mind." In recent years good working conditions, adequate pay, decent hours, and interesting work have attracted girls like Louise Jaissle to nursing.

In two weeks Nurse Jaissle would graduate with her class at Lenox Hill and be awarded the pin and black stripe for her cap which signify that she has successfully completed her course. The past three years had prepared her to perform delicate tasks and exercise the kind of judgment that until recent years were the exclusive prerogatives of doctors. During the war necessity dictated that many complex functions be allocated to nurses, and the results justified what had been considered a risk. Today the training of the professional nurse qualifies her to perform these services, with great timesaving to the doctors.

Louise Jaissle has been trained to administer medication subcutaneously, intradermally, intramuscularly, intravenously, rectally, by inhalation; she can give patients therapeutic baths, massages, and special exercises; she is able to change surgical dressings and irrigate body cavities. She has mastered the intricacies of equipment used for patients who require tracheotomy or "iron lungs," and administering complicated tests is as much a part of the routine as taking temperature was thirty years ago.

Louise Jaissle is typical of the 30,000 nurses graduated annually from the country's 1125 accredited nursing schools.[1] A highly selective nursing school such as that of Lenox Hill accepts only about 65 per cent of those who apply for admittance. A high-school diploma is required, and pre-entrance tests are given to find out if the applicant has an aptitude for nursing.

In her second year Louise Jaissle spent only fourteen hours a week in the classroom. She gravitated from a medical ward to surgery, to a clinic, to pediatrics, to the psychiatric clinic. She scrubbed for tonsil removals and learned to pass the Hurd retractor, the wire snare, the scrapers, the Fisher knife, at the proper moment without prompting from the doctor. During her final years she assisted nurses and doctors in cases that required advanced medical treatment. As part of her basic training she spent exciting weeks in the obstetrical department and also became a junior member of the operating-room team.

The total cost of her three years' training, including tuition, uniforms, books, and spending money, amounted to a little more than $1,500. But when she donned the uniform of a graduate nurse she would receive a salary of $270 a month. And, like the other 150 graduate nurses and 156 student nurses at Lenox Hill, she could live in a large, comfortable home—complete with swimming pool and clubroom—adjoining the hospital.

---

[1] These and other statistics in the article are for the year 1956—Eds.

"I think I have the best job in the world," she says. "Nursing is one profession in which we don't have to compete with men. Nursing is never dull or tedious. More girls should come into our profession—they'd love it, too!"

Old Battle-Ax

ANONYMOUS

->»«<-

At the head of the whole nursing corps in a hospital is the superintendent of nurses. She is the boss, and what she says goes. She has got where she is only after years of devoted duty. Many difficult and some-times tragic experiences have made her seemingly tough and hard. But if she is the stuff of which great nurses, like old Battle-Ax, are made, she is a woman compounded of humor, understanding, and tender-ness.

EVERYBODY AT ST. ANDREW'S HOSPITAL, from the famous surgeons down to the orderlies, cooks, and scrub women, called her the Battle-Ax. Behind her stiff-starched, solid old back, of course. Never to her face!

Years ago, before I enrolled as a raw, romantic little proba-tioner at St. Andrew's, a large general hospital in Fairview, a flippant young interne had sent her a bright new fireman's ax as an anonymous offering on the first of April, with an at-tached card which read, "To the old Battle-Ax. Give it to 'em in the neck!" Instead of resenting the jest, the Battle-Ax, who had a shrewd sense of humor of her own, improved upon it, for she had the gift framed in a shadow box and hung in her outer office as a grim reminder to all to watch their steps. We watched them.

Her real name, obviously—as well as that of the hospital

—cannot be told here, but Sarah Jane Hill will do. Sarah Jane
Hill, R.N., superintendent of St. Andrew's Hospital and also
superintendent of nurses. She ran both services, which was
rare. She had enormous responsibility, enormous power. Students and supervisors and head nurses, orderlies, telephone
operators, cooks, and night watchmen jumped at her word of
command. She was the top boss, the big shot, absolute czar,
and she ruled with an iron hand.

Glancing back over the years, I can see the influence of the
Battle-Ax upon my career. First, crude little probationer. Then
student and graduate R.N. A year in the psychopathic ward
of a big public hospital. Free-lance nursing in private homes.
Five months on twenty-four hour duty with a mental patient
—a wealthy manufacturer with a homicidal urge. At night I
had to sleep in the same room with him and keep the door
locked so that he couldn't escape. Every time his bed creaked,
I jerked wide awake. Even now a creaking bed makes me
start. Finally, superintendent of a hospital. And looking back
over those early beginnings I can see the strong hand of the
Battle-Ax shaping the shy, ignorant girl that I was, like a raw
lump of protoplasm, kneading and hammering and beating me
into a design. A painful process. But I learned about hospitals
from her.

"It's just like a jail! I feel as if I were in a chain gang! I'm
going home!"

Pretty little Rose Donovan, who came from my own home
town, was bawling her eyes out on my bed. It was our first
week as probationers at St. Andrew's. Forty of us, mostly
small-town or country girls eighteen or nineteen years of age,
with a smattering of older ones. Two teachers and one sloe-
eyed divorcee like a sulky flame, who hated and despised men,

and told you about it every chance she got. Personally, I thought she liked them too well.

St. Andrew's, a fine old private hospital, built when the city was young, on the lake front, and now surrounded by docks and warehouses, was a gray-stone structure grimy with soot; its bleak outlines, seen at twilight and dawn, reminded one of a jail. And the iron discipline which the Battle-Ax maintained was like a vise clamped into the raw flesh. Rules, rules, rules! Rules for rising, rules for eating, rules for going to bed. Every waking hour parceled out by rule. All lights out in the nurses' home by 9:30 P.M. No talking in the corridors. Placards on doors, "Silence! Night Nurse." One late leave a week. No overnight leaves for probationers. No familiarities with internes, orderlies, or male employees. We couldn't take a free step without falling over a "Don't." And then fines, forfeits, reprimands.

And so Rose Donovan decided she didn't care about being a nurse, after all. "You're foolish to stick it out," she said. "No three-year prison term for me! I'd rather be a scrub woman and call my soul my own." She left that afternoon.

But it was when we first went on the wards that the real tug of war came. One girl fainted and packed her trunk for home that night. The first day I couldn't choke down a single mouthful at lunch. I had had to make a bed containing a man who had been blackjacked for fifty cents. The first week my fingers trembled whenever I touched a patient, and I had wild, jumbled dreams at night.

Of course we had daily classroom work, the ward instructors were right over us, supervising every step of the procedures, and the charge nurse jacked us up between times. But even so, during those first weeks we were nothing but a rank nuisance on the wards; and one of the convalescent patients screamed bloody murder when Sue Meadows, a new probie, gave him a third-degree burn with a hot-water bag; and later he wrote a letter of complaint to the board. Sue was another who didn't make the grade. She's married now, with four children. . . . Remember that hot-water bag, Sue?

With the acutely sick we were always under strict supervision; but we had to get our training, and the Battle-Ax believed in weeding out the unfit early in the game and in giving us the baptism of fire. She had a gift for appearing at the psychological moment, and she was here and there and everywhere at unexpected times. A kind of electric current ran around the ward when we saw her large, massive figure looming suddenly in the doorway, her heavy face, impassive as a priest's, forking a look out of her small, deep-set eyes which took stock of the whole scene.

"Battle-Ax!" somebody would mutter, and we fell on our jobs like fiends. Sometimes she only glanced in, but occasionally she entered, looked on at some medication, or lifted a two-hundred-pound sick man as gently as an incubator baby, shifting him to a more comfortable position, or stood chatting with the patients. Sometimes these visitations occurred daily for a week; in that case they were storm signals; occasionally the squall passed harmlessly overhead, but at other times the lightning struck.

There was Miss Carr, the divorcee who protested too loudly that she hated men. Why she selected nursing as a career was a dark mystery, for she loathed waiting on the sick and constantly shirked her work. Her morning and evening toilets of the patients were a hasty lick and a dab; she talked to them about her troubles when they had troubles of their own. She was consistently dishonest in her charting, and encouraged social attentions from patients, internes, and male attendants. It was her habit to slip out in her street clothes, carrying her uniform wrapped in a parcel, for a stolen jamboree, and then appear later, dressed for duty, with a plausible excuse. And in the ordered rush and scramble of a busy hospital these excuses were not always X-rayed and analyzed. Moreover, she was crafty in placating head nurses and in shifting blame. The rest of us looked on at these scandalous proceedings but kept our own counsel. The Battle-Ax did her own policing and did not encourage spies.

"It's a wicked shame!" Celia Dunbar exclaimed indignantly to me one night. "When I relieved Miss Carr on the babies' ward today, half a dozen of the poor little mites were howling their heads off because they had not been changed—and yet she had charted that care. When I spoke to her about it she laughed and said, 'Let the brats bawl! It's good for their lungs.' Maltreating a baby! If it happens again, I'm going to speak out. I don't care if it is tattling."

But Celia was not driven to the disagreeable duty of reporting a fellow probationer for negligence, for in due course Miss Carr reported herself. She overstayed her late leave one night —excuse, her watch had stopped. At lunch Miss Carr gaily informed us what her line of defense would be. First offense. Terribly sorry and ashamed. Loved nursing, loved St. Andrew's, loved Miss Hill. A flood of penitent tears. She rehearsed the scene with gusto and made a bet that she could outsmart the old ogre and get off with a reprimand. But the Battle-Ax had started a quiet investigation of her own, calling probationers, head nurses, and supervisors; and when Miss Carr appeared, handkerchief to her eyes, she was blown right out of the landscape with one terrific machine-gun blast.

At St. Andrew's there was, as I have said, a rule banning flirtatious conduct.

Kissing, on such occasions, was a high misdemeanor and crime. Accordingly, when Celia Dunbar was caught in the hall by a supervisor and reported for this capital offense, it created a sensation. And there was still worse to come! For two days later she failed to appear on duty, and a hasty check-up of her room revealed the fact that her bed had not been slept in. Celia had stayed out all night. Without leave. Phew! Damaging deductions were inevitable. The student nurses were agog with excitement. Celia Dunbar!

Celia was a slim, gay, larky girl with glossy dark curls, wide gray eyes with long lashes and sooty shadows underneath, rose-petal cheeks, and a wide, laughing mouth. The patients adored her, for she had an instinctive gift for bedside nursing, and the masculine contingent on the staff swarmed around her like bees. When she held a baby in her arms, Dr. Deems on the maternity service, unmarried, would stare at her fixedly and a dreamy, faraway look would come into his eyes. She had that effect on men. During her numerous absences in the students' infirmary—for she was always catching colds—the internes inquired anxiously after her, and her room was loaded with flowers. And when this happens to a student nurse, the girl in question has It. Celia had It to the nth degree. The odd thing, under the circumstances, was that the other nurses liked her, too, for usually when a girl is a favorite with men, the members of her own sex begin to sharpen their daggers.

By this time we had settled down solidly into harness, and the rigid discipline which had chafed us so at first had become, through habit, as comfortable and easy as an old shoe. For the pressure on us was terrific. Drive, drive, drive. Jumping into our uniforms like firemen in the raw dawn, snatching a hasty breakfast, on the wards for eight hours, running up and down stairs, lifting heavy patients, pulling around beds and shifting cumbrous screens; and in addition to this eight-hour day of hard manual labor two and three hours daily of class work, so that night found us, with aching backs and throbbing feet, glad to flop into bed.

But not Celia! Her suitors kept her busy double time. She began to look pale, lose weight, and the sooty circles deepened under her wide gray eyes.

One day the Battle-Ax summoned her to the office. That was the first call. The same night, at supper, Celia told us, laughingly, that the Battle-Ax had told her she must choose between being a nurse and a play girl. But she kept right on being a play girl, and she did not slight her work.

"Now, Mrs. Jones," she would say to the bad postoperative case who had nearly lost her baby and her life, "I'm going to stay overtime tonight and give you a manicure, so that when your husband comes he'll see what a lovely wife he's got. And how about a dash of rouge and a lipstick?"

And Mrs. Jones would be lured into forgetting her pains and her grievance that her poor darling little incubator baby was being fed with a nasty dropper by a cold-hearted nurse in a mask, as she chatted with Celia, while over in the reception room of the nurses' home a furious young interne who had an early date with her was raging under his breath.

But she was always catching colds; she developed a hacking little cough. An X ray was taken of her lungs. No lesion. Everything okay. But the doctor read her a stiff lecture about silly young idiots who tried to burn the candle at both ends. It was shortly after this that the high misdemeanor occurred and she was summoned to the superintendent's office. No one knew what took place at the formidable interview, but at its close Celia fled weeping to her bedroom, and the interne, who had likewise been summoned, emerged with a scarlet face.

"What did old Battle-Ax say?" Miss Carr, avid with curiosity, approached Celia after supper in the lounge—for this happened before Miss Carr was dismissed for the good of the service.

Celia gave her a level stare which said clearly, "None of

your business!" and turned scornfully on her heel. Miss Carr shot her a look of frozen hatred, for she liked the interne herself. Two mornings later it was discovered that Celia had been out all night. Excited groups gathered in the corridors, disregarding the "Silence! Night Nurse" signs, and Miss Carr's tongue wagged venomously all that day, and was only checked by Celia's unexpected return for supper, radiant in a new hat, new furs, and a brand-new wedding ring. Of course it was the interne.

"I just dropped in," she explained gaily, "to tell you that Harry and I are married. Miss Hill knows all about it. In fact, she advised it herself. She told us," Celia laughed, "for heaven's sake to get married and get it over with, so that Harry could put his mind on his work. She said," Celia ended triumphantly, "that I had a real vocation for nursing—but I'd better keep it inside the family circle. And Harry thinks so, too!"

It was shortly after Celia's adventure that I began to have troubles of my own—troubles so acute that they nearly wrecked my career. Their center and source was Miss O'Day, head nurse on my ward. She was a tall, harsh-featured woman in her forties, autocratic and overbearing, a stickler for forms and procedures, and without an atom of justice in her bones. She took an instantaneous dislike to me the first day, and nothing I could do pleased her. I was dumb, awkward, inefficient, lazy, slow. She criticized my work, ridiculed me before the patients and doctors, elected me to the worst backbreaking chores on the ward, kept me overtime, so that I was late to classes, and declared repeatedly to all and sundry that I would never make a nurse in the world. Why, I couldn't even make a standing bed!

The pressure that winter in the hospital was appalling. An epidemic of flu had caught the city in its full grip and St. Andrew's was crammed to the roof; beds down the aisles of the general wards, nurses and attendants sick; and those who escaped were run off their feet. Miss O'Day dogged my steps like a starving timber wolf, and I added insomnia to my woes. Of course I could have complained and begged to be shifted to another ward. But Miss Hill did not encourage complaints and she made short work of the complainers. Learning to adapt ourselves to different personalities she held to be an intrinsic part of our training, and we were expected to take potluck with head nurses as well as with patients. And so, despite Miss O'Day's persistent efforts to goad me into open rebellion— which she would triumphantly report—I decided to stick it out in silence.

"You're foolish," said Freda Hansen, the student nurse across the hall from me, one night as she gave my aching back an expert alcohol rub. "She's a born bully and she's spoiling for a fight. Well, then, give it to her! She'll ride you until you do."

"It's because she's trying so hard to make me fight that I don't want to," I replied. "It would work to her advantage, not mine. Besides, I have a theory that Miss Hill uses Miss O'Day as a kind of acid test; if a student can stand her personality, she can stand the most cantankerous patient in the world. It's a trial of strength."

"You poor fish!" jeered Freda. "You give me a pain in the neck. No cantankerous patients in mine. Life's too short. When I get out of this prison dump, I'm going to hand-pick 'em. Rich, with sweet dispositions! Unattached gentlemen preferred."

"Gold digger!"

"Sure I'm a gold digger!" she retorted stoutly. "Why not?" She was one of the best student nurses on the wards and later she threw over a fine institutional position to marry for love a penniless grocery clerk with t.b., took him out to Arizona, and turned him into a successful rancher. . . . Remember those early ambitions, Freda?

The crisis with Miss O'Day arrived unexpectedly one afternoon. Martha Laidler, the other probationer with me on Ward 4, general medical, had gone off duty leaving some of her medications unfinished. Absorbed in my own work and not responsible for her tasks, I did not even note her departure. I was down at the end of the ward, easing a heavy patient into a more comfortable position, when I heard Miss O'Day's rasping voice:

"Miss McCoy!"

I glanced up. Miss O'Day, accompanied by Miss Hill and Dr. Bruno, was standing by one of Martha's beds.

"Why didn't you give this patient her medication?" Miss O'Day demanded angrily. "It was due an hour ago." Dr. Bruno eyed me severely. Miss Hill's heavy poker face never changed. "Do I have to watch over you every minute of the time? Come here and do it at once."

I came forward slowly. Something tightened around my heart. Here was my chance for reprisal. Here was my opportunity to expose and depose the tyrant before Miss Hill, for it was an established rule that one student was not responsible for another's work. Each had her own set tasks.

Moreover, I had not yet had that particular medication in classwork and I did not know the exact procedure. My position was impregnable. I was sorely tempted to make a break for freedom. Miss Hill still watched me, impassive as a Buddha. Something within me decided against it.

I said, "Yes, Miss O'Day. I'll do it right away."

She took the last word. "You should have done it long ago!"

She moved on to the next bed with Dr. Bruno. I crossed to the ward instructor, who was sitting at her desk. "Will you please supervise this medication?" I asked in an undertone. "I've not had it in classwork and I'm not sure of the procedure. It's Miss Laidler's patient."

Miss Hill had remained chatting casually with the patient in question, but her ear was cocked in our direction. She watched while the medication was given, and then she drew me aside.

"The first time you've given that medication?" she inquired blandly.

I nodded. I knew she was giving me an opening to complain.

"Then she's not your patient?"

I shook my head; I was still raging inside.

Miss Hill regarded me impassively.

"Miss O'Day is an excellent nurse," she stated after a pause.

I did not consider her such a world beater, but my opinion had not been asked, and so I stood silent.

"This is a heavy ward. How would you like," she plumped it out suddenly, "to shift to the maternity service for a while under Miss Lucas?" Now, Miss Lucas was the best-loved graduate nurse in the entire organization, and it was like asking if I'd enjoy being transferred to heaven out of hell. But there was a joker in the offer, for she added dryly, "That is if you're finding it too hard here?"

Translated, that meant if I was finding Miss O'Day, the excellent nurse, intolerable. She was giving me another opportunity to squeal, testing me out, and an affirmative reply would mean that I was a weakling who couldn't stand the gaff.

I admired her craft in spite of my cold fury. I shook my head. "Thanks, Miss Hill. It's all right here." The lie almost choked me.

"That's fine!" she replied heartily "I'm glad you like it!" She rustled briskly away. And so I was committed to a further term of penal servitude by my own act.

That night, when Freda heard the news, she was so furious with me that she refused to give me a rubdown; she called me the world's champion jackass who deserved all I got. And I gloomily agreed with her.

The next morning on the ward Miss O'Day met me at the door. But it was a changed Miss O'Day, cordial, brimming over with the milk of human kindness. She greeted me like a long-lost sister.

"Why on earth didn't you tell me that wasn't your patient?" she chided affectionately. "But you acted exactly right! Miss Hill was very pleased with you!" I began to see daylight. The Battle-Ax had put a flea in her ear. "You should have heard the things she said! She told me she offered to shift you, but that you liked my service so well you refused. Atta girl!" And she gave me a warm elder-sister hug. My prison term was over.

I never had another instant's trouble with Miss O'Day. And in time I even came to see that she was indeed an excellent nurse.

After my graduation, a full-fledged R.N., I kept in touch with Miss Hill. Several years later, at the termination of my five months' twenty-four-hour duty with the mental case, I determined to return to Fairview for a rest. My nerves were in rags. I wanted to loaf, to get a permanent wave, buy some new clothes, go to some concerts, and forget that creaking bed. Accordingly, I wrote to Miss Hill, stating my intentions and giving her my Fairview address. Upon my arrival at the hotel I was informed by the clerk at the desk that Miss Hill had telephoned twice; I was to go right over to St. Andrew's without a moment's delay. The lady sounded urgent, he said. So, without even stopping to wash my hands, I caught a taxi and was soon outside my former chief's door. But upon one thing I was firmly determined: I would not take another job until I had a few days' rest.

As I passed through the outer office, I noted a muscular young white-coated orderly seated under the famous ax, nervously twisting his hands. It was a familiar gesture in that room! I smiled. In the inner sanctum I found Miss Hill at her desk. She nodded briefly. "Now don't sit down! I have a job for you." She glanced at her watch. "You'll just have time to make that four-thirty train." And then she explained briefly that a superintendent was wanted immediately for a new hospital in Lacy, a neighboring city. She had been consulted and had recommended me.

I gasped. Superintendent of a hospital! It was what I had always dreamed of! But to be rushed off without clothes, without a rest—

"Well," said the Battle-Ax crisply, "make up your mind, if you intend to catch that train. If you don't want the job, say so."

"I do!" I burst out, and I stammered my thanks.

She waved them brusquely away. "Just see that you live up to my recommendations," she said dryly. "And remember what a hospital's for. Now, run!"

I ran.

FROM THE JUNGLE
TO THE SLUM

Damien the Leper

BY JOHN FARROW

->>><<<-

One of the most moving and inspiring stories in the
history of nursing is the one that follows. Born
Joseph de Veuster in a Belgian hamlet in the year
1840, Damien assumed the name by which he is
known when he became a priest twenty years later.
Still later, a young monk of twenty-three, he wrote
to the Superior General of his order, explaining that
his elder brother, also a priest, could not take his
place as a member of an expedition to the Hawaiian
Islands because of illness, and asking to substitute for
his brother. The request was granted, and Damien
sailed for Hawaii. Arriving there, he was given a
small island parish. It is at this point that we pick up
the story of his devoted service to the lepers of
Molokai.

LEPROSY HAD BEEN FIRST OBSERVED [in Hawaii] in 1853. Ten
years later it had spread to such an alarming extent that the
authorities realized that some measures would have to be taken
to segregate the afflicted and to fight the disease. Efforts in
this direction were at first pitifully inadequate. A small receiving station was established near Honolulu, but such an uproar
was raised by citizens, who dreaded the proximity of the
lepers, that land was purchased on the island of Molokai in a
peninsular region, bounded by the sea on three sides and
sufficiently isolated to satisfy the most timid. In 1866 one

hundred and forty lepers were sent there, not as patients, but as *colonists!*

Land was given to them, along with the essentials needed for farming. Then they were left to fend for themselves. They, those people with rotting limbs and horribly diseased bodies, were expected to till the soil and thus, according to the ingenious plan, be self-supporting and no longer a burden to the government. Of course the absurd scheme was bound for failure, and it was a failure that meant indescribable suffering and a fearsome death to most of the unfortunate victims. All suspected of the disease were ordered to report to the proper officials and prepare to go to the settlement. But the unsavory reputation of Molokai made this decree unpopular. The natives, always a family-loving people, could not understand why they should give up loved ones, whom they were quite willing to nurse and care for.

Damien's district was not exempt from the trouble. Just about this time he reported home that

"Leprosy is beginning to be very prevalent here. There are many men covered with it. It does not cause death at once, but it is rarely cured. The disease is very dangerous, because it is highly contagious. . . ."

Within a month after he penned these ominous words a doctor and four police officials arrived in his village and in a conspicuous place posted up the cold and tersely worded announcement:

ALL LEPERS ARE REQUIRED TO REPORT THEMSELVES TO THE GOVERNMENT HEALTH AUTHORITIES WITHIN FOUR-TEEN DAYS FROM THIS DATE FOR INSPECTION AND FINAL BANISHMENT TO MOLOKAI.

The priest watched while the officials went about their grim and formidable task. For the next few weeks the village was a place of sadness. Whole families journeyed in from the outer districts to deliver a son or a husband, a wife or a daughter, to the white men in obedience to the law. They spread their mats in front of the church and there, in dejected clusters, waited for the final parting. With heavy heart Damien performed his priestly duties, hearing confessions, giving absolution, and administering the Sacraments.

As on the other islands, there were some who did not submit to their fate with peaceful resignation. One man whose wife was said to have the disease took to a deserted ravine and there from behind an improvised fort defied the authorities. From an unknown source he had procured a rifle and ammunition. When the police attempted to advance on him they were met with warning shots and a threat that if they persisted the aim would be better the next time. A siege commenced; after a few days the officials made plans for a concerted rush, and it was certain that blood would be shed. Not wanting to see this happen, Damien interceded and begged that he be allowed to try to visit the determined native and persuade him that his opposition was useless. The officials, after warning the priest that whatever he did was at his own risk, granted the request. Immediately Damien commenced the ascent to the native's stronghold. He made no attempt to conceal himself, not even when there was a savage, angry report of a rifle and the terrifying ricocheting on the rocks about him. Three times the gun spat, and then in the silence that succeeded Damien, still climbing, shouted, "It is I, your friend, Kamiano." There were no more shots, but when he reached the level of the stony rampart he was confronted with mistrustful eyes and a pointed gun. The woman was standing behind her husband. It was to her that he first addressed his pleas, but the man interrupted angrily. White men wanted to imprison his wife for the crime of having a disease which they themselves were responsible for, having brought it to the Islands. There was no answer for him except the cold, uncomforting wisdom of statistics and science. For six long hours Damien sat trying to explain the necessity for the system of segregation. He talked with un-abating fervor. The reason for his eloquence was not a belief in the merits of the leper colony but that he knew that if he failed in his arguments there were guns waiting in the valley below, guns that would probably blast life away from these two bewildered beings, this husband and wife who asked only to be left alone and together. He used this attachment as a further argument and promised that if they acceded to the law there would be no attempt at any punishment for their attempts at frustrating the authorities and that the husband would be allowed, unmolested, to accompany his wife to the settlement.

His persuasions were successful. At dusk that evening, just as the police, apprehensive for his safety, were making plans for an attack, they were surprised by the approach of the priest and the couple. Damien informed the officials of the conditions under which the natives had surrendered. It is to the credit of the police that they kept his promises. There was no attempt at any retribution or punishment and the husband was per-mitted to stay with his wife and join the melancholy con-tingent.

The lepers sailed and the more pleasant tasks of his parish occupied the priest again. His thoughts followed them across the sea, and prayers were said daily at his altar for their welfare.

A Father Leonore had at this time completed a new church at Wailuku, on the Island of Maui. This parish was the scene of a large influx of laborers, brought there to work the rapidly

growing sugar plantation. The bishop, realizing the impression
that a large and colorful ceremony would produce among
them, made arrangements for a numerous array of parish
priests to assist at the dedication.

After the rites he addressed his clergy, praising them for their
progress, but also telling them of the problems that remained
in the vicariate. At such a discussion notorious Molokai could
not be overlooked. When the bishop spoke of the dread place
his voice became gloomy. Three priests had at various times
relinquished their regular duties to make short stays; but such
visits, before the strictness of the new board of health regulations, would have to cease. In the future any man who went
to Molokai would have to remain there for the rest of his life.
As the bishop said this, his voice faltered. Even he could not
demand such a sacrifice of anybody.

However, there was no need for him to voice a further
appeal. No sooner were his words ended than four priests, one
of whom was Damien, sprang to their feet and pleaded to be
allowed to live and work among the lepers.

The superior's eyes dimmed with tears as he gazed at the
four faces, each glowing with earnestness and sincerity. It
was a hard decision to make. He looked at each of the four
young countenances that were now so ardently turned to him,
knowing well the one he picked would lose its fresh healthiness
before the savage inroads of the incurable scourge.

Damien could see his superior's indecision. "My lord," he
said, indicating his younger colleagues, "here are your new
missioners. One of them could easily take my district. . . ."
He pleaded that experience such as he already possessed would
be needed at the settlement. There could be no doubt but
that this was the man for Molokai. The episcopal hand fell on
Damien's shoulder.

"This employment," said Monsignor Maigret in a low voice

and speaking with difficulty, as though conscious he was pro-
nouncing a death sentence, "is of such a nature that I would
not have imposed it on anyone, but I gladly accept your offer."

The affair was settled. Although everybody present knew
that Damien had selected for himself a martyr's death, there
were no attempts at speeches or laudations of any kind, save
perhaps a few silent handclasps of farewell.

A steamer was waiting to take Bishop Maigret to Honolulu.
It was decided that Damien should accompany him. Thus,
one hour after the decision that had changed his life, the priest
was once again on the sea which always, for him, was the
prologue to new and unknown experience. On arrival in
Honolulu Harbor it was discovered that a batch of fifty lepers
was being shipped that very evening to the colony. The opportunity could not have been more favorable to the priest.
Once again a sudden decision was arrived at. Without even
time to purchase or collect any belongings other than one extra
shirt and his breviary, the priest and his superior, who decided
to remain with him until he reached Molokai, transferred to
the other steamer.

The gangplank was lowered, the hawsers were cast off, and
as the breach widened between the ship and the wharf, a chorus
of agonized cries rose high as the doomed and the ones who
they were leaving gazed on each other for the last time. In
fragrant clouds *leis* of flowers fluttered to the water in futile
sad observance of an old custom which says that whoever, on
leaving Honolulu, casts fresh blossoms upon the harbor waters
is certain to return.

In the dim, chill hour that precedes dawn the ship fetched
up off the portion of the coast (Kalawao) where the lepers
were to be landed. As there was no protected wharf a boat
had to be lowered. The two priests clambered down the

lurching flanks of the steamer into the lifeboat and then, with other passengers, were rowed to the shore. It was dark, and a faint haze, adding to the dim veil of the hour, obscured the coast, making it difficult for Damien, who peered through the grayness, anxious to glimpse the place where he was to spend the rest of his life.

The rest of the passengers were landed and the boat waited, ready to take back the bishop who lingered in uneasy silence. It was a difficult moment for him. Although he had been prepared, he dreaded the final moment of parting; the leaving of the young priest on this unfriendly beach. His hesitation was broken by the coxswain of the boat shouting impatiently that he could not wait much longer. Unable to find words for Damien, the bishop turned to the gaping lepers who surrounded them.

"So far, my children," he told them in their own language, "you have been left alone and uncared for. But you shall be so no longer. I have brought you one who will be a father to you, and who loves you so much that for your welfare and for the sake of your immortal souls he does not hesitate to become one of you; to live and die with you."

He raised his hand in benediction, and Damien fell to his knees with bared head. There were a few hasty words of farewell and in a profound silence the staring crowd watched the bishop walk to the boat—that link with an outside world which for them had ceased to exist. Even the lowliest seaman of its crew, crouching over outthrust oars, was in their eyes surrounded with glamour. The coxswain shouted a hoarse command, blades dipped in the swell. Damien, with a sense of great solitude settling around him, watched the boat become smaller until it reached the side of the steamer.

There was a mournful hoot from the ship's whistle, the

vessel turned and, with rigging etched against the pale morning light, headed toward the open sea.

Farewell, indeed, it was for Damien.

He was alone and he felt his loneliness. It was hard to feel any kinship with the poor creatures that crowded about him.

There were a few whom the ravages of the disease had not yet blemished to a perceptible degree. The worst cases he was yet to see, for they were too crippled to walk the three rocky miles that separated their miserable quarters from the ocean.

The priest was escorted to the assortment of makeshift huts which, huddled together in wretched squalor, was called by courtesy a village. As in any other native village there were women and children sitting in front of their abodes but there was a grim difference here; the women whom Damien saw were not laughing or gossiping or engaged in busy domestic tasks. They sat still and listless. The children seemed equally apathetic.

The huts were primitive affairs, affording little shelter, and made for the most part of untrimmed boughs and branches leaned together and roughly thatched with long grass.

Not a corner of the dreadful place did Damien leave unvisited on that day of his arrival. He tramped everywhere, his heart aching at the pitiful misery that confronted him on all sides.

In those depressing surroundings Damien found one sign of a better influence in the shape of a small wooden chapel. To him, who was so full of faith, it must have been a welcome moment when he stepped across the threshold.

From the beginning he realized that in order to win the respect and confidence of the settlement inmates it would be necessary to show absolutely no fear or repulsion at their disease. There was no doctor at the colony, and he made it part of his daily routine to visit the bedridden cases and change their bandages and wash their sores.

The problem of food was not neglected. The original plan of the authorities had been that the lepers should farm and raise their own supplies. After the failure of this ridiculous scheme a small schooner had been sent to the island at irregular intervals with whatever provisions could be bought cheap in Honolulu.

Father Damien rapidly caused a change. Supplies were increased and a steamer with a fixed schedule soon supplanted the haphazard visits of a schooner.

Other necessities, such as clothing, bandages, and medicines, were also the subject of his incessant pleas to the authorities.

Another of his earlier objects of reform was the "hospital," a tumble-down shed where among scenes of unparalleled horror the friendless dying were deposited to spend their last hours in unheeded misery. Damien rebuilt the building, installed cots, persuaded a few of the more healthy lepers to work as nurses, and personally washed and bandaged the sores and wounds of each inmate. This latter task he did every morning. It is interesting to note that as late as 1887, just two years before his own end, he was still engaged at the same task.

The days went by. If their passage was slow and made tedious with the uninterrupted repetition of his work, or if because of that same reason they sped by with merciful haste, no one was ever to know. It seems that surely there were times when even he must have paused, overwhelmed with the apparent hopelessness of his position.

Not one of the reforms established by him was accomplished with ease, and, having been established, not one would have survived a week without his aggressive support.

He lived, of course, with the utmost simplicity. Two meals

a day were his limit: a late morning meal, usually consisting of rice, meat, coffee, and a few "hardtack" biscuits; and in the evening he would "take what was left at dinner, with a cup of tea, the water for which I boil over a lamp. I only take two meals a day. It is rarely I taste anything between. You see I live very well; I do not starve and I am not much at home in the daytime."

After darkness he would light the lamp and read his breviary; then, perhaps, he would spend a half-hour or so at his useful hobby of carpentering, or he might write to, or reread one of the precious letters from home.

Letters from his family were, except for an occasional religious paper, his only link with Europe. The demands of his own little world, whose boundaries began with the rocky precipices a few miles behind, were enough to keep him occupied. To him the plight of his lepers was infinitely more tragic than the distant drama of history.

The years marched on. Damien was yet in his thirties, still young according to the world's reckoning, but regarded as a patriarch by the outcasts of Molokai. He looked the part. In appearance he seemed at least ten years more than his actual age. Toil had thickened his figure from slimness to a broad sturdiness. Hardships and rigorous self-discipline had exacted an inevitable toll on his face. Gray was beginning to temper his hair. His eyes, already weakened through excessive reading during student days, were suffering from the continual glare of the tropic sun.

If laughter was rare to him it did not mean that he was of the lugubrious type who, on the basis of their own somber righteousness, seek to prevent the pleasures of others. He encouraged rather than frowned upon a pleasing custom that had come into being whereby a score or so of his parishioners would come and visit him every day while he had his evening meal. Squatting in a circle around him, for he ate outdoors, they would regale each other and him with noisy stories and anecdotes. Good-humored arguments might take place, a guitar perhaps would tinkle and always, sooner or later, songs would be chanted. The hour was in the late afternoon, just before dusk, when the long shadows cooled the island and the oblique rays of the sinking sun, with a final brightness, made the treetops dance in a golden shimmer. These gatherings grew to be such popular functions that they acquired, in the native language, the definite and poetic name of "Time-of-peace-between-night-and-day," and as the light faded and Damien sipped his tea before the friendly eyes of his audience, he would sometimes be forced to answer innumerable questions about his own country and village, but more often he would be allowed to remain silent while the others talked. The Hawaiians like to talk, and the lepers were no exception to this racial trait. With a folklore that is exceedingly rich to draw upon there was never any scarcity of legends. Damien, who enjoyed the ancient tales, spent many a pleasant hour listening to the exploits of the early Hawaiian heroes.

After he had finished eating Damien would brew a kettle of tea over a small lamp. As six battered cups were all he possessed it would become a matter of boisterous competition among his guests to decide who was to drink with him. His pipe would be lit, and everybody was free to borrow it for a few puffs. He showed the same hospitality to all and in everything. The door of his hut was never locked and as he was absent most of the day he let it be known that anybody who so wished could enter and rest on his bed. By this time he seems to have been absolutely without fear as far as the disease was concerned. Having won the lepers' confidence, he adhered to his policy of never showing repulsion or disgust at their ailment.

When in 1881 the then ruling monarch of the Kingdom of

Hawaii, Kalahaua, accompanied by his chamberlain and commissioner of immigration (both Americans) and a suitable retinue, set out on a tour of the world, the royal duties were assumed by the king's sister, the Princess Liliuokalani, who, as heir apparent to the throne, had been proclaimed regent during his majesty's absence.

It was only natural that the attention of such a woman should be turned to notorious Molokai. Damien's name was not unknown in Honolulu, and reports of his courage were even beginning, much to his dismay, to spread to more distant countries.

When the regent made known her intention of visiting Molokai the officials were profoundly surprised, even shocked. But she was not to be dissuaded. Two weeks after her decision, flanked by a numerous party, she embarked aboard the steamer *Lehua*.

Damien had worked feverishly in making preparations for his distinguished guest. When the *Lehua*, presenting a brave sight with new paint glimmering in the morning sunlight and with the large crimson-and-gold royal standard fluttering splendidly from her main-truck, dropped anchor off Kalaupapa landing, her passengers could see a crowd of some eight hundred lepers, all of the colony able to walk, drawn up on the beach to receive them. The sashes and banners of the burial associations had been utilized for the occasion, and of course the band was in great evidence. Near the landing stood a triumphal arch festooned with wild flowers; around it the priest had mustered the less terrifying of his charges into two ranks, to form a guard of honor. The children were placed to scatter flowers along the pathway of the royal procession.

Great and happy and sincere was the commotion as the princess was rowed ashore. Cheers were given and her name shouted with wild enthusiasm as the band blared the national anthem. The ovation continued as she set foot on the beach, and after having greeted Damien was escorted by him through the garlanded arch, past the guard of honor, to a dais that had been especially erected for this moment.

Onto the platform she stepped, a tall woman with a majestic appearance suited to her birth, wearing a black dress unadorned save for a sprinkling of flowers around the neck. Visibly moved by the welcome, she held up a hand and the cheers gradually died away to an expectant silence. She gazed upon the sea of disease-ravaged yet cheerful faces that we so eagerly turned to her and so obviously waiting for the words that never came, for try as she could the princess was not able to find voice. Her lips trembled and tears flooded her eyes, and turning to one of her staff, she mades a gesture for him to speak in her stead.

The schedule of the visit called for only one hour ashore but she insisted on remaining the entire day, with the priest showing her almost every part of the settlement, but beyond his simple explanations and her questions there was not much conversation between them. The peasant-born priest from Belgium and the daughter of Polynesian chieftains seemed to understand each other well without many words.

She told Damien it was hard to believe that anyone should stay in this tragic place of his own free will.

Her words were a tribute, but he seemed puzzled.

"It is my work," he explained with simplicity. "You see, madame, they are my parishioners."

Before replying, her eyes roved from him to the pitiful crowd that followed close behind.

"Your parishioners," she said softly, "and my people."

It was night before the anxious captain of the *Lehua* was informed that his royal passenger was ready to return. And it was a fine night. High above the tall, dark outline of the island precipices rolled a majestic bank of clouds from behind which spilled the glow of a full moon; a veil of stars curtained the rest of the sky; the sea was flat and on the beach the dancing flames and shifting shadows of festive bonfires made the beauty complete.

The leavetaking of the princess was inexpressibly sad. The lepers chanted *oliolis*, melancholy recitatives that, like the sagas sung by the bards of ancient Ireland, told of the glories and victories of the ancestors of the royal house of Hawaii. Sometimes all would sing in chorus, sometimes the women would wail alone, or it might be that the men would carry the refrain for a few minutes; the chanting never ceased until the steamer had sailed. Nor was music the only ceremony. Flanking the princess as she walked to the landing were men carrying lighted *kukui* nuts bound in ti leaves, torches that blazed and flared and gave off eddying clouds of white smoke. The burning of those nuts was one of the zealously guarded symbols of the ancient royalty and was a distinction granted only to personal retainers. Solemnly, and showing their pride at being allowed this privilege, the leprous torchbearers stood as erect as their disease allowed them, grouped in a half circle, a sad parody of a military formation, while their princess said farewell to the priest.

The moment was not without its note of gallantry. As she stepped into the waiting boat she extended her hand to Damien who, with a sudden impulse, bent low and kissed it.

The oars dipped and the boat surged forward, and every time each oar touched the water a shower of phosphorescent sparks was kindled. The chanting rose in volume, and Liliuo-kalani, silhouetted against the sky and sea, standing in the stern sheets of the little boat, waved good-bye to her subjects.

"*Aloha*," she cried. "*Aloha*" . . . Then, sitting down and disregarding the presence of the seamen and her attendants, she wept uncontrollably.

When the ship arrived in Honolulu the newspapers were filled with enthusiastic praise for the princess. Every detail of the trip was printed. Damien was the subject of a flood of glowing adjectives.

The pace of his work never slackened nor did his consideration for his charges lessen. Always impatient with the ways of officialdom, his wranglings with them now increased in number and vehemence.

This harsher side of him was revealed only to ordinary men, for his ill-temper never touched the lepers. To them he always remained the same, a kind father, sometimes stern perhaps, but always just and understanding and ready to help. Whatever he did, he did for his lepers. Their life was his life; he had made it so since he first put foot on the island.

Then he had been a young man, splendid in health and burning with zeal, to whom no obstacle was too large to overcome. But now, after twelve years on Molokai, he seemed, to the interested eyes of a visiting official, "an embittered old man." This was in 1885, when he actually was only forty-five years old.

That same year, on the morning of the first Sunday in June, he was celebrating early Mass in the chapel at Kalawao with his customary fervor, chanting the Latin in his deep, steady voice and showing no other emotion than his usual devotion. In fact, during the entire ritual of that morning he did nothing to indicate that the Mass might be different from the many he had celebrated before.

It was a hot day. In the sultry, crowded interior the congregation, all of whom were invalids in varying stages of the disease, probably welcomed the relaxation that comes with the end of the Gospel. Perhaps, even, there were a few that, with a torpor induced by the heat, might have been inclined to drowsiness as the priest, standing before the altar, divested himself of chasuble and maniple in preparation for the sermon.

But after he had advanced to the sanctuary rail (he had no pulpit), and began to talk, all signs of lethargy among his listeners quickly vanished. There was a sudden shocked stir, for instead of addressing them with the usual *My brethren*, he had said, slowly and significantly, *We lepers*. . . .

It was his way of telling them that he had contracted their disease.

"Why don't you rest, Father Damien?" one of his parishioners asked.

"Rest?" he retorted. "It's no time to rest now, when there is so much left to do and my time is so short!"

No doubt was there as to whether he had the disease. A few months previous to his dramatic announcement he had, while shaving, upset a kettle of boiling water on his bare foot; although the scalding liquid had seared his skin there had been no pain. Lack of sensibility is one of the first stages of leprosy, a symptom which he, of course, instantly recognized. Disturbing as this knowledge must have been, he nevertheless made no mention of it until Dr. Arning, a German physician, came to the settlement.

When the two men met on the beach and were introduced by an officer from the steamer, the doctor, who was an enthusiastic admirer of Damien's work, was astonished and chagrined to find the priest seemingly ignoring his proffered hand; surprise, however, gave way to concern when Damien, as they walked to the village, excused himself for his apparently unfriendly act by saying, in the most matter-of-fact manner, as though it were of little consequence, that he believed he had contracted leprosy.

The doctor made a careful diagnosis.

"I cannot bear to tell you," he said, "but what you say is true."

His distress was so evident at being forced to deliver such a terrible verdict that the priest assured him: "It is no shock to me for I have long felt sure of it."

With astounding energy he embarked on new enterprises. Perhaps he realized that the eyes of the entire settlement, and afterward those of a far wider audience, were upon him, but a new mood began to envelop him. Hitherto he had always been what is known as a serious man, but now he made it a point always to have a smile and to be cheerful on every occasion. Where, with his sick charges, he had been kind to the children, nursing, feeding, and teaching them, he now joined in their games, and it became no uncommon sight to see a dozen of the pitiable urchins frolicking around the priest, shouting and laughing, as he walked from his labors to his hut. Formerly with his hammer and chisel he had made only the most practical articles but now, if he had an hour's leisure, it would be passed by fashioning a crude toy. And in Honolulu the Sisters received requests for dolls and dolls' clothing.

As he crossed the threshold of his last year the high standards set by his restless, eager mind, the same standards that had served to make him feel that even his most prodigious accomplishments were never enough, goaded him into a whirl of frantic endeavor.

His forty-ninth birthday passed and he calmly began to prepare for death.

"I would like to be put by the side of my church," he told his assistants, "under the stout old tree where I rested so many nights before I had any other shelter."

It seemed to be the happiest period of his life, those last few months that were the threshold to his grave. With the certainty that his work would go on, a great tranquillity had come to soothe his restless nature and he was content for the end. He made his will, leaving what few belongings he had to be disposed of at the bishop's discretion. "How happy I am to have given all to Monseigneur!" he told Father Wendelin. "Now I die poor, having nothing of my own."

Memories occasionally occupied him. He talked of the past, of his early days at the settlement, of the bleak morning on which he had landed. "They are all gone," he said, referring to the lepers who had met him on that day. "And I shall be seeing them soon." Sometimes he talked of home; he lived his life over again and wondered whether they remembered him at his first parish.

Near midnight, on the eve of Palm Sunday, he was given Holy Communion for the last time; it was evident he could not survive much longer, and as the news was made known, an anxious, silent crowd gathered around his house to wait in melancholy vigil. Life persisted in him during the entire Sunday. For the most part he was unconscious, although occasionally his eyes would flicker open and he would try to smile at those who watched by his bed. As earthly things slowly receded from his vision, he seemed to see two other figures in the room, one at his head, one at his feet, but he did not say who they were.

Candles were lit that night. In the early hours of the morning he died, the end coming as he had wished it, without a struggle, as though he were falling asleep.

He was dead, but the bell that tolled his requiem, the bell he had fastened with his own hands on the tiny steeple of St. Philomena's, sent an echo that was to be heard around the world. Damien and Molokai suddenly became familiar names in every country as editors, in an enthusiastic chorus of sympathy and eulogy, spread the news of the priest's death.

The universal pity that had been stirred by the priest's sacrifice did not cease with the newspaper laudations. The world now realized that, while he was gone, other lepers re-mained, dying and living in the same shameful distress as he had found on Molokai.

Damien might be dead, but his story was not finished, nor is it yet, for his death marked the beginning of a great cam-paign to stamp out the disease and to make happier the lives of lepers.

In the Australian Bush

BY SISTER ELIZABETH KENNY

->>><<<-

With Salk and Sabin vaccines we now have powerful weapons for winning the battle against polio. But in the early part of the present century the causes and cure of the disease remained a profound and baffling mystery. Physicians all over the world were attempting unsuccessfully to cope with the problem. It remained for a young nurse in the Australian bush to discover, almost by accident, a method of treatment which later was to be accepted, after many battles and much discouragement, by reputable physicians.

I WAS TWENTY-THREE when I first encountered the disease that had baffled medical science since the days of the Pharaohs, the disease known as infantile paralysis.

One late autumn evening I drove up to the door of the humble dwelling of an employee of a cattle owner. I had been there just six months before to bathe and dress the warm limbs of the newly born that had come to gladden the hearts of the parents. I was expecting nothing more serious than the usual teething trouble or an upset stomach as a result of improper feeding. The shy young stockman, or cowboy, who had summoned me, had given me no details.

Nurses everywhere, I imagine, feel a strangely mystic link between themselves and the baby at whose birth they have officiated. They have guided the mother through the valley of shadows and have felt the first rose-leaf touch of the little body. Thirty years ago the young nurse bore the responsibility of both lives. Without assistance, with none of the modern conveniences, in the crudest of settings, we were called upon to act in every emergency and to bring all the comfort we could to the sick. Now, even in the most remote parts of Australia, an expectant mother can be brought by plane or swift motor ambulance to a clean, well-equipped hospital, where all that modern science can provide smoothes the way for both mother and nurse.

In those days, the days of which I speak, the only available help was usually many miles distant. But a certain sense of security was always mine when I saw the campfire burning in the yard and a saddled horse tethered to a nearby tree. There was something reassuring in the sound of a fresh young Australian voice singing some well-known song. I knew that horse and man were ready at a moment's notice to travel many miles for help that might be sorely needed. The same songs have since been heard on the rocky steeps of Gallipoli, in the mud of Flanders, on the sun-scorched sands of the African desert, and among the hills of ancient Greece—songs sung for freedom and the protection of the mothers of the men who sang them.

During my brief stay at the cottage six months before I had grown to love the little two-year-old sister of the new baby boy, and as I rode into the yard I expected to see her come running out to meet me. But all was quiet. The setting sun shed its soft light on the autumn flowers that surrounded even the least pretentious of Australian homes—great masses of bronze and white and pink chrysanthemums and dahlias. But the silence disturbed me. The shy youngsters usually swarm out to greet the bush nurse, and I was full of fears when the frantic mother, only a year older than I, opened the door to me.

There were four children in the family, but it was the little girl, my special pet, who was ill. She lay upon a cot in the most alarming attitude. One knee was drawn up toward the face and the foot was pointed downward. The little heel was twisted and turned outward, or abducted, as we say. One arm lay with flexed elbow across the chest. Any attempt to straighten a member caused the child extreme pain. The little golden-haired girl who had gladdened my former stay in this humble home was indeed very sick, and with an ailment that was unknown to me.

For the moment I felt beaten, since I did not know what to do until I could get the necessary medical advice. This must come by telegram. The nearest telegraph office was several miles away. There was nothing for it but to ride out, send my message, and await the answer. The waiting seemed years instead of hours, and during that interval a very agitated father of seven children came to me with the appalling announcement that his ten-year-old son and his four-year-old daughter had been taken with what he called the "cow disease," and neither of them could stand or walk.

"They went lame yesterday, just like the cattle have been doing for the past two or three weeks," he explained, "and today they can't move."

The distance between the two homes was four miles.

In my anxious suspense the reply to my telegram was anything but heartening. It read, "Infantile paralysis. No known treatment. Do the best you can with the symptoms presenting themselves." It was signed by Dr. Aeneas McDonnell.

Within the space of a few days three more cases were reported to me, making six in all. I shall deal here with only the first case, as it was typical in respect to both the symptoms and the treatment which I employed.

Fortunately, perhaps, I was completely ignorant of the

orthodox theory of the disease. It had not been encountered by any of the members of the medical profession with whom I had been associated. In those remote days it had not been prevalent and if it occurred at all it must have been left unobserved by the country practitioner. I felt as if I had been confronted by a blank wall, but panic plays no part in the training of a nurse.

The obvious agony of the little golden-haired patient called for immediate action of some sort. The cruel shortening of the muscles affected, the wild fear expressed in the once-laughing blue eyes, the tenseness and the terror of contact even with the loving arms of the almost distracted mother, were sufficient to wring the heart of anyone who witnessed them. My family upbringing and my feeling of utter helplessness prompted me to close my eyes and pray for divine guidance.

I set to work at once to relieve the mounting distress that was evident in the whole being of the disease-racked child. I saw the little girl's efforts to protect the painfully contracting muscles from stretch that would increase the pain, and from my knowledge of muscle structure I was aware that if this contraction could not be overcome, deformity and perhaps other most undesirable complications would result. I knew the relaxing power of heat. I filled a frying pan with salt, placed it over the fire, then poured it into a bag and applied it to the leg that was giving the most pain. After an anxious wait I saw that no relief followed the application. I then prepared a linseed-meal poultice, but the weight of this seemed only to increase the pain.

At last I tore a blanket made from soft Australian wool into suitable strips and wrung them out of boiling water. These I wrapped gently about the poor tortured muscles. The whimpering of the child ceased almost immediately, and after a few more applications her eyes closed slowly and she fell asleep.

Oh sleep, Oh sleep, I thought gratefully. Nature's soft nurse!

After a short while, however, the little slumberer awoke fretfully and cried out, "I want them rags that wells my legs!"

And so the little girl of the Australian bushland unknowingly spoke her approval of a treatment that was one day to become the subject of much heated debate among the learned members of the medical world.

It was not long afterward that I had an experience which I feel impelled to include in this narrative, because it is a strong defense of the most maligned race on earth, the Australian aborigines. Wherever my wanderings have taken me, I have always heard the black natives of Australia described as the lowest form of humanity, possessing all of its vices and none of its virtues. I remember how, as children, we used eagerly to wait and watch for the yearly "walk about," as they called it, of the Kookabookerra aborigines when they would leave their hunting grounds and come in to visit the various homesteads on their annual begging tour. Their race has almost vanished from the earth, and as a respectful salute to them I must here set down an episode that brought me close to at least one member of these people.

In my remote nursing area I was called to the bedside of a twelve-year-old girl whose father was miles away at a shearing shed. The mother some time before had been thrown from a horse, had incurred several fractured ribs, and was depending on her small daughter to look after the house and the two younger sons. The sudden illness of the little girl had naturally brought fear and confusion to the household.

I saddled my horse and started out in the heavy heat of the late afternoon, keeping the sun on my right shoulder, as I had been directed, until I came to a traveling stock route. After some involved maneuvers I finally saw the blossoming wattles where I was to make a sharp left turn into the forest. By the time these miles had been covered, the sky was blackly overcast by a regal Australian thunderstorm.

The birds and the shy animals of the bush thereupon must have beheld something strangely new to them—an unclad human being. For, to keep my clothing dry, I immediately got down from my horse, disrobed, made a bundle of my clothes which I placed on a stump; then, unsaddling my horse, I set the saddle atop the bundle and over that threw a waterproof blanket I carried with me. I, myself, garbed like Eve—who never was faced, I am sure, with the problem of finding a dry outfit when the one she possessed became drenched!—sat topping everything on the stump, enjoying a wonderful shower bath while my horse turned his back to the storm. I recommend this mode of ablution to anyone who is not bashful in the presence of gum trees, birds, and the inquisitive koala bear.

When the rain ceased, I dressed and hurried on my way.

Arriving eventually at my destination, I was greatly disturbed at the condition of the little girl. Her abdominal pain seemed to indicate appendicitis, and my first thought was to get a messenger if possible. The nearest neighbor was three miles away, but there was a stock road nearer by upon which there was one chance in a hundred that someone might be passing.

My first act, then, before making any examination, was to open the door of the cottage, step out into the night, and deliver the Australian call that is known from the Gulf of Carpentaria to the Great Australian Bight. Standing on the stump of a tree, I called "Coo-ee-ee," which means, "Come to me!" It may mean, "Come and eat your food!" or "Come and share my sorrow!" or "Come, you are wanted!" But its urgency is ever "Come to me!"

After the third call I stopped to listen in the faint hope

that I had been heard. There came no answering voice, but in the great silence I heard the soft clap-clap of the hands of a lubra—Australian negress—from the clearing beyond the scrub, and the faint, monotonous chant of the aborigines to the accompaniment of their curious instruments, the digeree-doo. A corroboree was in progress!

Fear seized me, for I had heard weird tales of dire happenings to those who had interfered with the corroboree. I stood transfixed for a short space, and suddenly the voices ceased. The silence that almost hurts descended upon the bushland. With dread great in my heart, I hastily returned to the house and bolted the door behind me.

Upon examining the little girl, I felt my blood literally run cold. True enough, she had symptoms of appendicitis, but she also had the symptoms which a short time before had grown so familiar to me and which, when reported, had been diagnosed as infantile paralysis.

I knew that if I were wrong and the child really had appendicitis, the application of hot foments would be disastrous, resulting probably in a rupture of the abscess and almost certain death out here in the remote bushland. How I longed at that moment for means to send out a message seeking advice!

Suddenly my heart stood still. The family dog had risen from the floor with a warning growl toward the door. He had heard someone approaching. I knew that any white man would herald his coming with the responsive "coo-ee." But the ears of the bush dwellers are attuned to distinguish noises, and listening I heard the sound of one footstep followed by the tap of a peg. I breathed a sigh of relief.

I knew that Chief Waddy Mundooee, as he was known to his tribe, had come to help. Some time before I had seen this black trying to hobble around with one leg half gone. The loss of his leg remained a sacred secret with him, but I had arranged to have the stump attended, and had also got him a useful peg leg. I had thus acquired his eternal gratitude. When he arrived back among his people with the amazing limb, he became known immediately as "Waddy Mundooee." "Waddy" means wood, and "mundooee" means foot.

I was not afraid to open the door to Waddy Mundooee, who straightway greeted me with, "White fella Mary wantum something. White fella Mary in trouble."

Out of sheer gratitude I could have thrown my arms about Waddy, but I was deterred by the fact that he stood almost stark naked in the moonlight, surrounded by his braves. In keeping with the tribal custom, his ribs and cheekbones were painted terrifyingly white, while ornamental feathers stuck to the dried blood of gashes in his legs, self-inflicted for the purpose. Around their waists Waddy and his braves wore strings with natty appendages of opossum tails.

Waddy's messenger, wearing a red tablecloth I had tossed out to cover his nakedness, mounted my horse and rode off with the telegram I had hastily prepared asking for advice on the child's abdominal condition. In good time the warrior returned with a wire from Dr. McDonnell to the effect that abdominal muscles were frequently affected in infantile paralysis, and to treat them accordingly. I am happy to say that the little girl made a very rapid recovery.

Since that long-gone day I have frequently come in contact with patients who have had operations for appendicitis only to discover subsequently that they were suffering from infantile paralysis.

The aborigines of Australia are not the insensate animals that many ethnologists would make them out to be! They may be dirty, they may be lazy, but they are capable of displaying a heroism on occasion that would put many a white man to shame. I know of one young black prisoner who was being taken to jail by a policeman. In fording a river, the police horse got out of his depth and threw the officer into the treacherous stream. The young black boy jumped from his horse, smashed his handcuffs on the stump of a tree, leaped into the river, and saved the life of his custodian.

In more recent years some German fliers in attempting to fly to Australia crashed on a barren part of the west coast of our continent and were found emaciated and only half alive by a tribe of blacks. The tribe brought water in their bark coolamans, or buckets, and gave them drink. They also caught fish and cooked it for them, and when they found the fliers too weak to masticate the fish, they performed this service for them as well. Then they prepared bark stretchers and carried them to the nearest white man's residence.

When I saw Dr. Aeneas McDonnell some time later and told him how I had treated my young bush patients, he stared at me and asked,

"Do you mean to tell me they recovered?"

"Why, of course!" I said.

He looked incredulous at first. "Elizabeth," he said finally, "you have treated those youngsters for symptoms exactly the opposite of the symptoms recognized by the orthodox medical men of today."

"You told me to do the best I could with the symptoms that presented themselves," I reminded him.

"Yes, I know," he said thoughtfully. Then he fetched from his library some impressive-looking tomes that dealt with this baffling disease. What I discovered in their pages left me speechless with astonishment. It simply could not be that I, in contraposition to wise authorities, had blundered upon a treatment that had met with success!

"But—they don't say anything here about *spasm*," I managed to point out. "And that's what I saw—and treated!"

He gave me a long, troubled look. "The way before you is going to be hard," he observed prophetically. "You are going to know heartbreak and humiliation. Sorrow will be your lot from this day forward. But if you have the courage to carry on, a great reward will be yours. The great cities of the earth will bid you welcome."

Hospital of the Queen's Heart

BY PRINCESS ILEANA

->>><<<-

Princess Ileana, the beautiful daughter of Queen Marie of Romania, was forced by Communist pressure to leave her native land and now resides with her children in Massachusetts. Early in 1944, while still in Romania, she journeyed to the small town of Bran in the Carpathian Mountains, where she owned a small castle inherited from her mother. The country was in an uproar. Wounded soldiers were everywhere. Ileana decided that the greatest assistance she could give would be to open a hospital. Despite almost incredible difficulties, she managed to do so, and served there herself as a nurse and general factotum. The patients in this little out-of-the-way spot in the hills were utterly unlike those one would be apt to encounter in a big city, but their problems were those of sick people everywhere. Princess Ileana gives us fascinating glimpses of them in the following adventure.

VERY EARLY ONE GLORIOUS FALL MORNING, even before I had arrived at the hospital, a gypsy family, mother, father, and little daughter, appeared in the hospital courtyard and stood expectantly, waiting to be let in and their needs inquired into. Sister Ginia, the night nurse, brought them into the hospital and established them in the waiting room. Then she went to get Dr. Puscariu, and just as he appeared, a short while later, I arrived, glowing and buoyant from my short, brisk walk down from the castle in the crisp, chilly morning. I was full of energy and well-being, eager for my day's work.

The gypsies raised their hands to their lips in a shy peasant gesture as I came in.

"*Bine ai venit*—welcome to you," I said. "This is your daughter? What is wrong?"

"She is sick with her knee, Highness," answered the mother. "We waited a long time for it to get better, but it did not. So we have brought her to you. We have carried her for many days' journey."

The parents were basketmakers and mushroom gatherers. They were filthy and slovenly. The father was spare and tall, as the gypsy men often are, bearded, and wearing a tattered tunic and trousers which were bound about the calves of his legs with cords. He had thrown a piece of old carpeting about his shoulders for warmth. I cannot describe the mother as being dressed. She was covered with layers of smelly rags from which the colors had long since disappeared, and they were tied with a rope about her spare middle. She looked a hundred years old, so wrinkled and weatherbeaten was she, although I knew she could not have been much older than I.

But the little daughter was one of the most enchanting beings I have ever set eyes upon. She was about twelve years of age, small-boned and delicate; her small oval face was perfectly modeled. She had jet-black hair which was twisted about her head in a braided coronet, and her eyes were large, violet-blue, fringed with black eyelashes as thick as ferns. How she was ever produced by these two I could not imagine. I looked at her, fascinated—one rarely sees such flawless beauty and perfection in flesh and blood. Obviously her parents felt the same way. They completely adored her.

Unlike her parents, she was decently dressed in a red skirt wrapped tightly about her little hips and a silver-embroidered blouse. Around her head was swathed a white scarf, and a dark-blue wool cloak fell from her shoulders. She looked like something that had fallen out of a fairy tale; she was a lost-princess thrown in among beggars.

Puscariu and I took her into the dispensary and lifted her onto the examining table. The parents followed and stood nearby, their anxious, adoring eyes fixed on their daughter.

We drew up her skirt. The sight that met our eyes was sickening. The knee was swollen to twice its normal size, and from several places at once oozed yellow, evil-smelling matter.

Dr. Puscariu, after a few moments of examination, picked her up and carried her into the X-ray room. We made several plates, the anxious parents standing in the doorway, peering in awe and a little fright at the fearsome machine, yet entrusting their angel confidently to my care and protection.

Then we turned the child over to the nurse to bathe and put to bed, the parents still in close attendance, silent, dignified, watchful yet confident. Puscariu and I studied the X rays. Without any doubt at all this was tuberculosis of the bone.

"You'll have to tell the parents—not I," he said dryly. "More than likely the girl's leg will have to be amputated."

I was filled with dismay at the prospect of bearing such tidings, but as I turned away from the X rays I knew that it had to be done. There was no mistake in our diagnosis.

What a way, I thought, to start such a glorious day. I had come with such joy and zest to this day's work, and now I found myself plunged into tragedy, and the news I must give to these simple people would be a crushing blow.

I called them into the waiting room and sat them down. Sit in my presence? Indeed, yes—I wished it. They did so, stiff and ill at ease. I explained as well as I could what the matter was with their daughter's knee. Using simple language, I told them about the rottenness of the bone inside the knee, and how the poison of it was seeping into the child's blood, slowly working its way through her body, and that in order to save her life perhaps we would have to take her leg away.

The mother, horrified, covered her mouth with her shaking hands, and then turned to look at her husband sitting impassively beside her, his eyes upon me. Together they shook their heads in stunned silence. After several moments she found her voice.

"No, no, Altetza," she faltered. "Do not cut off her leg. It is not possible to. What would poor people like us do without legs? She must keep her leg. She really needs it very much. She cannot earn a living without it. We cannot keep her without a leg."

How well I understood her—I knew the absolute, utter poverty of the gypsies. Actually, their bodies were all they possessed. To deprive a gypsy of a limb is to deprive him of even more than a necessity or a prized possession. It is to take away a part of his life.

Once more I explained, searching for even simpler language, and I reminded her that, after all, it was her child she loved, not her child's leg. Surely, I said, if it was a choice between dying or remaining alive with only one leg, it was better for the girl to live, even though crippled.

"Do you not understand," I went on, "that your daughter is going to die if nothing is done for the knee? There is nothing we can do to save her except to operate."

"Yes, yes, I do understand you," moaned the mother. "But please be kind to her and do not cut off her leg!"

I explained patiently that it wasn't that I wanted to cut off her leg. In fact, I greatly wanted not to. I tried to make her understand that it wasn't my idea, nor was the decision mine. It was the result of examinations that the doctor and I had made, and the pictures that the machine had made of the bone inside the knee. It was they that indicated that the leg might have to come off, and I was only telling her what the examination and the X-ray pictures had revealed.

"Surely," I finished, "you and your husband love your child more than you love her leg!"

"Oh, yes," agreed the mother distractedly. "We do. We do understand. Still, Domnitza," she pleaded, "we will be very grateful to you if you will please not cut off her leg."

Tears of desperation sprang into my eyes. How could I ever make her understand that it wasn't dependent upon me whether or not the child would keep her leg? I had nothing to do with it! Once more I went through the entire explanation.

The woman again listened closely and obediently, then she glanced at her husband, sitting mute and observant. He shook his head and she turned back to me. They spoke together, urgently but very respectfully.

"Yes, we understand what you say. We do, and we trust you, Highness. But just the same, please, we would be so grateful if you do not cut off our daughter's leg."

I had run out of arguments. There was nothing more I could add to my explanations. I finally assured them that we would do our best. I told them as plainly as I could that even if we did not amputate they must know that her leg would be stiff, and it would remain that way for the rest of her life.

They rose, looking at me with suffering eyes, saying nothing, accepting my judgment.

The doctor and I made further examination of the girl's knee. She was one of the sweetest creatures I have ever had anything to do with. She was patient and obedient; she did whatever we expected of her without protest, and, in all our study of that unfortunate knee, never once did she cry out although we must have hurt her very much.

Finally, Dr. Puscariu decided there was a very slight chance that the leg might not be amputated, that scraping the diseased bone might be sufficient, and a knitting together of the knee bones thereafter be possible. But we couldn't know certainly until we had opened the knee.

On the day of the operation I explained all this to the mother.

"Please," she said, "may I be with my child while you operate?"

I was disconcerted by the request. My immediate impulse was to say No with great finality. But I caught myself in time and said that I would ask the doctor who was going to do the operation.

I thought the idea was mad, but Puscariu was wiser than I.

"Let her come," he said. "You know, if we don't allow her to stay with us, she may think that we are doing mischief to her daughter. She'll be happier if we let her stay, even if she doesn't understand what is happening."

"But that's just it," I protested. "How will she stand the sight of it? It is going to be horrid to watch."

"Put her far enough away from the table," he advised. "You will find in the end that it is better so."

So I returned to the mother and told her that the doctor had given permission for her to be with her daughter if she would stay quietly in a corner of the room while we operated. I would tell her what was going on, and I promised to tell her the truth.

"That I know, Domnitza," she said simply.

We dressed her up in a sterile gown over her rags, and tied sterile gauze about her head, tucking up her lanky locks. We settled her on a high stool in the corner of the operating room. Then Puscariu, Badillo, and I turned to our job of scrubbing. Sister Heidi brought in the little patient and put her on the table. She smiled at the mother and they exchanged a few words, but true to her promise the gypsy woman remained where she was.

Badillo administered the anesthetic, and the child's eyes remained fixed on me, above the ether cone, until they closed in unconsciousness.

I felt dreadfully disturbed. There seemed to be a ridiculous great sob mounting inside me, entirely unprofessional and very upsetting. I had become greatly attached to this beautiful gypsy child, and I felt a kinship, a compassion, and respect for the mother who did not understand, who feared for her child, yet trusted me with the blindness of an animal. I caught myself up sternly. This was a job that had to be done, I told myself. I must think of the operation, not of my feelings. Enough of this sentimentality over the little girl lying before me and her mother sitting like an anxious good child on her stool, her hands in her lap, in the corner over there.

We began. The intense light of the lamp . . . the draped white sheets . . . Puscariu across the table, remote . . . his precise, deliberate hands . . . the shining knives . . . the scalpel that bit deeply into the bone . . . then the knee flexed. A few incisive thrusts and the bones were separated. Matter flowed; there seemed to be quarts of it. Sister Heidi mopped it up. More knives . . . more chiseling, deep, deep in . . . and thank God, we reached healthy bone.

Full of gratitude, I looked up momentarily, my hands still occupied, and called over to the motionless mother.

"The leg is all right. We will not need to cut it off."

Her expressionless waiting face lit up with joy. She uttered no word of relief or thanks to us, but slipping down off the high stool to her knees, she made the sign of the cross and unashamedly addressed herself to God, thanking Him aloud that her child's leg had been saved.

We went on with the operation, listening to her humbly as we worked. She was quite oblivious of us. Then she rose and clambered back onto her stool, folded her hands again in her lap, and relapsed once more into immobility, her eyes upon us.

When we finally wheeled the child out of the operating room and took her back to her bed in the ward, the mother followed silently, a little way behind us so as not to be, perhaps, in the way of the great doctors and the wonder-working Domnitza. Quietly, without invitation, she sat herself down beside her daughter's bed. She studied the sleeping girl's face for a moment and then turned to me, and, for the first time in the days I had known her, I saw her smile. Her weatherbeaten face was rapturous, illumined, completely transfigured. I was startled to see shining out at me from beneath the deep-cut, aged network of lines and dullness of expression her daughter's radiant beauty. Almost shocked, I knew that once—perhaps not too many years ago—she had looked like this fairy child.

Leaving her there beside the bed, I went out of the ward with mixed feelings. I was grateful and glad that the operation had gone so successfully, and I was full of admiration for the devotion of the gypsy mother. But I was suddenly afflicted with sadness that the delicate, unearthly beauty of this young child was destined to be obliterated, that she would become like this crone, her mother, in a few short, aging years of the exposure, physical hardship, and continual childbearing of the gypsy woman's life.

The child recovered after long nursing and care, and one day the following spring the three of them, the silent gypsy father, the devoted mother, and the daughter who limped painfully now as she walked, but on her two legs, crossed the hospital courtyard and the bridge, turned down the road, and vanished back into the mountains whence they had come.

I recall the girl's beauty yet with unbelief and pleasure, and instantly thereafter her mother's dull, spiritless, furrowed countenance appears before me, out of which the daughter's beauty had shone incredibly for a moment when she smiled, and then died down again like a flame into its ashes.

A young man, married for only three months, came to us with a long history of stomach trouble, suddenly grown worse. After examination we felt sure it was cancer. When we opened him we found cancer indeed, and so far advanced that Puscariu knew further intervention was useless. We closed him up without doing anything.

The patient's mother and young wife sat in the waiting room during the operation, and once again it was my heavy-hearted duty to be the bearer of bad tidings. So I went to them. They rose anxiously as I came in. They were peasants; the girl had graduated from the University of Bucharest and had taught school for a year or two before she married and came to a village near Bran to live.

I greeted them, said briefly that the patient was still under anesthetic, and we sat down together. I wondered a little frantically how to begin, and then I began in the middle, for I could think of no preliminaries.

"Look," I said earnestly to the girl, my hands nervously tightened into fists in the lap of my white apron. "You do love your husband, don't you?"

She nodded, her eyes fixed on mine.

"And you've been happy together? Your marriage is a good one?"

Her eyes lit up instantly. "Oh, yes, Domnitza," she said quickly. "We are very happy."

"Well, my dear," I went on, "you will have a chance to prove how much you love him. You are going to have to love him as you never did before, and in a much harder way."

She sat very still, her eyes still on my face.

"The operation on your husband has not been successful. In fact, it was hardly an operation at all. Your husband has cancer, so badly that we cannot do anything for him."

"Is he going to die?" she interrupted in a small, steady voice, agony in her eyes.

"Yes." I made no qualifications. She had asked a straight, courageous question, worthy of a straightforward answer. "But you can do something wonderful for him before he does."

"He need never know the truth. If you love him enough you can make him believe that all is well with him, that the operation was a success, and he will get well. He is not going to live very long, and these last months of his life are in your hands. You can make them whatever you choose—gloriously happy or full of misery.

"Today we did our best for him in the operating room. It amounted to just exactly nothing. Everything, now, is up to you."

She heard me through, her eyes serious and comprehending. Tears trickled down her face as I ceased speaking.

"I understand, Domnitza," she said. "Thank you very much. I will know the things to do."

The mother leaned back against the wall while her daughter-in-law and I talked. In peasant fashion, she had covered her mouth with her hands, and now she stood up, glanced at the icon, and crossed herself.

"If this is the will of God," she said, "the Lord giveth and the Lord taketh away. We will make his last days happy."

None of us lied to the young man; we said nothing either way, but he took for granted that the operation had been a successful one. Every day during his convalescence his wife came to visit him. She brought him flowers and little nonsensical gifts, and their laughter sounded through the ward as they opened them together. Everyone shared their fun. There seemed to be no shadow upon them. She played her role admirably.

But when she left the ward after carefree, loving farewells, I was always waiting for her in the passage. She used to lay her head against my shoulder and sob silently in my arms. I did not try to speak comfort to her for there were no words to be said, but she knew that I understood her ordeal, and that I loved her.

We duly discharged her husband, and they went home together. He lived for six months. Soon after he died, his wife went to Bucharest to resume her teaching, but first she came to Bran to tell me the outcome of her tragic, loving guile.

"We had all the happiness of a long married life rolled into those months," she said. "Because every hour might be his last one, I tried to make each one as perfect as I could. It wasn't hard, for really it all consisted of little things—not hours or days, but moments. You can always take care of the moments! And then I discovered that I was doing it for myself, for my own pleasure and satisfaction. I cannot tell you how our happiness grew, Domnitza—and our love, so fast and so deep—in so short a while. Perhaps because there was no time for silly little quarrels, or my wanting my own way, or wasting precious time in foolish things that don't matter.

"I never knew that there was such happiness in the world. I'm certain that I would never have found it otherwise—only through the loss that I knew was going to come.

"Domnitza"—she leaned toward me earnestly—"why do we need to be on the edge of the grave to learn this? Just you think—how wonderful if he and I could have had the joy for many years that we had for a few months! But would we, if he hadn't been so ill, and you hadn't taught me to put him before myself?"

I was silent, for I was thinking, Who knows?

She answered her own question. "I think it is a question of knowing that such a marriage is possible, and then working at it—taking the trouble and the pains to make it turn out."

We had an unremitting struggle to prevent patients from eating food brought in to them surreptitiously by their families. The ways and means they found of hiding it were varied and often original, and our game of finding it was often exasperating and sometimes hilarious. One of our chores at the end of visiting day was to make a routine search for it, for, try as we might to persuade them, the patients would never admit to having any. We looked beneath bedclothes, under mattresses and pillows, under the bathtubs, on window sills behind the curtains, in the windowboxes, and even in the wastebaskets. We collected the food, located its owners, scolded a little, labeled it and put it in the pantry, to be given at mealtime. However, once in a while we were outwitted, and a new hiding place was found.

We had with us for a while an old peasant woman whom we operated upon for cancer of the stomach. She was the most cheerful old woman I have ever known. Nothing worried her. She had a brown wrinkled face like a leftover apple in the spring, white hair that surrounded her head like an aureole, for her head kerchief was always slipping off, and a merry, dry, cackling laugh. To judge from her casualness and the scant attention she paid herself one would think that the operation was of no more importance than a scratch on her finger.

The operation went well, her condition was good, she was obedient, and her progress was uneventful and unremarkable until her third day. On making rounds that morning we discovered her sitting bolt upright in bed, her rumpled, blue-striped hospital johnny unbuttoned, happy and very pleased with herself. She was thoroughly enjoying pickles which she was eating out of a half-emptied bottle.

Mild and gentle Dr. Puscariu exploded in wrath. For once he hit the ceiling, and very effective he was, too. Who was responsible for this outrage? A patient eating pickles on the third day after a stomach resection, indeed!

We took them away from her and made her lie down again. She was in tears, like a greedy child who has been deprived of forbidden jam. I coaxed her to tell me where the pickles had been hidden and how she got them, for the usual ground had been gone over the evening before in our customary search for hidden victuals, and nothing had been found in her bed.

At last, with sniffles and sobs, she confessed that her family had hidden them in the stove in the center of the ward—it was summer and the stoves were cold. She had got out of bed, crossed the room, taken them out of their hiding place, and back to bed with her—she did so like pickles for breakfast!

I will add, since I myself am one of those persons of inquiring mind who always want to know the end of a story, that the old lady was none the worse for walking about and eating pickles when she should have been flat on her back and having broths. She recovered duly and returned to her mountain cottage, her peasant constitution as ironclad as before.

Another old peasant woman who afforded us great amusement came to the hospital with cancer of the rectum. The operation was successful and she was our guest for six months —and when I say "guest" I am being quite literal. She came from a dreadful little shack in the mountains; she had no family and no means whatsoever. She had lived all her life in the roughest and crudest of surroundings. When she came to us she hardly knew how to use a bed, she had no appreciation at all of such cold and repellent things as sheets, and she viewed the bathroom with awe and suspicion.

But before she left us she became a lady. She complained to me if the nurse had not done her hair properly, or if her sheets had not been changed. She kept her bedside table orderly with a precision that was mathematical. She wished her hospital bedgown to be fresh and unrumpled; she preferred the pink stripes to the blue. We discovered that she took her johnny off at night after the lights had been put out, in order to keep it unwrinkled, for we had not enough of them for the patients to change every day. She became absurdly fussy and demanding, and niceties hitherto completely unknown were matters of great importance to her. Her pretensions were a source of continual amusement to us, and the news of her latest foible was a daily conversational tidbit in the staff dining room.

Finally she recovered and left us to return to her hovel on the mountain. One day she made the trip back to the hospital to visit us and to bring what she could to pay for her operation and care. Clutched in one hand were four leeks, freshly pulled from the earth which still clung to their roots, and in the other hand a pound of goat's-milk cheese. Of her hospital vanities and airs there was no trace. She had reverted!

Christmas came. We made ready for it with our usual joy and anticipation. My children came home from school for their holidays, as children do everywhere at this season. The convalescent soldiers went out one gray, wintry afternoon to cut down the beautiful symmetrical fir tree they had picked out weeks before for the hospital's Christmas tree. Singing carols, they dragged it back over the snow, several ropes tied to it, each man hauling on one. The very act of singing and listening to Christmas carols is a kindler of joy. Our soldiers' voices carried clearly through the keen, early winter twilight, and we heard them coming long before they reached the courtyard. We went to the doors to listen and felt our hearts warm and lift to the familiar airs. Thus we heard the first carols of the season—always an event—and we felt that Christmas had been ushered in.

We set up the tree in a ward which at the moment was empty. Patients and staff shared in trimming it; we used chains of colored paper and bits of ribbon cut in strips and pasted in links which the children and the bed patients had been making for weeks, gilded nuts, and apples hung from strings. Precious hoarded candles tipped each branch, waiting to be lit.

I had a useful gift of clothing for each member of the staff, and for every patient we had secured a small icon and prayer book and a sewing kit. The sewing kits came from the American Junior Red Cross—I wondered if the children who contributed them ever imagined how much pleasure they gave.

The Glee Club under Dr. Puscariu's direction had been practicing the old carols. We cut pine and fir branches and decked the wards with them; their nostalgic scent overpowered and banished the usual soap-and-antiseptic hospital atmosphere. As Christmas Eve approached and our small preparations were complete, every one of us felt the same thrill and expectancy that we had known on the other Christmases in happier times. Oppression notwithstanding, Christmas was still magic—it had not changed.

On Christmas Eve I laid aside my familiar red uniform and its white apron and coif and I put on a silver evening gown with a little clinging train. I took my remaining jewels out of their hiding place—my mother's beautiful sapphire-and-diamond diadem, my diamond bracelets, the great diamond cross hung on my grandmother's ropes of pearls, my diamond-and-ruby earrings. I put them on.

How strange and unfamiliar I looked, staring back at

myself from my dressing-room mirror. I knew that I was looking at a ghost from the past as I surveyed my splendor. (Did I know it was the last time? How did I know? . . .)

The children came clamoring into my room, dressed in their best, and we gaily started out, crunching down the dark, snowy village street to the hospital and the Christmas Eve party.

The staff and the ambulatory patients had assembled, and there was a gasp of pleasure when I took off my fur coat and head shawl and my shining gown, glittering jewels, and the diadem appeared. The nurse they knew and loved had turned into a *domnitza* of the past. They were delighted; they knew I had done my best to honor them by wearing the finest I had, the splendor and prestige of yesterday—theirs as well as mine—which I was sharing with them once again. I was not out of place in this guise, here in my country hospital with my simple people. My magnificence was not a gesture of superiority; indeed, thus I was more a part of them than ever.

Sister Lorie had dressed up her fat little daughter as a diminutive Father Christmas, and the other tiny children ran about as small Christmas angels, in little white nightgowns and white-and-gold paper wings which sometimes hung askew.

We began our Christmas party with the reading of the story of the Nativity according to St. Luke. And then followed the distribution of gifts, interspersed with carols. The staff and patients together presented me with a huge bouquet of my favorite flowers, freesias. Today, when I find freesias in a florist shop and smell their overpowering sweetness almost giddily, I am transported back into that white-walled room full of the Christmas fragrance of evergreen and burning wax candles, its warm orange curtains drawn across the windows shutting out the night and the threatening new world. The great Christmas tree mounts toward the ceiling, its candles blazing, and about it are grouped these people, my people—the excited children with their shining faces, Dr. Puscariu and his family, Dr. John and Dr. Lucy, Barbu, the gardener, Captain Boeru, Maria, Anna and her Josef, Badillo, Max, dear Noelle who had come from Bran-Poarta for the celebration, Ioana and Vasile, never far apart, usually hand in hand, all the nurses, Rosa and the other patients—dear, familiar, lost faces all, wreathed in smiles, turned toward me in affection and comradeship. . . .

I moved among them, distributing the gifts with the merry assistance of my children, and then we went through the wards to the bed patients, accompanied by the carolers and all the others of the staff. Eyes lit up as I came in my glittering finery. They called me their Christmas princess, and there was the same tone of affection and possessiveness in their voices as they said it that was in the "Domnitza!" "Domnitza!" of everyday demands and urgencies and needs.

Afterward we had our simple Christmas feast—little cakes, *cozonac*, our traditional, tall-loaved holiday bread, and wine. There were more carols, dancing to an accordion and fiddle played by two of our soldiers, and then we said our good nights.

My heart was filled to the brim as my family and I walked home that Christmas Eve. The children were chattering in excitement around me, and I politely, absently, answered them, but within I felt an almost holy silence. Danger, privation, anxiety, we of Spitalul Inima Reginei shared them together, yes, but we shared more than these. We shared love and dependence upon each other, the good companionship of hard work and mutual trust. We had the best part of life. Ah, I was a wealthy woman, I thought. I had the love and trust of true and simple people. I knew an unbreakable bond with them—the service of others.

As I walked, I lifted my heart to the still white stars in that cold, black winter sky. "Glory to God in the highest, and on earth, peace, good will to men," we are told the angels sang in a sky full of glory that first Christmas Eve. But I could only say silently, my heart so full of gratitude that it was near to breaking:

"Thank you, God—oh, thank you!"

Nurses on Horseback

BY ERNEST POOLE

→»«←

We come closer to home in this description of how
one of the most famous nursing organizations in the
world, the Frontier Nursing Service of Kentucky,
began. It is the story not only of one devoted leader,
Mary Breckinridge, who was responsible for it all,
but also of many fearless and tireless women such as
Hannah O'Driscoll, the Irish nurse who came to
serve the poverty-stricken mountaineers. Not least,
it is the story of college students who act as horse
couriers during their vacations. The experiences of
all of them are worthy to stand with the greatest in
the nursing tradition of service to humanity.

DOWN IN THE KENTUCKY MOUNTAINS snow was falling, late
at night, in a lonely region cold and still, the giant beech trees
white like ghosts, and the small cottage on the hillside dark, its
occupants asleep. But a dog began to bark inside as a voice
called up from the trail below:

"Hello, nurses! Hello, hello!"

A window was opened, a nurse looked out and saw a man
in an overcoat with a lantern on a shaggy mule.

"That you, Mr. Rainey?"

"Yes. My woman's punishin' mighty bad. We didn't aim
to ask you to ride out on such a turrible night, but—"

"That's all right. I'm used to it. I'll be right down," the
nurse replied. And a few minutes later out she came, dressed in

a heavy sheepskin coat and boots and breeches, forty-pound saddlebags over her shoulder, and a layette under one arm. She quickly saddled her horse in the barn, threw her flashlight on the leather gear to make sure of girths and straps, then mounted; and following the man down a steep path to the snow-covered trail, she was off on a three-hour ride to the log cabin in the hills where a child would soon be born. And she took it all as a matter of course. She was used to it. It was part of her job. She'd been out on scores of nights like that. For hers was one of the nine stations of the Frontier Nursing Service, and that is the kind of service they aim to give to the mountaineers.

"If the father can come for the nurse, the nurse will get to the mother," they say. And so they have done, no matter what the weather. Trained nurse-midwives in the hills, on call at all hours day and night, they ride to lonely cabins to bring new life into the world and save the life already there. It means hard riding on rocky trails, up icy slopes where the mountaineer may have to get off his mule with an ax and chop out the ice ahead; and in the floods of early spring the nurse may have to swim her horse over swollen rivers and creeks. She rides with heavy saddlebags packed for all emergencies and with a "hurricane lantern" or torch, for in the cabin there may be no light but that of the open fire, and no doctor will be there. Two lives will be dependent on the nurse and her alone.

Mary Breckinridge, the woman responsible for it all, had been away on a speaking trip at the time when I went down; but from Lexington that night she came up with me by train; and getting off at daybreak at Hazard, a big mining town hung with smoke in sluggish columns, through which I caught glimpses, on steep hillsides close about, of coal mines, breakers, miners' cabins, we breakfasted in a lunchroom and then set out by automobile for her home, some twenty-five miles away.

Our road wound in and out through wooded hills of slate and sandstone, with almost perpendicular little fields of corn and rye. The sun rose and cleared the mists and clothed the hills in rich warm russets, leaving blue and purple shadows in the deep-cut creeks below. And all the mines were left behind and we passed rough log cabins now, with stout sandstone chimneys and split-oak shingles on their roofs, with tiny barns and corncribs, white geese and chickens, pigs and mules. We met a boy in a dismal old car, which had apparently broken down. He had bought it, he informed us, for five dollars and a pistol and half-a-dozen bushels of corn. We passed others on the road, men with miners' lamps in their caps, others with rifles, hunting squirrels. Quiet people, tragic people. Our young driver was the last of a family long engaged in one of the bloody mountain feuds. I thought of feuds and moonshiners and the stories of John Fox. But my attention soon returned to the gracious woman at my side.

A fine-looking woman of middle age, rather short of stature, her strong, appealing, sensitive face lights up in a quick, wonderful smile, and her voice, so low at other times, becomes dynamic when she speaks of "seeing through" the present to the future of this work for frontier mothers and babies and children all over the land.

She comes of one of the oldest and most noted families in the South. When she was a little girl, Mary Breckinridge lived for twelve winters in Washington and later for about two years over in St. Petersburg, with French and German governesses. Later she went to a Swiss school and then to one in Connecticut. From the public men who came to her father's house in Washington, the growing girl heard many discussions of big national questions that affected rural life, and she came to feel that the health and welfare of the people on the soil were vital to the progress of our whole American civilization. To prepare herself for service, she took the stiff training as a nurse at St. Luke's Hospital in New York.

World War I began and she went to France with Anne Morgan and worked hard for several years taking care of small French children. But her thoughts kept coming back to Kentucky and to the mothers and children among the Kentucky mountaineers. For she had long known of the urgent need for doctors and for nurses there.

When she had come back home, she proposed to make a demonstration of what intelligent nursing could do to safeguard the lives of mothers and children on our many forgotten frontiers, to point the way to other such regions all over the United States.

In the counties of Leslie, Knott, and Owsley, covering a mountain region of about a thousand square miles, she made a survey of conditions affecting the plan she had in mind. With a population of twenty-nine thousand there were only three little towns of from two to three hundred inhabitants each. All the rest of the mountaineers lived in lonely cabins and shacks scattered along the rivers and up the creeks and branches that made deep cuts into the hills. Those narrow canyons were their homes. A few of the men went away to work in the coal mines and on the railroads outside, but the greater part stayed in the hills.

The women and children helped in the fields, looked after the cabins and the livestock, raised a little garden truck, and drew the water and cut the wood. The women made wonderful "crazy quilts," and some of the men made splint-bottomed chairs, and a few old crones still carded and spun and dyed the wool for homemade clothing. In the hills the game, so plentiful in the days of Daniel Boone, had long ago been shot away. In the streams the fish had been dynamited by men who came in from the mining towns and made their river hauls at night. For most of the people in the hills corn pone and potatoes and pork were their food, three times a day, year in and year out.

Poor people, desperately poor. More than 99 per cent were white, Americans of the old stock, come once from England, Scotland, and Wales. Some of them were Presbyterians. More were Baptists. "Holy Rollers" some were called. Many had no religion at all. An old people on an old frontier. Gone was most of the vigor and hope of their forefathers, the pioneers, but not their pride. Slow-moving, quiet, low-voiced men, they were quick to shoot when they felt that their rights or their honor were concerned. Moonshiners fought sheriffs and families fought families, sometimes until all the men in each family were dead.

But they could be hospitable to a stranger at the gate; and though some were suspicious at first, the rest liked Mary Breckinridge. They knew her name. She was of their kin. So they took her in. Scores of nights she slept in crowded cabins, sometimes having to share a bed. And rising with the family long before the daylight, often as early as two o'clock, she breakfasted on pork and corn bread and saddled her horse and rode away. Using on her many rides thirteen horses and three mules, she rode nearly seven hundred miles, watching, questioning, listening, giving help and advice to sick mothers and children, learning where the midwives lived, and making long trips to their cabins and shacks far up the rougher creeks and branches.

"Granny women," the midwives were called, because nearly all of them were rugged, gnarled old mountaineers. One of them was the county jailer. Practically all the rest worked with their men upon the soil, looked after the mules and chickens and hogs, and cooked and washed and spun and wove. Most had raised big families. One old woman had "raised eight and lost about as many more." Between them were wide variations both in cleanliness and intelligence. Only four of the fifty-three had information out of books. One had been "a pure scholar" in her day and "knew all the words in the blue-backed speller." Most could neither read nor write, and what midwifery they knew had been learned by watching other old crones.

Though some were silent at the start, the rest of them soon opened up and told Mary Breckinridge what they had learned. They had not begun their practice, it had been thrust upon them. As neighbors they had been called in.

"Somebody had to be around to cotch the babies," one of them said.

Two had "cotched" their last babies at ninety. One said she had delivered about seven hundred and sixty in all, and another over a thousand. She could tell by marks she had made in a book. They had begun on cows and sows. Most of them had no equipment. When called to a delivery, they knew they would find in the cabin hog's grease to use on their unwashed hands; and that, they told her, was enough. They rarely had a doctor's aid, for it took physicians in towns outside from six to twenty hours on horseback to reach such patients in the hills. For her services, the "granny" charged only from two dollars to five.

Into a crowded cabin she came; and there, whenever possible, she kept her patient out of bed. In most cases the crisis took place on the knees of the father of the child or with the mother standing up. Most of the mothers worked in the fields right up to the time of confinement and were up again in three or four days, or even a few hours. And this worked fine, the "grannies" said, with young mothers of fourteen;

but "old mothers" of twenty-two, who had borne half-a-dozen babies like that, began to show the effects of it all. So things went wrong, lives hung in the balance. And the midwives then recited ancient "spells" from the Bible or laid beneath the bed an ax, edge up, to stop a hemorrhage, or treated the patients with teas they had brewed from herbs made out of barks and roots, more often with tea made from soot. Or they labored hard with greasy hands, called in old quack doctors, who knew no more than they did, and together they would work all day and on all through the tragic night.

And though the average midwife claimed that, in most of her hundreds of cases, she had saved both mother and child, she remembered those cases that had gone wrong, for they were haunting memories.

So Mary Breckinridge learned about the conditions she would have to meet. In order to prepare herself, since there were no midwifery training schools for nurses here, she went to London and took the training at the British Hospital for Mothers and Babies; and she supplemented that by a first-hand study of the work of the famous Queen's Nurses, in England and the Scottish Highlands, trained nurse-midwives.

Then she came back home again; and mustering her own resources and those of her relatives and friends, and taking counsel from physicians and experts in public health, and with the backing of the Kentucky State Board of Health, she carefully made her plan of attack. And in May 1925 she formed her organization, to provide trained nurse-midwives for neglected regions, to work in cooperation with the nearest medical service and public-health authorities, to deliver women in childbirth and safeguard the lives of little children, to care for the sick of all ages and take measures to prevent disease, and to work for economic conditions less inimical to health.

In the little village of Hyden, which was the county seat, she opened the first nursing center, herself and two trained nurse-midwives in charge.

They had no easy, quick success, for some of the mountaineers at the start were suspicious of such "brought-on women"—which means women from outside. But in saddle in all weathers the three workers found their way to hundreds of rough cabins, made friends with the children, cared for the sick, gave help and advice to the weary mothers and to others big with child, and when the time of crisis came, brought their babies into the world in ways unknown up there before. Small comforts, rest, and cleanliness. Exhausted mothers from their beds saw women cleaning, washing, scrubbing, doing things for babies and children. The news of it began to spread by word of mouth all through the hills. And the response of the county, from Hell-fer-Sartin to Hurricane creeks, over Thousand Sticks Mountain and Owl's Nest, was such that in the first four months more than five hundred mountaineers, nearly all of them women and children, had registered as patients.

Another center was soon built, on the Middle Fork River, five miles away. Wendover, she called it. She has lived there ever since. And one evening during my stay she told me this story, which illustrates how she established relations with her mountain neighbors there:

"A twelve-year-old boy, with heart disease, came to our clinic one winter's day. He belonged to an impoverished branch of the old Morgan family, proud of the men who gave their names to Morgan's Riflemen in Virginia in the Revolution, and to Morgan's Raiders later in the Civil War. Both his parents were long since dead and he had been taken in by a neighbor; and though he did not complain, the little chap was thin and pale, and his hands and feet were always cold. In the two-room cabin where he lived he could never get near the fire, he said, because there were so many 'least ones' there. So I asked him to stay with us for a while. Then he showed he was of Morgan stock by asking us if we would 'back a letter'—which means write—to the man who had given him a home. 'He was good to me,' he said. Then he pulled a nickel out of his pocket—all the money he had in the world—and gave it to me, saying: 'If you bust this nickel, you can git a stamp for that thar letter.'

"I meant to keep him here until I could take him down to Lexington for the hospital treatment he required. Later, among our patients, I found others who needed such care, an expectant mother and three small children. But just at that time the ice broke up and the Middle Fork River rose in a surging muddy tide, roaring down the narrow valley, burying the wagon road. It might be a fortnight till I could take my patients out by wagon, I learned; and the woman's case was too urgent for that. So, with the small Morgan boy, the woman, and the three little children, I crowded into a small flat-boat, piloted by a tall mountaineer. Standing with long pole in hand, he steered the whirling little craft for ten hours down that angry tide, avoiding ugly rocks and logs and shooting rapids by the score. Early that evening we came to a point where we could land and make the rest of the journey by wagon with a team of mules, up over a steep mountain trail and down to the railroad, in time to catch the late night train. The Morgan boy had been quite unperturbed by the dangerous river ride, but he'd never seen a train before and when the locomotive headlight came flashing around the bend, suddenly he clutched my arm and whispered:

" 'Won't it git us, ma'am?' "

"The mountaineers are not the kind to beg," she told me. "They're poor but far too proud for that. They're the kind who suffer in silence and won't appeal for charity. And though most of the money for each center has been given by people outside, the mountaineers have done all they could.

The help was not given in money, for little of that is seen in the hills. But land was donated, and lumber and labor. A widow sent her oldest son to help haul logs with a team of mules. For one center volunteers gave twenty-seven hundred feet of timber "on the hoof," and others offered to cut it and haul it to the sawmill, where the sawing was done free by various other volunteers. During the sawing the mill blew up and one of the men was badly burned. Twenty-four men in relays carried him on a stretcher over a long mountain trail to the nearest nursing center, where nurses dressed the ghastly burns that covered half his body.

"You women are mighty good," he said, "and if I get out of this, I'll help put up your house for you."

He died of his burns soon after that, but the other volunteer helpers kept on; and, with their aid and generous contributions from people outside, the new center was soon built. Others have been added since.

The directing center is at Wendover, a comfortable two-story log house set high up on one steep slope of a narrow valley. From a beech forest it looks down on the Middle Fork River beneath. The water was low when I was there, and women were washing clothes in the stream; but in spring it rises into a muddy, raging flood; and water, too, comes rushing down the gullies in the hillside, and bulwarks and channels of concrete are needed then to protect her home and the other buildings along the slope—cabins and small cottages, living quarters, offices, dispensary and clinic room, an apple bin and stables and barns. There is also a tiny blacksmith shop, for the horses must be shod. And fuel for the cold weather comes down a long wooden chute from a little coal mine up the hill.

The regular staff of the Service includes assistant directors, supervisors, relief nurses, nurses, and a physician in the small hospital five miles away, and nurses in the field. At Wendover there are secretaries, too, and the couriers, girl volunteers, who from cities north and south come in to help at various times during the spring and summer and fall. Without roads or adequate telephone, and only one slow daily mail, which arrives on the back of a mule, there is need as vital as life and death for quick communication, and the couriers meet it as best they can. Up early to feed and groom their mounts, often they are in the saddle all day and until late at night. Over the winding mountain trails, up rocky creek beds to the gaps, and down steep, treacherous paths they ride, carrying news and messages, guiding doctors and visitors, and taking out on horse or mule back patients who need hospital care. During my stay at Wendover a sick horse arrived from one of the centers, "mailed in," slowly led by the local postman on a mule. And this was a frequent occurrence there. The two girl couriers got to work. One was a Smith College girl. For guidance they had a couple of books on the care of horses. Between them they spent the night in his stall and so managed to pull him through. The nearest graduate "vet" was at Lexington, nearly two hundred miles away.

A boy of sixteen, from a northern school, came down about three years ago and worked as a courier all one summer. He became an expert in transporting future mothers over mountain trails on mules. As a crowning achievement, toward the end of his service he brought a woman, who was to have twins, eleven miles on muleback to the hospital for her confinement, for she was to be a difficult case. It took him four hours to make the trip, for the lady had to be handled with care. Because she had several other children, it was hard to persuade her to come; and she agreed only when allowed to bring her "least one" along on the mule. So, as he afterward remarked:

"There were practically four of them. Some job for me and for the mule!"

For an emergency case of childbirth, all other work is put aside. If need be, the whole organization centers quickly on that case. And a wonderful record has been the result. Up to December 1931 the Service had delivered more than a thousand women in the district, with the loss of only one mother at childbirth, and she was a hookworm cardiac! There was one other, a *mitral stenosis,* who died in the hospital eighteen days after delivery. Deliveries are still performed by the old native midwives, too, but their activities have waned, while the work of the Service has increased. Unfortunately most deliveries come in the winter months or in early spring, when the trails are almost impassable. Here is what one field nurse wrote in a routine report:

"A big flood Friday and Saturday smashed everything along the river on both sides. At nine o'clock on Friday night a man came for me from Wolf Creek. He had to swim down the road and we couldn't get back the way he came, so we went up Hurricane Creek on the most terrific trail. We had to swim Coon Creek four times and he waded up to his neck nine times. Reached his cabin at midnight, delivered the baby early next morning. Got home in the afternoon and was just dozing off when another call came. Had to take a boat this time. The river was so swift, the boat skimmed past the landing like a piece of driftwood. Landed safely below the ford in the M's bottom field, and reached the cabin that night. At 2 A.M. I caught an eleven-pound boy."

"We have been having a fruitful time," another nurse reported. "Five babies in three days, and one false call, and a sixth baby two days later. In three days I had about four hours' sleep. Two fried eggs and a spoonful of rice to keep me going for fifty-two hours. One case lasted thirty-one hours. Slow but steady progress all the time. It was bitterly cold. The wind blew down the chimney and kept filling the cabin with smoke. No windows, so we all sat in darkness around the fire, the smoke making our eyes burn."

They get calls from outside their districts, too.

"Set of twins just arrived at the center," a nurse reported not long ago, "their father bringing them on a mule and driving a cow in front for their keep. They are from outside our territory but we could not refuse them. The mother had died in giving them birth. They were five months old and weighed less than seven pounds each. After a hard struggle they are really beginning to pull up."

Here is one more story, from the center at Possum Bend. On a snowy Christmas Eve, with the anxious man who had come for them, both nurses started out for his home; and though the distance was only six miles, it took three hours to make the trip, because for the greater part of the way they had to wade their horses in darkness up through chilly waters amid great boulders and snow and ice, in the gulch called Hell-fer-Sartin Creek. From there by a branch of the creek they came to the steep, rocky slope known as Devil's Jump, where they dismounted and led their horses up the slippery trail to the cabin. The man took the horses to the small barn and the nurses carried their saddlebags and the layette into the house. Its single room was lighted by a little coal-oil lamp and a log fire in the hearth, and the walls were thickly papered with picture pages from magazines. A couple of neighbor women were there. In the huge iron kettle water was already boiling and one of the beds had been made with clean sheets, and there was a large assortment, too, of crazy quilts, both old and new for since her marriage at sixteen Sally, the mother, now twenty-six had been known as "the sewinest an' workinest woman on the creek."

For three long hours, with barely a cry, she went through her agony; and a little after midnight the first Christmas baby on Hell-fer-Sartin Creek was born. When told that she had an eight-pound girl, Sally looked at her daughter and said:

"I reckon she's a right pert young 'un."

Meanwhile Sam, the father, had climbed by a ladder into the small loft to tell the news to four little boys in the one big bed up there. And one by one their heads peeked down.

"What shall we call her?" Sally asked. A nurse suggested Noel Mary, and Sally seemed greatly pleased with that. Though urged to stay and "take a night," the nurses decided to go home. One of them would return next day, and one of the kindly neighbor women offered to stay there all week, to "do for Sally" in the house. So, after Merry Christmases and cups of good hot coffee, the nurses mounted and rode away. The storm had cleared and the moon shone down upon the snowy hillsides. A lovely world for Noel Mary. They reached home before the dawn.

Responding to such treatment, "the little old woman" of the mountaineer has learned to "set a heap of store" by these skilled nurses who come to her aid. With few exceptions, the native girls still marry in their early 'teens and the quick succession of babies and the hard, grinding life they lead turn some into little old women indeed by the time they are twenty-five. Both her love of the children she had borne and her dread of having another were put by one mother into these words:

"I'd ruther have another than lose one!"

For delivery and the care that is given long before and after birth, the mountaineers commonly pay not in money but in labor or kind—fodder for horses, skins of "varmints," chickens, eggs and vegetables, quilted "kivvers," or splint-bottomed chairs. A nurse told me of one mother whose fifth baby had been born after the death of her husband, and whose eldest son, aged ten, rode into the center on a mule, with a splint-bottomed chair that he had made.

"I aim to bring you more," he said, "till the baby is all paid for."

"Mac," the Scottish nurse, told me the story of Nancy, the gallant nurse from Ireland. Hannah O'Driscoll was her real name but she had always been called "Nancy," so the nurses called her that. Born in 1892, at Skibbereen in Ireland, she served three years at Malta and Constantinople during World War I, and for several years after that with the Queen's Nurses in Manchester. She worked hard and she worked well. Her superior over there wrote of her "ability, devotion, tact, and friendliness." But Nancy liked to move about this wonderful world and see new things, so later she came over here; and after working for a time in a maternity hospital up North she learned of the Frontier Nurses through one of them, a friend from Scotland, who had served with her in the war. And in the fall of 1930 Nancy came down to Kentucky.

"She was shy with new people at first," said her friend, "but then her quick humor came bubbling up and the new people soon were her friends. And she worked so hard, and loved it so down here, that she made a quick start. Had she ridden? we asked her. Oh, yes, she had, over in Ireland long ago. And she didn't like a tame horse, so she took Dixie at the start; and the wilder he was, the better she liked him. Falls didn't trouble her in the least. The very first time she went out with me he threw her and she broke her nose. But on she got, and we went to my case. All she had was a nosebleed, she said. When we got home and found she was wrong, she looked at her nose in astonishment and laughed at it.

" 'Oh, is it broken?' she said. And I remember a night in December, a pitch-dark night and freezing hard. About ten o'clock a young man of nineteen came up to the hospital on a mule, and called to me: 'Hello, hello!' His wife was about to have a baby. She was my case and I told him I'd come; but while I was getting ready, Nancy came in and heard about it.

" 'I'll just come with you! Wait!' she said. And a few minutes later we started out.

"We had to go six miles to Bull Creek. It was pitch dark, as I said before, and my horse stumbled on the trail and threw me, tore my face a bit. I looked for Nancy but she was gone, so I mounted and went on. And I'd been on the case for over two hours before she arrived. Riding behind me, she explained, she had taken a wrong turn in the dark and Dixie got lost on the mountainside.

" 'We kept coming to a cliff, and up he went each time!' she said. 'And I knew we'd been up that cliff before but I just let him take his way!'

"On he went through the thick woods. And she lost her hat and cut her face on the branches overhead. When she got to the case at last and saw that my face was bleeding, too, she burst out laughing. Then she got to work and helped me. A fine, quick worker, Nancy was. But Dixie grew sick of the cold outside, so he slipped his bridle and home he went. And after the baby had been born and the mother all attended to, we rode back together on Bessie, my mare, down Bull Creek all ashine with ice, for the weather had cleared and there was a moon. We got home for breakfast at six o'clock."

"Tell me more stories about her," I said.

"Oh, I haven't any stories," answered "Mac." "Only just bits in the day's work."

"Give me some more bits," I urged. "What else did Dixie do with her?"

She didn't keep him very long. He was sent back to Wendover and Nancy was given a fine black horse, named Raven. She rode him all the rest of her life. Raven likes to kick up a fight when other horses were about. While I was with Nancy once, on a case, we heard a great crashing of wood outside and looked out and saw Raven and Toby, my horse, kicking out at each other, hind to hind, and smashing and pulling the picket fence down. It was all we could do to get them apart.

"Raven was wild but a splendid beast, and Nancy surely loved that horse. She loved to go down steep places, too. I remember a call we had, early one morning in the spring, in a very heavy rain. The river was up, in such a tide, you couldn't possibly swim across, so Nancy and I went up over the mountain and down by a muddy trail, so steep that our horses kept sliding. Back on their haunches they would go, and I'd hear Nancy's ringing laugh through the rain. Her service cap was over one ear and the layette, wrapped in a heavy brown paper, was tucked bulging under one arm. When we came to the roaring old river below, three men were waiting, with a small flat-boat. In we got, with our saddlebags that weighed nearly fifty pounds apiece, and the layette held up over our heads, to keep it out of reach of the waves that kept splashing into the boat. Down the river for three miles we dashed, shooting rapids through the rocks; and though of course we were drenched to the skins, Nancy considered it all grand sport! We landed at a schoolhouse and took mules to Henry Couch's. There we crossed in another boat and reached our case in time to catch a nine-pound boy at noon.

"Nancy worked hard and she worked well. And she kept such accurate records of every case coming under her care that, when our superior checked them up at the time of her death, she found not an omission or mistake. But hard as she worked, she took it lightly. Her sense of humor was never far off. When an anxious man would come for her, off she would go with him to his wife and work all day on a desperate case; and then she would come home in the dark; and when we'd ask her where she'd been—

" 'Oh, accompanied by the curate,' she'd say. She loved to hear songs on my Victrola. When Harry Lauder was singing one night I said I'd have only Scotch tunes in heaven. And then Nancy said to me: 'But you'll play the Irish ones for me, Mac!' She was a beautiful dancer, too. And she had a big book about flowers in which she used to press and dry the wild flowers she found on her rides. She had another book on stars, and she would go up to the top of the hill and look at them on a clear, still night. The people liked Nancy and she liked them—although she saw them just as they were, the good and bad, the weak and the strong. She faced life in all its situations. And no matter how ugly it might be, she was always interested.

"I remember one wild Sunday night. There'd been some stabbing over a feud and a man half full of moonshine came galloping up here on a mule. His friend had been stabbed five times, he said, and once just below the heart. We saddled our horses and went on the run. Our guide was using only one stirrup. With the other he kept beating his mule. When we got to the place, a crowd came running, and by the cabin stood a man, ringing a cowbell.

" 'Help!' he kept shouting. 'Somebody help!'

"We hurried in and found a young wife wringing her hands. Her husband lay bleeding on the floor. We managed to stop the bleeding soon and made him more comfortable until a doctor could reach the spot. But Nancy then got interested in an old couple sitting there. The granny told how, when she was young, she grew jealous of her husband and ripped out his insides with a knife. And the two old people both laughed at the memory till the tears rolled out of their eyes! 'It cost all the money we had in the world but it was worth it!' the granny said. And Nancy watched in a curious way these specimens of humanity. 'Yes, I suppose it was,' she said. 'You see? They're that kind of people,' she told me on the way home at the end of the night. 'It takes all kinds of people to make a world—and what a funny world it is!'

"But though she knew life both good and bad, it was the good that she believed in. 'That's the realest part of the world,' she said. All over the district the children were crazy about the 'red-haired nurse.' Often I've seen her riding home with six 'least ones' on her horse, three before and three behind. She always *carried* her service cap.

" 'Why do you take it?' I asked her once. 'You never wear it.'

" 'Oh,' she said, 'I think the world of my fine cap. I just don't want it on my head!'

"She had lovely red hair and she liked to let the wind have a chance to blow it about. But she was so shortsighted she couldn't see things on the ground. Once I saw a snake down there.

" 'Look out,' I called. 'There's a copperhead!'

" 'I don't see any snake,' she said.

" 'He's right down there in front of your horse!'

" 'I'll just have a look!' she said. And before I could stop her, off she jumped. He struck at her but she sprang aside, and then she said admiringly: 'Oh, is that a copperhead?'

"Another time, on a windy day, we were riding down from a ridge and Nancy was ahead of me. All at once she stood up in her stirrups and began to wave her cap.

" 'What are you doing that for?' I asked.

" 'Can't you see? It's a patient—waving to us from across the valley,' she replied. I looked.

" 'Oh, no, it isn't,' I said. 'It's a man's shirt out on the line.'

"But they often did wave to her, all the same, and come out to chat when she rode by; and whenever they needed a nurse, they would ask for the redheaded one. They liked her and they liked her work. She was straight as a die with those she served, and never spoiled them. Indeed, she bullied them instead. But they came by scores to her clinic at Cutshin. The clinic there was her own idea. We warned her against it at the start, for Cutshin was a long way off, in a lonely district of the hills, and to get there your horse had to climb up over some of our steepest mountains and ford the river twice besides. More than once, with my heart in my mouth, I watched Nancy swim her horse over the wildest river in spring. Nothing could keep her away from her clinic. The mothers and children over there had no other medical care. They needed her. And that was enough. They gave her a room in a cabin and she brought curtains, a table and chairs, and made a nice little clinic there. And men, women, and children from miles around used to gather once a week and crowd around that cabin door. Roars of laughter came from inside, with Nancy's voice talking fast through it all. Joking and talking as she worked, she made it for them and for herself 'a marine holiday,' as she said. So her clinic kept growing month by month.

" 'If anything should ever happen that I couldn't go,' she said, 'you'd go with Toby, wouldn't you, Mac?'

" 'What do you mean?' I asked her. She only smiled and tossed her head.

" 'Oh, you never know in this world,' she replied, 'what's going to happen from day to day.'

"Now and then, as time went on, she began to have a pain in her side. She made light of it and went on with her work, and she rode away one morning without ever telling us that she was having another attack. She had not only her clinic, that day, but three maternity patients to examine before and after birth. The two prenatals weren't coming just right and Nancy was keeping an eye on them. Her pain must have grown to an agony—but still she kept on about her work and didn't get home till the edge of the dark. Our local committee of mountaineers was coming to supper here that night, but Nancy went up to her room.

" 'I feel pretty bad,' she told me. 'Please ask them to excuse me tonight. I'll just have some tea and go to bed.'

"The next day she was so much worse that the doctor examined her and found that she had appendicitis. The surgeon from Hazard came over and operated right away, but he found that, on her last ride, she had ruptured her appendix. For days and nights she lay in the shadow. Some of us were with her all the time and the doctor barely left her side. She begged me once to go and see those two prenatals. I went and came back and reassured her. They were doing fine, I said. Then I spoke of Raven, her horse.

" 'I'll never ride him again,' she said. But most of the time she lay still and fought for the one slim chance she knew she had. Hour by hour, though, she grew worse, and in her delirium she rode Raven down the cliffs and swam him over swollen tides and went into cabins and talked to her patients. Her thoughts kept flying out to them, to the mothers and babies most of all, and she tried to get up and go to them. Between her spells of delirium she insisted on giving directions about each case to the nurse who was relieving her. Not once did she ask anything for herself.

"Many of her patients came here after she was gone. Pearl Lewis came, with tears in his eyes.

" 'I don't feel like I ever want to come to Hyden any more,' he told me. 'She saved my woman.'

"So many others felt like that. Over at Cutshin the fathers are building a clinic in her memory. When she died, she was taken down to Lexington for burial. Nearly three hundred mountaineers followed the stretcher on which she lay as she was carried down the winding path, through the village, and so to the motor road. Behind her rode a part of our corps —but first of all, just behind the bier, walked slowly Raven, her black horse, with stirrups crossed over the empty saddle— just as they do in the army, I'm told."

For Nancy's life had been the kind that Stevenson was thinking of when he wrote in one of his books:

"Life is a thing to be dashingly used and cheerfully hazarded. It's an affair of cavalry."

Labrador Nurse

BY B. J. BANFILL

→»«←

From the Kentucky hills to the ice-bound coast of
Labrador may seem a far cry, but there is startling
similarity between the lives of Mary Breckinridge
and Sir Wilfred Grenfell, the English doctor and
missionary who spent his life in service to the inhabitants of the bleak peninsula. As superintendent of the
Royal National Mission to Deep Sea Fishermen, he
established nursing and medical missions along the
coast, among them one at Mutton Bay. To Mutton
Bay from Australia came Nurse Banfill. Her experiences during several winters have been compressed
into the following adventure, which describes excit-
ingly the hazards of nursing the sick while snow and
ice hold the land in their grip.

THE LAST STEAMER of the fall brought our winter supplies.
These were all we'd have until next June or July, when the
ice and sea were sufficiently open for the steamer to enter the
harbor again. It was absolutely necessary to check each
precious piece of freight on the manifest as it was brought
from the hold. Muffled in dickie and sealskin boots from scalp
to toe, chilled to the marrow, I stood on the windswept *North
Shore's* deck. At intervals we managed to step inside and warm
our limbs until someone stuck his head through the door and
shouted, "Your freight bes next, the purser wants that yous
be ready to check." At five o'clock the last piece had been

struck off the list. Uncle John informed me that he had stowed all our freight, as fast as it was unloaded, in his kitchen, away from dogs and frost. "Wes can't land freight at the Station until high tide at midnight," he said.

Stiff and cold, I swung down the rope ladder and jumped into Uncle John's boat. The captain shouted, "Raise anchor. All hands forward." A sailor hauled up the rope ladder, the engine started, and sailors hauled the anchor rope and wound it around the great iron posts on the deck. Uncle John shoved his boat away from the wash of the propeller and the *North Shore* swung westward while the crew shouted, "Have a good winter! See you next spring!"

And we replied, "Merry Christmas—to everyone!"

On the way home I made up my mind to have fifty winks of sleep before midnight. The cold air had made me very drowsy. More asleep than awake, I did dressings for patients who had waited two hours for my return, ate a hot supper, and crawled to bed. At eleven-thirty, Annie, the housekeeper, shouted. "There be the putt of Uncle John's motor!" Out in the darkness we caught sight of the flickering light of his lantern swinging in the stern. By now the wind had teeth. Two boatloads of freight drew into the wharf and anchored at our rocks. These rocks were slippery, steep, and treacherous, so I got out extra lights to take to the men. A drizzling, sleety rain greeted me when I opened the shed door. Uncle John fastened our lantern to a high post which lighted up the rocks between the boat and the Station, then he stretched a plank from the boats to the rocks. Knee deep in the chilling, briny water, regardless of cold and fatigue, with sleety rain slowing progress, the men went back and forth carrying loads of freight up to our kitchen. Under their heavy loads it was impossible for them to see all the trip holes in the rocks so I walked ahead flashing light in front of them.

The only means of summer transportation over land is a homemade carrier which consists of two poles with slats across them. If the load is extremely heavy, it takes one man at each end of both poles; if lighter, only two men are needed. Patients, seals, coal, and all types of freight have to be carried this way.

By three o'clock in the morning the kitchen resembled a junk shop. When the men had finished their mugs of hot coffee and thick hunks of bread it was four o'clock. We went to bed until eight, then we started to pack away our year's supply of precious food. Fresh eggs would not be strictly fresh, and butter might be slightly off flavor, but eggs are eggs although overripe, and butter is butter no matter how strong it smells or tastes. We felt rich, almost luxurious, as we contemplated our full cupboards.

The disappearance of the last steamer around the point was a signal for all routine to change. Sometime during the night summer melted into oblivion and winter took its place. By noon winter supplies were being moved into the homes where they would be safe from hungry dogs and destroying frost. For weeks nets and traps had been drying on the rocks; now they were carried inside ready to be repaired during some winter blizzard. Potatoes, meat, lard, oatmeal, flour, and vegetables in huge quantities were put into a primitive cellar, a hole under the kitchen floor.

As the weather grew colder, last-minute boatloads of wood were thrown up on the rocks to be moved later by dog team over the rocks to the homes. Sealskin boots replaced rubber ones, summer clothing was packed away, and heavy woollen socks, waterproof dickies, and mittens appeared.

Almost every home has an outside summer kitchen in which the people live during the summer. Now, cookstoves, tables, chairs, dishes, and cupboards were moved into the winter kitchen. This inner room is the fisherman's sanctuary and living quarters until spring. Wood, komatics (a wooden sled, on which a sitting box is securely roped), dog harness, frozen seals, water buckets, and slop pails stay with the dog food in the summer kitchen.

Just as man's routine changed so did the harbor: barren black rocks and cold, green, lacy whitecapped water disappeared, for during the next afternoon goose-feather snow fell steadily. By night the hillside was a world of sparkling, fleecy, white beauty. The water was a pudding mess of "slob"—ice and snow mixed and similar to unformed ice in an ice-cream freezer. Later this changed to a glare sheet of solid ice and, still later, to a soft, white-padded carpet. Winter in deadly earnest would soon be upon us.

All large boats require from ten to fifteen men to haul them from the water, over sand and rocks, far enough from the shore to prevent a tidal wave or huge, floating ice cakes from destroying them. Boys scurried through the village hunting for men to "gang up" to haul boats to safety. And in less than a week summer was forgotten as the winter routine of dog teams and komatics was established.

The seventh of November, after a busy day, a quiet evening seemed possible, so I lighted the fire in the fireplace. The telegraph operator came with a message from the doctor. "Can you go on an emergency case? I cannot leave."

The call had come from the east more than a hundred miles down the coast. The doctor was tied up with a maternity case, I learned later, so had wired for me to answer this call. Winter was upon us; nearly all the boats had been hauled up. The round trip would mean approximately two hundred and twenty-five miles, with several nights aboard a boat. At this time of year distance is difficult to compute. One has to reckon with the sea and the weather. We might make ten or we might make fifty miles in one day, or there was a possibility that we might not make fifteen miles and have to turn back or be stranded several days anywhere along the coast.

No cabin boats were available in Mutton Bay. I wired to two other villages but was unsuccessful. No man would dare risk the trip in an open boat, because if we should get caught in a storm, we should certainly freeze to death. After trying for two hours with no luck, I had to wire the doctor, "No cabin boat available."

At eleven o'clock that night he wired back, "Cabin boat located. Boatman willing to attempt trip at daylight tomorrow. Will call for you." This meant a night's delay in starting to answer an emergency call.

The next morning, swathed in woollen undervests, sweaters, leather jacket, waterproof dickie, woollen socks, and rubber boots, I waited for the boat. By eleven o'clock I resembled a parboiled wild goose and was beginning to grow anxious about the boatman.

At noon another wire came from the doctor: "Terrific sea in Harrington makes travel impossible today." Our water, only thirty miles away, was calm and peaceful. When he learned that we were not in the grip of the storm he wired to me again.

This emergency case should have had medical treatment the previous Tuesday. It was Friday, the patient was suffering agonies, and even if we wired instructions there was no available equipment to relieve him.

On Saturday morning I got into the same paraphernalia and waited. At one o'clock the boat docked and I went aboard. It was Mr. James, the bird inspector, with his son and boat. Many times, over almost impassable seas, he had risked his life to save someone else's life. That day the wind was with us and the boat sailed along like a graceful swan. We made six miles an hour until darkness set in at five o'clock. About four o'clock Mr. James said to his son, "Soon we must find a sheltered cove where we can anchor for the night."

Sunburned, grimy, fascinated, steaming in woollens, and at the same time shivering with cold, I enjoyed the trip. Sometimes I stood beside the boatman on the open deck and at other times I huddled close to the cabin stove. Once, for fifteen minutes, Mr. James let me take the wheel.

As twilight approached Mr. James and Tom discussed the merits of each cove. Would a sudden northern blizzard sweep through that cove? Were there any dangerous shoals hiding beneath the water in this cove? Would the anchors hold here? What about this one? Always the same questions until I began to wonder if any cove would have all the required points. Then we ran into one which met Mr. James' approval and he shouted to Tom, "Drop anchor."

We had one cabin, approximately six by ten feet, in which there was a stove, table, two berths, a swinging lamp, two men and me, plus our extra clothing, wood, food, and supplies, but with absolutely no privacy. Mr. James knew that this was my first long-distance, close-quarters, non-private, minus-necessities trip, so casually he remarked, "Tom and I will go out on deck while you get ready for bed."

Quickly I stripped off a few outer layers, crawled under and among blankets, snuggled down, turned my face to the wall, and shouted, "All right." The two men climbed into the other narrow bunk and loud snores soon told me that weariness had been forgotten. In a very short time I was sound asleep. My last thoughts were of woollen odors and a feeling of being cooked alive, because my feet nearly rested on the stove which Mr. James had crammed with wood before he crawled into bed.

At four o'clock in the morning I awakened shaking with

cold and felt the dampness penetrating through every bone. My blankets had slipped to the floor. As quietly as possible I tugged at them; from under a mound of deerskin Mr. James' muffled voice asked, "Are you cold? I will get up and light a fire." With chattering teeth I replied, "No, I'm all right, only the blankets and I parted company." Quickly he jumped across, tucked me in, and crawled back into his berth. Again all was quiet, and the gr-whish of sonorous breathing told me that he was asleep. Like a cradle on the deep we swayed with the sea's rhythmic motion. Once more warmth crept into my body and I slept.

At five-thirty the men crawled out and Mr. James said, "You do not need to get up yet." Their breakfast, a large mug of boiled tea and a huge hunk of bread and butter, did not take long. The teapot was shoved to the back of the stove to be reheated again and again during the day. At seven o'clock Mr. James stuck his head through the door and shouted, "Better crawl out and have a mouthful before we get into loppy water." He knew my weakness as a sailor and how much better a seasick person's stomach operates if there is something in it when that awful feeling strikes.

I dashed some cold salt water on my face and was wide awake. The cabin reeked with multifarious boat odors, so I took my biscuits and a dish of dry cereal and made a quick exit to the fresh air on the open deck. It was one of those fine mornings with the invigorating tang of sea blowing across the water. There was a nip in the air as we cut our way through the waves that made it a joy to be alive. We dived deep into the watery trough, heaved forward, then rose onto the crest of the next whitecap, spanked down onto the green foam, then struck loppy water. The boat rolled to its side, was tossed high in the air, then righted itself and lurched forward. The water was icy green and the air was icy cold. In fact, everything from sea to sky, including myself, was green and icy. With a final lurch we planked onto calm water.

Mr. James was not familiar with the dangerous shore and reefs beyond Old Fort, so we stopped to pick up a pilot. By the time Tom had thrown the anchor overboard, Mr. James was over the edge and pushing off in a kinoo toward the shore. In a few moments he returned with a pilot. As I have said before, along the coast everything and everybody is interested in everybody else. This man heard our need, closed his local store, and came to help us. He might be gone for a day, two days, or a week, but he would not take a cent for his services.

When the men cast anchor in the harbor of our destination, a blinding blizzard struck and snow fell all night. Had we been one hour later, we would have had to anchor outside indefinitely.

It was now Sunday afternoon. I took one look at Mr. Gadly, the patient, whose agonizing groans could be heard all over the home, and immediately knew that, without a couple of days' treatment, he would never live to reach a doctor or hospital. For several days he had been delirious from pain so I gave him a strong sedative and started a series of wires to the doctor, a hundred miles away. Over the wires we diagnosed and the doctor prescribed. When the patient was fairly well under the sedative, I started treatment and by seven o'clock that night he was rational and comfortable. By paracentesis I released ninety ounces of fluid. Lest he collapse if I continued, I stopped treatment temporarily and let Mr. Gadly sleep for several hours before releasing more.

The temperature was dropping and the ice was catching in the tickle, so Mr. James and Tom slept aboard their boat in order to move it frequently to prevent its being wedged into an ice block.

Monday evening the weather turned much colder and Mr. James came ashore to inform me, "If yous wish to get out this fall we will have to leave at daybreak. If not, my boat will freeze solid and we will not be able to move until next spring."

Often it is hard to get telegraphic connections—particularly when they are urgently needed. I tried for several hours to reach the doctor for advice, then gave up and decided this was a time when I would have to depend on my own judgment. I explained the situation to Mrs. Gadly and left her to make the final decision. My heart ached for these people, but I could not give them much comfort or hope. The husband-father could not live long at home. He might die at any moment along the journey or he might not survive an operation. Coast mothers and wives have to face many stern realities with fortitude and calmness. I could not remain away from my station and Mrs. Gadly could not leave her children, telegraph office, and post office to accompany her husband. He would have to set off on this uncertain trip with me, a stranger, in attendance.

I had a long talk with the family and explained that we could not guarantee anything. Also, that for the greater part of the trip we would not have any contact with the land for hours, perhaps days, and that we would have to travel with the weather and the sea. They knew what all this involved. I could assure them that God was with us on land and sea and that His great love would care for us wherever we were if we trusted ourselves in His merciful hands. After prayers and consultations, Mr. Gadly and his family felt that we should make an attempt to get him through to the hospital. We assured them that, God willing, we would get him there.

Late that night the men made a stretcher that would go through the cabin door and was large and strong enough to balance across a small kinoo on the way to the waiting motorboat.

Early Tuesday morning I gave Mr. Gadly a strong sedative and sent another wire to the doctor, informing him that we were starting for the hospital but we were unable to wait for a reply. I promised Mrs. Gadly that whenever there was an office where we stopped I would send her a message so that she would know how her husband was standing the trip.

We carried Mr. Gadly downstairs and placed him on the handmade stretcher, which the men carried to the water's edge and balanced across the kinoo. As we cut our way through shimmering ice to the boat Mr. James remarked, "What a perfect day! We should be able to reach some harbor where we can lift the stretcher ashore into a friendly home."

At four o'clock that afternoon Mr. James again remarked, "What an ideal day!" To which Mr. Gadly replied, "God has been with us to give us this day." At four-thirty, like a thunderbolt from a blue sky, a blizzard swooped down on us. The force of the gale swung the boat about and a wild sea faced us. In a few moments the boat was coated with ice and snow.

Mr. James shouted to Tom in a tense voice, "Nothing to do but find some sort of shelter and that quickly. The anchors will not hold here." Hastily Tom lashed everything to the deck. Like a hammock, the cabin lamp swung from side to side. The boat pitched forward, lurched backward, and then rolled broadside, all in one moment.

Outside was inky blackness that one feels rather than sees. A feeling of pending danger filled my soul. The sound of the waves grew louder and closer. I felt a dark blanket drawing itself around and over us. As we swayed, rocked, and plunged in the semishelter, we could hear the weird, unearthly roar of the sea and wind, followed by the loud boom of the breakers as they broke in fury against the rocks. Through that eerie darkness those booms sounded like angry cannons answering each other out of the depth of nowhere. As one died away in the distance, the next boom roared at its heels.

It was a ghastly business. Here we were, and here we stayed until two o'clock the next afternoon—an emergency patient facing death, every moment counting, not a relative aboard, no means of communication with land, and frequent treatments requiring a sterile needle and syringe. A swaying wood stove and a sliding basin in which to boil my sterile equipment did not help matters.

Wiry, wizened, tough, and more than sixty years of age, Mr. Gadly gazed patiently and courageously about the cabin. He had known all the hardships encountered in a life spent on the sea and he accepted his fate without complaints. His was an inner calm as he lay there awaiting his fate. His serene patience inspired me with a confidence and a strength which spurred me to do my best.

Outside, the foredeck was icy, wet, and slippery with briny spray swishing from every side, while overhead it was wild, black, and stormy. At ten o'clock the lines began to strain, so the men put on their waterproofs and went out to tighten them. When they returned, their rubber clothing left trails of icy salt water on our cabin floor. Their red faces dripped with salt water. A constant drip, drip came from the cabin roof as water slowly soaked our blankets and mattresses.

Bedtime came. The men spread a deerskin and blankets on the floor of the cabin for me. In this way I was within reach of Mr. Gadly without having to disturb the other two men. If they had slept on the floor and I had taken the berth, I should have had to climb over them every time I had to treat the patient. There was little room for extra feet to move about on the floor, but it was dry and free from drafts.

Mr. James was loath to have me sleep on the floor while he and Tom took the only bunk, and it was only after much expostulating that he gave his consent.

At last the night ended and daylight came. I heard a foot

slipping over the edge of the bunk and thought Mr. James might have forgotten I was on the floor. "Watch out for my head," I called up to him. Carefully he threaded his way to the stove, stoked the fire, stuck his head out to feel the weather, came back, and crawled into his berth. "She still blows. We cannot move," he informed me; then once again rhythmic snores echoed through the cabin.

My cramped position during the night, the motion of the boat, the odors, and the dampness made me stiff and seasick. I gave Mr. Gadly his breakfast and made him as comfortable as possible. From experience I knew that nothing but food would relieve that empty, retching feeling in my stomach but, being Scotch, I disliked to waste our good and treasured food. However, in desperation, I finally was willing to sacrifice it. My breakfast acted as a stomach lavage. No sooner was it down than it was up and I felt like a new person. After another hearty breakfast I was ready for anything. I must confess there swept over me an intense longing for city conveniences or even the black veil of privacy on the open deck.

All forenoon we huddled in our swaying, dripping, cozy but wet shelter as the boat creaked, groaned, and rocked. Mr. Gadly dozed while Mr. James slept, but with one ear and one eye open. Tom read jokes from the *Reader's Digest* and I knitted on a sock for the Anglican guild bazaar.

At two o'clock Mr. James, apparently sound asleep, landed on his feet and exclaimed, "She's stopped!" I never knew how he felt the storm cease and wakened at the exact moment, but a fisherman can be asleep one moment, while a blizzard rages, and wide awake the moment it stops. As suddenly as it had come up, the storm abated, the wind went down, and the sea subsided. The sea on this part of the coast is like some women—erratic, whimsical of mood, uncertain of temper, and capable of producing furious storms without warning. Just as quickly it can become as gentle as a lamb. The men unlashed everything. Mr. James took the wheel and we were on our way. Mr. Gadly appeared brighter and a little stronger. Since he had been a seaman all his life he was not seasick so he had enjoyed his food, and that gave him strength.

Just before darkness settled we reached a harbor and, because Mr. Gadly required considerable treatment, the men went ashore to sleep in order to give me more room to work. Before going, Mr. James left me wood for the stove and fresh drinking water, then casually remarked, "Here is my police whistle. If you feel the anchors giving way or the boat drifting out to sea, blow three blasts and I will row out to you."

Tired as Mr. James was, once he was asleep in a non-swaying bed it would probably have taken a bomb to waken him. But with him on guard ashore and with the police whistle dangling about my neck, I felt perfectly safe.

Worn out from his treatment and the long trip, Mr. Gadly did not get to sleep, even with a strong sedative, until four o'clock in the morning. The harbor was rough, the boat heaved and tugged at the anchor chain, which clanged against the side of the boat and made sleep impossible for me. Once in that eerie watch the stillness was broken by a ghastly thump against the boat. Mr. Gadly drew himself up on to his elbow and whispered, "Is that Gabriel thumping on the wall? Has he come for me?"

The morning was radiantly beautiful. There was not a ripple on the clear, sparkling water which was so transparent that the images of the underbrush and rocks on the shore formed a double picture and it was hard to distinguish where the shore line ended and the water picture commenced. A soft breeze stirred the grasses at the water's edge. Gulls silently skimmed the glassy water or balanced on one foot on the edge of the kinoos which were anchored to blocks of wood in the harbor.

Morning brought the men back on board and with them a sick woman with her newborn baby to go with us to the hospital.

We went around the point and, as if to speed us on our way, a brisk breeze sprang from nowhere. Just a week from the day the emergency call had reached the doctor we docked at the Harrington Mission wharf. Dr. Gray greeted us there and I turned the patient over to him. Soon Mr. Gadly was in a hospital bed under the care of doctors and nurses. A great weight of responsibility rolled from my shoulders.

A few hours' break from duties and routine work always proved a great treat. When one worker visits another on the coast, hours pass like minutes. For dinner a delicious goose, browned like a Christmas turkey, awaited us. This, after several days of boat food, was so wonderful I have not words to describe it! A tub bath and three hours of unbroken sleep in a stationary bed, minus woollies, for the first time since the previous Friday, was heavenly.

The following day was the doctor's birthday and the matron had planned a dinner party at the hospital. If the mail boat on which I was to return to Mutton Bay could get away in the afternoon she would advance the party to noon. The mailman assured us that the western mailman would not be back in time for him to leave that afternoon. In order to have more time to visit, the matron loaned me one of her uniforms and I helped with the patients. Just as the lunch bell rang word came that the mail boat would leave for Mutton Bay in an hour. There was just time to have a hurried lunch, say good-by to Mr. Gadly, and row across to the mail boat. With my heart at the evening dinner party and my body on the boat, we headed homeward.

A lovely coast afternoon faded into a brilliant starlit evening. The northern lights sent great shafts of radiance leaping

to the zenith where a curtain film changed from vivid green
to orange as it rolled across the sky too swiftly for our eyes to
follow. Lying on the deck, I watched the awe-inspiring and
flaming beauty of the borealis light up the sky from east to
west while mare's-tail streaks danced from north to south.

Day by day the weather got colder and we added more
blankets to our beds, another layer of newspapers beneath our
mattresses, and pulled on an extra sweater when we went
outside.

A coast winter's morning always presented a challenge. At
six o'clock, from under a mountain of blankets, encased in
woollens, turtlelike I would stick out my head, give my nose
a tweak to make certain it was not frozen, then draw back into
my shell to recover from the shock. In a few moments I would
gingerly stick out one bed-socked foot, then another, shiver,
then finally emerge completely. Now the real ordeal commenced as I side-stepped a snowdrift to close the ventilator,
if it were open, then leaped back to the icy linoleum. Quite
frequently I did not open the ventilator because tiny mounds
of snow sifted under and over the sills bringing plenty of fresh
air with them.

Two feet from my bed a stovepipe came up from the office
coal fire. Before retiring I placed my water jug, tooth paste,
and washcloth beside the pipe. Many times the water and
paste were frozen solid.

At four o'clock one morning my foot struck something wet
and cold. On investigating I discovered that my hot-water
bottle had leaked and my blanket was crisp with frost. In
training we were never warned not to freeze patients with
hot-water bottles!

Just before Christmas an emergency call came from a village
six miles away. "The dogs had her down," was the message.

That would probably mean that a child had fallen among the dogs and may have suffered twenty or thirty bites. I left by dog team as quickly as possible.

My guess proved to be right, and I spent several hours treating the wounds and calming the frightened little girl. I left directions and dressings with the mother and at two o'clock in the afternoon we set out for home. At three o'clock a Labrador gale showed in the offing. Far out at sea we could see black clouds rolling in, gathering force as they approached. The wind swept past us at forty miles an hour. Tom mushed, first with one foot then the other, in an attempt to urge the dogs to greater speed. He ran beside them shaking his snake whip and shouting, "Eddy-up, eddy-up." I had to turn around and ride backward so that the cutting wind could vent its force against my back. At five o'clock wet, blinding snow filled the air and clung thickly to our hoods and dickies.

Suddenly on the brink of an open glade our dogs halted. Tom, with a quick jerk, unhitched the traces. With a leap the dogs were over the glade onto floating ice. When they were safe on the other side they stopped, sank to their haunches, lapped snow, and rolled over in the drifts. Tom snatched up the pivot rope and shouted, "Hang on. Don't move. For the love of life, don't lose hold of the komatic." With a sickening shudder I realized why he had shouted, "Stick to the komatic." One second in the rushing water below us and I would have been sucked under the ice. Before I had time to think he jerked the nose of the komatic and it dropped with me on it onto the opposite floating ice.

Tom rehitched the dogs and urged them on faster. The gale was rapidly approaching when we came to a narrow dog trail rounded in the center and sloping to icy sides. For three hundred feet the trail ran along within one foot of open, roaring rapids. As if by instinct, the dogs entered this trail, slowed down, and cautiously felt their way. They seemed to know that one misstep would mean instant death. As they clawed their way along, a front paw would skid from the rounded center and dangle over the rushing water. With a scramble, the dog would frantically claw himself back onto the path, only to find his hind paw over the treacherous edge. One by one the dogs reached the safe trail again and without stopping they looked back, as if to say, "We did it!" Then they strained their shoulders into their harnesses, lowered their heads into the oncoming storm, and raced on.

Coast dogs are a mixture of savagery and love. Given a chance they might devour a person in a few moments, yet the same dogs will undergo hardships and suffering, extreme cold and hunger, in an attempt to take one to safety.

Just as we reached the station, the gale struck like the roar from a dozen cannons. The building shook, windows rattled furiously, and snow drifted into the kitchen. For a while it seemed as though the rafters would not hold against the fury of the storm. It was a wicked, wild night. Any babies ready to come into the world or any split heads would have to wait until morning.

Mother Alphonsa

BY VICTOR ROBINSON

➤➤》《《◀

As we have seen, the heroines of nursing may spend their lives in little-known corners of the earth. But they are just as likely to be as near to us as around the corner. Our next three adventures tell about nurses who have worked among the poor and diseased of a great city. Mother Alphonsa had been born Rose Hawthorne, the gently nurtured daughter of Nathaniel Hawthorne, the writer. Like many another noble woman, she became imbued with the desire to serve those who through the circumstances of life were unable to help themselves, and in doing so achieved deep and lasting satisfaction for herself.

THE WOMAN WHO STANDS in the harbor of New York, facing the sea with upraised torch, welcoming the ships from every shore, is named Liberty Enlightening the World: on the base of her statue is inscribed one of the noblest sonnets in the English language, appropriately written by a woman of New York, named Emma Lazarus. The genius of Emma Lazarus flowered early: in her youth her poems were commended by William Cullen Bryant and admired by Ralph Waldo Emerson; her prose was praised by Turgenev. Miss Lazarus, absorbed in general culture, had not been interested in the historic problems of her people. She knew Greek and Latin, but not Hebrew. Ancient Hellas fascinated her; Palestine bored her. Despite the reproach of the poet Stedman and the remonstrance of John Burroughs, she kept aloof from Jewish themes. In the 1880s, however, the czarist persecutions and pogroms brought swarms of Russian Jews as refugees to New York, and the ardent Hellenist was transformed: the Hebraic fire awoke within the soul of Miss Lazarus. She studied Hebrew, and wrote the fervent appeals which made her known to the world as a leading apostle of her race.

In the literary salon of Richard Watson Gilder and his wife Helena de Kay, the poetess Emma Lazarus met the poetess Rose Hawthorne Lathrop. It was a meeting of two gifted women, one of pure Sephardic stock, the other a richly endowed child of the Puritans, Rose Hawthorne Lathrop, "the Rose of all the Hawthornes," the daughter of one of America's foremost novelists. The friendship which developed between these two women was intense and brief, for the youthful Jewess, who had been adored in the studio home of the Gilders, abruptly disappeared from its soirées. Emma Lazarus, in her prime, was stricken with cancer.

Mrs. Lathrop learned of another case of cancer: a seamstress, operated upon in a hospital and pronounced incurable, was shipped the following day to Blackwell's Island. The daughter of Nathaniel Hawthorne could not help contrasting the two cases: she grieved deeply for the quenched genius of Emma Lazarus, but all her pity went out to the seamstress. Both died of cancer, yet in circumstances that were vastly different. Miss Lazarus was surrounded by loving relatives and affectionate friends, attended by private doctors and nurses, with every comfort that wealth could procure, every alleviation that science could furnish; the nameless seamstress, sensitive and refined but penniless, died in the hell of an almshouse on Blackwell's Island, friendless and alone. The story haunted Rose Hawthorne Lathrop, and she, too, disappeared from the world.

A new Dominican religious, to be known in time as Mother Alphonsa, lived in the slum heart of the Lower East Side of New York City. Tall visitors to her little flat looked to the nun like eagles in a canary cage. The nun established in her tenement the most exclusive of organizations: only the destitute with incurable cancer could enter. It so happened that Alice Huber, a Kentucky girl, read of Mother Alphonsa's work among the cancerous poor, and decided to pay her a visit. She found herself in the midst of extreme poverty: the rain leaked through the ceiling; the walls were filled with bugs; the dying patients were loathsome. Unbearable disgust overwhelmed Alice Huber, and she felt she could not endure this misery and ugliness for a single afternoon. Before she said good-by, Miss Huber looked again at the nun who wore a nurse's dress, for the nun-nurse had taken a course in the New York Cancer Hospital: she was beautiful and cheerful and happy, and diffused a wholesome joy among her patients. Alice Huber, destined to become Mother Rose Huber, remained forever with Mother Alphonsa, "her earliest companion and her chosen successor." The nameless seamstress had not died in vain: Rose Hawthorne Lathrop was Mother Alphonsa.

Mother Alphonsa founded the Dominican sisterhood known as the Servants of Relief for Incurable Cancer. As her work expanded, she moved from 668 Water Street to 426 Cherry Street, which she named St. Rose's Free Home, after the first saint of the New World, Rose of Lima, Peru. The work grew year by year; the little house on Cherry Street was closed, to be replaced by a modern fireproof hospital on the corner of Front and Jackson streets from whose roof can plainly be seen the Statue of Liberty in the great harbor. For the first time accommodations were available for male patients in the new building. Without distinction of race or creed, of color or sex, there was only one passport to St. Rose's Free Home: poverty with cancer. Mother Alphonsa placed Mother Rose Huber in charge of the new building, for she was occupied elsewhere.

With the opening of the new century, Mother Alphonsa established the Rosary Hill Home in the village of Hawthorne, New York. An old, cancerous German woman had been sent to the almshouse on Blackwell's Island, as the wives of her sons could no longer tolerate her presence; she was brought to the Home, and though rescued, she remained embittered; with her Lutheran prayer book in her lap, she set her aristocratic old face in an inflexible mold and would not even look out at the sunshine. One of the Sisters, fertile in expedients, remembered a splendid secondhand donation, a handsome, black-satin dress. She gave it to Grossmutter to put on, and then asked her if she would walk out in it. Up jumped Grossmutter from her chair, and wandered through the garden. After that it was necessary to watch her, for even when the weather was cold and damp, Grossmutter would fumble her way down the stairs and steal out-of-doors in her satin gown.

At the Rosary Hill Home were summerhouse and greenhouse, and many buttercups and daisies, with fields of goldenrods and asters; here life was prolonged by care and every nursing comfort, and the last days were spent in a haven of peace; the patients learned that the flowers did not shrink at their approach, nor did the ducks and chickens shudder at their half-eaten faces and awful stenches; the trees bore fruit for them, and Mother and the Sisters loved them; they were outcasts of society because of their terrible affliction, but they were honored guests in the Home. They were human enough to know their privileges, and the poorest of them made many querulous demands, often unreasonable or impossible of fulfillment, yet in the face of pain and disfigurement their jests and laughter resounded through the Home. The Rose Hawthorne Lathrop in Mother Alphonsa had not forgotten the use of words, and she said, "To see a destitute, incurable cancer patient full of delight and crying out in thanksgiving and contentment is a remarkable sight indeed." During the last thirty years of her life this remarkable sight was seen many times by all who witnessed the work of the good hands of Mother Alphonsa.

The Woman Who Never Gives Up

BY JEROME BEATTY

→》《←

One of the most famous names in the history of nursing is that of Lillian D. Wald, founder of the Henry Street Settlement, the first of the American public-health services. Miss Wald died in 1940 shortly after this story of her life was written. It is not too much to say that the movement she began, which has grown steadily in the succeeding half-century, is one of the noblest monuments erected to the memory of any man or woman of our time.

A GREAT MINISTER who planned to preach on Unselfishness could do no better than to use as a text the life of Lillian D. Wald, a woman with a backbone of tempered steel and the courage of all the lions in Africa. Other noble men and women have devoted their lives to those who suffer from hunger, illness, and injustice, but few have won as many battles.

While her fame is great among social workers, the average person is less familiar with her name than with the institutions she created—the Henry Street Settlement in New York, the Visiting Nurse Service, and the Federal Children's Bureau, which she conceived and helped persuade President Taft to inaugurate. She originated public-health nursing services in schools, in isolated sections, and for policyholders of life insurance companies. She has been called "the greatest single contributor to the public health of America."

Once someone thought it would be a stimulating idea to tell

how many lives had been saved by Lillian Wald, directly and indirectly, and how many hungry and sick the world over had been cared for through her influence. The figures included hundreds of thousands of underprivileged in Russia, South Africa, and China. But they were never issued. "Miss Wald would have been furious," said an executive.

Lillian Wald was properly educated in Miss Crittenden's English and French Boarding and Day School for Young Ladies and Little Girls. Influenced by relatives who were physicians, she went to New York to become a nurse—in those days a strange profession for cultured girls to adopt. After three years of training she and another nurse were asked to go to the East Side to talk to mothers on the care of the sick. They agreed, with no suspicion of the almost unbelievable misery, filth, and disease they were to find.

One day Miss Wald was telling a group how to make beds. A child came, pleading for help, and led her to a foul tenement where in two rooms nine pitifully undernourished persons lived, most of them sleeping on the floor and in no need of lessons in bedmaking. The head of the family was a cripple who was out exposing his deformities as he begged for pennies. On the one bed, suffering from a hemorrhage, lay a woman who had not been touched for two days.

A self-respecting scrub woman might have fled, nauseated, but twenty-six-year-old Lillian Wald pitched in, bathed the woman, sent for a doctor and cleaned up the miserable rooms. Hours later she left, shaken by what she had seen. She and her friend, she declared, would promptly take care of cases like that. "Once people know of these frightful conditions," she thought, "they will contribute money to alleviate them and laws will be passed so such things cannot occur."

Lillian Wald had not learned that hearts as big as hers were hard to find, and she was dumfounded that people were lukewarm, even when she told of such cases as the mother and baby who died of infection because the midwife left in the midst of the delivery upon discovering that the twenty-one-year-old husband had only a dollar; and of the three children with typhoid fever, who lay in a room where a tired mother was "doing a wash" and who had no pillows to lie upon because they had been sold to buy food; and how the untutored mother, after the nurse had bathed and fed the children and through her quick skill turned them back from death, kissed the nurse's hand and cried, "Oh, God, is that what I should have been doing for my babies?"

"People like that," folks assured her, "*have* to suffer. Nobody's ever been able to do anything about it. You might as well give up."

Lillian Wald never gives up. Instead, she found a powerful ally in the late Jacob H. Schiff, and with his contributions, added to those sent regularly by her sympathetic mother, she established in 1893 in Henry Street the first Visiting Nurse Service in the world.

Jane Addams had founded Hull House in Chicago four years before. The social-settlement movement was spreading, but it was concerned primarily with furnishing recreation and education and relieving poverty. Charity clinics and religious bodies nursed only a few of the poor. Lillian Wald's idea was to help the sick of every creed and color. Nobody had thought of that before and although there was no precedent to help, neither was there red tape to hinder.

The Visiting Nurse Service grew rapidly. At the end of ten years figures were gathered to check the efficiency of Miss Wald's nurses on pneumonia cases, which test nursing ability to the utmost. In one year her group had cared for 3,535 cases, in homes, with a mortality rate of 8.05 per cent. In the same period the rate in four large New York hospitals was 31.2 per cent.

The Henry Street nurses never refuse to respond to a call. For thirty-eight years Miss Wald had a telephone beside her bed and all night calls went direct to her. She found that patients wanted to pay something, but that nearly half of them were too poor.

When the subject of her own salary came up, she said, "If I have executive ability, it is God-given and comes without effort and that I will throw into the pot. I am a nurse, and to the end will accept only the same salary as is paid to the others."

Visiting nurse services now are found throughout the world, many, even in China and Japan, conducted by former associates of Miss Wald. Secretly she liked to think she helped a little in the miracle of the Dionne quintuplets, for the late wife of Dr. Allan R. Defoe was a Henry Street nurse and the doctor told Miss Wald, "All I know about nursing I learned from my wife."

Throughout her life Lillian Wald did what had to be done, while others stood by and worried and wondered. Doing what had to be done, it was inevitable that Miss Wald should extend her activities beyond nursing and settlement work. Soon she learned that nearly every reform is opposed by selfish interests, and she rolled up her sleeves and fought. She had the faculty of making true friends in every stratum of society and when she went out for help to influence legislation, saloonkeepers joined bankers to help her.

Beginning with laws to clean the streets and remove the garbage, she moved to Albany as a leader in the war on sweatshops and bad housing, and to Washington to help improve the conditions of immigrants and attack child labor. Every move to help the underprivileged gained her quick support. She helped organize exploited women into unions and fed them when they were on strike. Once when she was with a wealthy friend who disapproved of her labor activities they saw a striker throw a stone through a window. "That's what you're encouraging," he reproved. "I don't like force," she said, "nor unrighteous strikes, but I have observed that about the only difference between people in trouble is that sophisticated ones engage lawyers, primitive ones throw stones."

Her darkest moment came when the United States was rushing into war. Miss Wald, the friend of all races, was one of the women who led 1,200 of their sisters in a parade on Fifth Avenue as a protest against war. She organized meetings, argued in Washington, fought furiously—and lost.

Small-minded women might have sulked, but Lillian Wald pitched in to protect her boys as best she could. Many of them she had helped to bring into the world. Her leading worker, with salary paid by the Henry Street Settlement, became chairman of the draft board so the draft would be administered justly. Many of her nurses were among the first to go, leaving her staff depleted. Still the women and children at home must be helped. Money for Henry Street was hard to get. One of her most generous contributors, because of Miss Wald's "unpatriotic conduct," refused to give one cent more. Others, smugly viewing her as a Red, rejected with caustic reproof her appeals for money.

The war ended, her nurses and most of her boys came home. The House on Henry Street operated efficiently again. Then came a broadside from the Daughters of the American Revolution, blacklisting Lillian Wald as a dangerous radical. To be called a radical disturbed her not at all. But she was terribly hurt because such a body of women, who, she believed, ought to be supporting her every step, should deliberately try to cripple her work.

Hearts were heavy in Henry Street; friends feared the

blacklist would affect contributors. Their fears were foolish. Letters and telegrams expressing confidence poured in upon her. Contributions increased. So great had been their accomplishments that Lillian Wald and Henry Street were not checked even for a moment.

At sixty-eight she was as attractive, as quick-witted, and as dramatic a storyteller as in the days when influential families sought her as a dinner guest, though—because of her effective methods of obtaining contributions—wealthy men good-humoredly groaned, "It costs $5,000 to sit next to Lillian Wald at dinner."

When she wrote an article about the Visiting Nurses nearly 10,000 impoverished persons wrote her, telling pitiful tales of uncared-for sick, and asking how nursing could be obtained. Miss Wald replied to every letter.

Peace, meaning rest and quiet, Lillian Wald brought to thousands—but, because of her great, unselfish heart, never to herself.

A Day with a Visiting Nurse

BY KIM ANDREWS AND
ALBERTINA P. JEROME

➤➤»«««

WHAT DO VISITING NURSES DO? What kind of people do they care for? For me, these and many other questions about the Visiting Nurse Service of New York were most satisfactorily answered by spending a whole day with a visiting nurse as she made her rounds—a rare privilege indeed.

At eight-thirty in the morning the center presented a scene of quiet concentration as each nurse studied her case record and mapped out with the supervisor her itinerary for the day. The more urgent cases were at the top of her list, but the whole day was planned for a minimum of travel. Sometimes it was necessary to call a doctor for instructions or to discuss a family situation with a welfare agency before starting out. In the meantime I had a chat with the supervisor, who explained how the center is operated and the method of keeping records. At last my nurse was ready and we began our tour, on foot, as this center happened to be in Manhattan and all the calls in the district were within walking distance. In widely scattered areas, such as the Bronx and Queens, the nurses use busses, the subway, or automobiles.

We first visited Mrs. L., one of our many diabetic patients. She lived in a basement back room of an old brownstone house where daylight and fresh air rarely penetrate. The room was cluttered and dirty—in fact, I wondered how she could even manage to exist in such surroundings. Sitting gingerly on the edge of a chair, I watched the nurse as she tried to teach Mrs. L. to give herself the necessary insulin shots. This lesson was followed by a detailed discussion of diet. To some of the suggestions the patient objected strenuously, crying out, "When I go to heaven, I'll take fifteen pounds of sugar with me!" Patiently the nurse continued the discussion until she was convinced that Mrs. L. would make an effort to watch her diet. "How do you know exactly what she should have to eat?" I asked after we had left.

"Well, of course we have learned in our nutrition courses what a diabetic should have, but, due to her foreign background, this woman has very definite taste preferences, so I talked with our nutrition consultant and she worked out a more acceptable diet. We often discuss families with her, especially the undernourished ones for whom she helps us plan meals to suit their nutritional needs as well as their pocketbooks."

"Pull your coat around you and keep it away from the wall," advised my nurse as we climbed five flights of dirty, rickety stairs, reaching our destination quite out of breath. The nurse knocked on the door and we were admitted by a tiny old lady living in a small but spotless room. Although the furnishings were meager, the pots and pans shone on the walls. Mrs. S., also a diabetic, was delighted to see us and was all ready for her injection, with water boiling on the stove to sterilize the needle. She was ready with her quarter—all she could afford to pay. After the treatment the nurse remained to chat for a few minutes, as this was evidently the high spot of the day for little Mrs. S. and she enjoyed playing the gracious hostess. When we had reached the street I asked, "Why didn't you discuss her diet with her as you did with the other woman?"

"Because, when I got the insulin out of the icebox I saw she had no food," the nurse replied. "One of her neighbors will be in later to give her something to eat, and she is the one with whom I discuss the diet."

On our way to the next case the nurse tells me about old Mr. B. who had been bedridden and ill for the past two weeks. His daughter, who worked all day, had been at her wit's end trying to care for the old man and in desperation had sent for her older married sister who lived out of the city. Because she had her own family to care for, the sister could not stay to help, but she remembered the Visiting Nurse Service of New York because she had attended one of our mothers' classes twenty years ago! She got in touch with our Service, the doctor was reached and orders obtained from him. By this time we had reached old Mr. B's. home and the nurse set about bathing him, changing his bed, and finally gave him a liver injection for his anemia.

"It must be tough lying there helpless and alone all day," I remarked after we left.

"Yes, and that's when little things get you down, too. I found out one day that Mr. B. was constantly pounding on the wall for a neighbor downstairs to come and raise or lower his windowshade. First he wanted it up so he could read, and then, when he was ready to take a nap, the sun would be shining in his eyes, so down it must come. Friend neighbor was getting rather tired of this routine, so we just tied a longer string to the shade, fixing it so he could adjust it himself. Even a little thing like that not only made him happier but cured the neighbor's frazzled nerves. Now she'll be much more apt to come running if he really needs help."

As we left that house a man stopped us on the street. He had a worried look on his face. "Say, Nurse, if there was a little boy in my store who got mumps, could I get it, too? Could the rest of the kids hanging around with him get mumps?" When told it was possible, he clapped his hands to his face and rushed off, exclaiming, "Gee, I'd better get them kids out of there!"

The nurse told me that on our next call we would find a highly excitable old lady, easily upset by small events. She becomes excessively annoyed at her neighbors, their children, dogs, leaking faucets, and so forth. To our surprise we found the door wide open, the whole family waiting for the visiting nurse. The central figure was the old lady, all dressed up to attend her granddaughter's confirmation. She knew, however, that she must have her mercuhydrin injection that day, so in spite of the mounting excitement which set her pulse racing, she waited for the nurse as patiently as she could. It did not take long for the injection, and we all started down the steps together. The little family, bound for the church, waved affectionately at the nurse as we started in the opposite direction.

"One more little lady and then we'll have lunch." We soon found ourselves in a "railroad apartment" and the nurse led the way down the long hallway to a big bedroom at the front of the house. Here Mrs. W. sat in a wheel chair in a sunny bay window watching the passing show in the street below. Bright little plants filled the side windows and a canary sang gaily in his cage overhead. When the old lady tried with difficulty to wheel her chair about, I saw that she was badly crippled with arthritis. I chatted with her a few minutes while the nurse went back to the kitchen to heat paraffin, a process which requires great care, not only because it is highly inflammable, but must be just the right temperature. When she returned, she dipped the old lady's hands into the paraffin— a treatment which would relieve the pain and help limber up the joints. After about twenty minutes this was removed. We wheeled the old lady back to her window and took our departure.

"How does she happen to have the best room in the apartment? Isn't that usually the living room?" I asked.

"Yes, it was the living room once, and Grandma was poked off in a dark little back room down the hall where she couldn't see a thing all day long. Since the family is away all day, her daughter and son-in-law working and the teen-agers at school, it just didn't make sense to me to waste that lovely sunny room, so I suggested that they move Grandma in there. Did that ever start something! After a while, though, they reached the point where they would consider the plan, and last week, when I called, much to my joy they actually had carried it out. They fixed up the front room as you see it now, repainted her old room, and made a nice little living room for themselves. Now the children can entertain their friends in the back of the apartment without fear of disturbing Grandma, and she is happy in her new role as reporter of neighborhood 'doings.'"

Now the morning had gone and the nurse led the way to a little restaurant which she said filled her requirements: good, inexpensive food, a clean restroom, and a telephone booth. After giving our order she called the center and came back with an extra case added to her list, so after lunch we started out again.

This home was more prosperous-looking than any we visited in the morning. The apartment was filled with old furniture, portraits in heavy gilded frames, ornate figurines, painted vases with artificial flowers, tapestries, and oriental rugs—all kept immaculately clean with the aid of a maid. Our patient, a beautiful white-haired old lady in flowing nightgown and negligee, looked as if she had stepped from one of her own old pictures. She was suffering from arthritis and the nurse was giving her a course of exercises to increase the motion in her joints. During the treatment Mrs. D. regaled us with tales about "the good old days." After she had had a vitamin-B injection she handed the nurse a ten-dollar bill—about three times the cost of the visit. The nurse started to give her the change but the old lady said, "Please keep it. Maybe it will help someone less fortunate than I who needs a visiting nurse and can't afford to pay anything." The nurse thanked her, gave her a receipt for the contribution, and we started on our way once more.

We had seen so many old people that I was beginning to wonder if the VNSNY had no other patients, but our next call brought us to the home of nine-year-old Tommy who had had polio. The nurse carefully explained to the mother the reasons for the prescribed exercises for his atrophied leg muscles. The boy, who had not been spoiled because of his handicap, responded beautifully to treatment. The nurse showed the mother how to continue the daily exercises in her absence. The three—nurse, mother, and boy—acted as if it were a game, the mother treating Tommy with a friendly roughness to which he responded good-naturedly. She showed that she had absorbed the nurse's teaching and we left feeling that the boy was really making progress.

As we walked along the nurse told me that premature babies are usually kept in the hospital until they have reached a required weight. In the meantime the hospital asks the VNSNY to investigate the home to find out if it is a suitable place in which to care for such an infant. Our next call was to be an "evaluation visit."

We found an overwrought mother recently returned from the hospital after giving birth to premature twins. Two small children, aged two and three, were very much underfoot and the mother was wondering how she could cope with this situation when not one but two babies would be brought home. The nurse sat down with her and helped her work out a plan. A relative who lived nearby might be persuaded to care for the older children for at least part of each day. The importance of rest and a nourishing diet for the mother was emphasized. Where were the twins to sleep? That, too, was worrying Mrs. M. They still had one crib but could not afford to buy another. The nurse showed her how she could use a bureau drawer on a table placed out of drafts. Where would she bathe them? Yes, she had a small tub which she had used for the other children. New bottles would have to be bought, and the nurse advised her what kind to get. She promised to show her about formulas after the babies were brought home. Mrs. M. asked many intelligent questions and gradually the lines of worry began to disappear from her face. The nurse left her apparently much calmer and with the promise to return after the babies have been sent home from the hospital.

Our next call was to be the last for the day, and the nurse told me about Mrs. C. who had polio six months after her baby was born, which left her with a paralyzed left arm. At home now with the baby, she was very anxious to care for him entirely by herself and the nurse was helping her to realize this goal. On a previous visit the nurse had given the baby a bath, but every time she instinctively started to use her left hand, Mrs. C. would say, "But you are using both hands—do it with one." Today the mother tried it herself with the nurse's help. After continuous practice she will probably be able to bathe the baby entirely alone. It was interesting to see the way Mrs. C., by putting the bottles between her knees, could adjust the caps and nipples. They had also worked out a plan for doing away with safety pins. Grippers were sewn on small pads and the diapers were folded and placed within them. By working together, many similar problems were being solved and Mrs. C. was happy in the knowledge that she could soon care for her baby alone.

On our way back to the office I said, "So this is what you do every day—carry that bag up endless flights of stairs and visit hundreds of people such as we have seen today."

"Yes, but not *every* day. For instance, tomorrow I'll be back in the center in the afternoon teaching a 'mothers' class."

"What is that?" I asked.

"A six weeks' course for expectant mothers is given in each of our fourteen centers, beginning every other month. In these two-hour sessions the mothers are taught how to prepare for their babies and how to care for them after they're born. They even practice bathing them, using lifesize dolls as models. Maybe you would like to play hostess at one of these courses. Often when we come in from the field we have so little time to get out all our equipment that it's a great help to have a volunteer set out the layettes, bathinettes, charts, and other things we use. They take the registration, too, and at the final class in the series make up the little diplomas for the graduating mammas. In fact, we depend so much on the volunteers that it is hard to get along without them when they all leave for the summer. If you could pinch hit for the next course, we'd certainly appreciate it. Speaking of volunteers—of course you probably know that they do all kinds of clerical work in the centers, too, so that we are relieved of a lot of paper work and can get started earlier on our rounds. The mothers' class is just one of my 'extracurricular' activities. Some of us are assigned either to day-care centers for children of working mothers or to nursery schools for children of preschool age, where we work for a few hours each week with the teaching staff. And then, of course, there are a number of conferences with our supervisors and with consultants from Central Office. So you see our days are far from monotonous!"

By this time we were back at the center where the nurse wrote up her reports and I discussed with the supervisor my day with a visiting nurse. My outstanding impression was the thoroughness with which the nurse gave care to all her patients, covering their immediate needs, sleep, diet and general hygiene. Completely at ease in each home, she was welcomed and treated as a friend.

ADVENTURES IN WAR

Florence Nightingale:
The Greatest Nurse

BY CECIL WOODHAM-SMITH

⟶⟫⟪⟵

When most of us think of nurses, we have an image
of well-educated young women, carefully trained,
devoted to the care of the sick and conforming to
the highest standards of their communities. It was
not always so. A century ago nurses were apt to be
illiterate and filthy slatterns, more often drunk than
sober, of doubtful morality, and coming from the
dregs of society. That all this has changed is owing
in very large part to the work of a single woman of
genius, Florence Nightingale.

Flo Nightingale was born in 1820, the daughter
of a wealthy and aristocratic British family. Her
early life was a round of suitors and parties and
foreign travel. Yet the suitors did not satisfy her,
the parties seemed empty, and only a desire to help
the sick could fully occupy her mind. Imagine the
distress of her family when they learned that she
wished to adopt a vocation which until that time
had been almost entirely the calling of women of
the lowest standards and class. The struggle was long
and bitter, but Florence finally had her way, becoming superintendent of the Institution for the
Care of Sick Gentlewomen in Distressed Circumstances in London. She completely changed the
Institution's routine. She wrote to a friend, "I
am living in an ideal world of lifts, gas, baths, and

double and single wards." She would have gone far, but it was an outside event, having nothing to do with nursing, which gave her her greatest opportunity.

That event was the Crimean War. What she accomplished is here described in the words of her biographer, Cecil Woodham-Smith. As Mrs. Woodham-Smith points out, she revolutionized the care of the soldier in war, and she changed the conception of nurses that the public had harbored. "Never again would the picture of a nurse be a tipsy, promiscuous harridan."

But Florence Nightingale's work was far from over. Returning to England, where she was the greatest heroine of her day, she devoted herself to establishing the profession of nursing on a scientific level. She wrote innumerable tracts on nursing. She advised doctors and nurses from every continent on the functions of the nurse, on the establishment of nursing schools and nursing departments in hospitals. Before she died in 1910, at the age of ninety-one, she had become a legend. No one before or since has played a role in nursing even comparable to hers. If you should be unlucky enough to be sick and lucky enough to have a nurse to care for you, you can bless the memory of Florence Nightingale.

To THE BRITISH PEOPLE the invincibility of the British Army was an article of faith. Waterloo was a recent memory, and it was taken for granted that the nation which had beaten Napoleon could not be defeated. But since Waterloo forty years of economy had run their course, and the army that had won Wellington's victories had ceased to exist.

But in the spring of 1854 confidence was complete. The Guards were a magnificent body of fighting men as they marched through London to embark. The crowds that cheered them did not know that behind these splendid troops, the flower of the British Army, were no reserves. They were doomed to perish, and when they perished, their ranks were filled with raw recruits made "pretty perfect in drill in sixty days."

The first operation was not to be in the Crimea. The British Army was to relieve Silistria, in Romania, then a Turkish province, where the Russians were besieging the Turks. A base was established at Scutari, a large village on the Asian shore of the Bosphorus, and in June, 1854, the British Army disembarked at Varna, in Bulgaria. Nothing was accomplished. A cholera epidemic broke out; the army became an army of invalids. The Allies then proceeded to the true objective of the war, the destruction of the great naval base recently constructed by the Russians at Sebastopol.

Though the plan of a descent on Sebastopol was an open secret and had been discussed in the press, it had never been officially intimated to the supply departments; consequently no preparations had been made. When the British Army embarked at Varna for the Crimea, there were not enough transports to take both the army and its equipment across the Black Sea. Thirty thousand men were crammed in, but pack animals, tents, cooking equipment, hospital marquees, regimental medicine chests, bedding, and stores had all to be left behind. Cholera still raged, and more than one thousand cholera cases were sent back to Scutari.

A week later the British and the French won the hard-fought Battle of the Alma, and the wounded paid the price of the abandonment of the army's hospital equipment. There were no bandages, no splints, no chloroform, no morphia. The wounded lay on the ground or on straw mixed with manure in a farmyard. Amputations were performed without anesthetics; the victims sat on tubs or lay on old doors; the surgeons worked by moonlight because there were no candles or lamps. And another 1,000 cholera cases were sent back to Scutari.

Of this the British public knew nothing. Nor did they know what awaited the wounded and the sick when they reached the base at Scutari. At Scutari were enormous barracks, the head-quarters of the Turkish artillery. These barracks and the hospital attached had been handed over to the British, and the British authorities assumed that the hospital, known as the General Hospital, would be adequate. The unexpected disaster of the cholera epidemic produced total disorganization. The first 1,000 cholera cases filled the hospital to overflowing; drugs, sanitary conveniences, bedding, doctors were insufficient.

When the men arrived at the Barrack Hospital there were no beds. They lay on the floor wrapped in the blankets saturated with blood and ordure in which they had been lying since they left the battlefield. No food could be given them because there was no kitchen. No one could attend to them because there were not sufficient doctors. Some of them lay without even a drink of water all that night and through the next day. There were no cups or buckets to bring water in. There were no chairs or tables. There was not an operating table. The men, half-naked, lay in long lines on the bare filthy floors of the huge dilapidated rooms.

Such scenes of horror were nothing new in the military annals of England; similar miseries had been endured by the British Army many times before. But these horrors had remained unknown. England rang with the story of Scutari because with the British Army was the first war correspondent, William Howard Russell of *The Times*.

Russell was an Irishman with an Irishman's capacity for indignation, and in dispatches published on October 9, 12, and 13 he furiously described the sufferings of the sick and wounded. "It is with feelings of surprise and anger that the public will learn that no sufficient preparations have been made for the care of the wounded. Not only are there not sufficient surgeons . . . not only are there no dressers and nurses . . . there is not even linen to make bandages."

The revelation burst on the nation like a thunderclap. The country seethed with rage. A letter in *The Times* demanded angrily, "Why have we no Sisters of Charity?"

It was read by Sidney Herbert, who in December, 1852, had been appointed Secretary at War, and was now responsible for the treatment of the sick and wounded. On October 15 he wrote to Miss Nightingale, inviting her to go to Scutari in command of a party of nurses, with the Government's sanction and at the Government's expense.

She had already acted on her own account and, without consulting Herbert, had arranged to sail for Constantinople with a party of nurses in three days' time.

She wrote to Liz Herbert: "I do not mean that I believe the *Times* accounts, but I do believe we may be of use to the poor wounded wretches."

This letter crossed one written by Sidney Herbert at Bournemouth on the following day, in which he formally asked her to take charge of an official scheme for introducing female nurses into the hospitals of the British Army.

Fourteen professional nurses who had experience of serving in hospitals were engaged; the other twenty-four were all members of religious institutions. The party was nonsectarian, nurses, insisted Miss Nightingale, were to be selected "with a view to fitness and without any reference to religious creed whether Roman Catholic nuns, dissenting deaconesses, Protestant hospital nurses or Anglican sisters."

Miss Nightingale refused to admit "ladies," as such, into

her party. All must be nurses; all must eat the same food, have the same accommodation, wear the same uniform, except the nuns and sisters, who were allowed to wear their habits. And the uniform was extremely ugly. It consisted of a gray tweed dress, called a "wrapper," a gray worsted jacket, a plain white cap, and a short woolen cloak. Over the shoulders was worn a holland scarf described as "frightful," on which was embroidered in red words "Scutari Hospital."

On Saturday morning, October 21, 1854, the party left London Bridge to travel via Boulogne to Paris. One night was to be spent in Paris and four nights in Marseilles, where in spite of official assurances Miss Nightingale intended to buy a large quantity of miscellaneous provisions and stores. From Marseilles the party were to proceed to Constantinople in a fast mail boat, the *Vectis*.

On October 27 the party sailed in the *Vectis*. She was a horrible ship, built for carrying fast mails from Marseilles to Malta, infested with huge cockroaches, and so notorious for her discomfort that the Government had difficulty in manning her. Florence, a wretchedly bad sailor, was prostrated by seasickness. She suffered so severely that when Malta was reached she was too weak to go ashore.

On November 3, still in atrocious weather, the *Vectis*, "blustering, storming, shrieking," wrote Miss Nightingale, rushed up the Bosphorus, and anchored off Seraglio Point next day. Constantinople, in the pouring rain, looked like a washed-out daguerreotype. On the opposite shore stood the enormous Barrack Hospital. Everyone was on deck, eager to see their goal. "Oh, Miss Nightingale," said one of the party, "when we land don't let there be any red-tape delays, let us get straight to nursing the poor fellows!" Miss Nightingale, gazing at the gigantic pile, replied: "The strongest will be wanted at the washtub."

The nurses disembarked, climbed the slope, and passed through the enormous gateway of the Barrack Hospital, that gateway over which Miss Nightingale said should have been written "Abandon hope all ye who enter here."

The vast building hid a fatal secret. Sanitary defects made it a pesthouse, and the majority of the men who died there died not of the wounds or sickness with which they arrived, but of disease they contracted as a result of being in the hospital. The wounded arrived and were placed in the building without food, bedding, or medical attention.

The doctors at Scutari received the news of Miss Nightingale's appointment with disgust. They were understaffed, overworked; it was the last straw that a youngish society lady should be foisted on them with a pack of nurses. Opinion was divided as to whether she would turn out a well-meaning, well-bred nuisance or a government spy.

However, on November 5 Miss Nightingale and her party were welcomed into the Barrack Hospital with every appearance of flattering attention and escorted into the hospital with compliments and expressions of good will. When they saw their quarters, the picture abruptly changed. Six rooms, one of which was a kitchen and another a closet ten feet square, had been allotted to a party of forty persons. The same space had previously been allotted to three doctors, and elsewhere the same amount was occupied solely by a major. The rooms were damp, filthy, and unfurnished except for a few chairs. There were no tables; there was no food. Miss Nightingale made no comment, and the officials withdrew.

While the nurses and sisters unpacked, Miss Nightingale went down into the hospital and managed to procure tin basins of milkless tea. As the party drank it, she told them what she had discovered.

The hospital was totally lacking in equipment. It was hopeless to ask for furniture. There was no furniture. There was not even an operating table. There were no medical supplies. There were not even the ordinary necessities of life. For the present the nurses must use their tin basins for everything—washing, eating, and drinking.

The party had to go to bed in darkness, for the shortage of lamps and candles was acute. Sisters and nurses tried to console themselves by thinking how much greater were the sufferings of the wounded in the sick transports. The rooms were alive with fleas, and rats scurried in the walls all night long. The spirits of all sank.

The doctors ignored Miss Nightingale. She was to be frozen out, and only one doctor would use her nurses and her supplies. She determined to wait until the doctors asked her for help. She would demonstrate that she and her party wished neither to interfere nor to attract attention, that they were prepared to be completely subservient to the authority of the doctors.

No nurse was to enter a ward except at the invitation of a doctor. However piteous the state of the wounded, the doctor must give the order for attention. If the doctors did not choose to employ the nurses, then the nurses had to remain idle.

For nearly a week the party were kept shut up in their detestable quarters, making shirts, pillows, stump rests, and slings—and being observed by her penetrating eye. The time, sighed one of the English Sisters of Mercy, seemed extremely long.

Miss Nightingale was first able to get a footing in the hospital through the kitchen. To cook anything at the Barrack Hospital was practically impossible. The sole provision for cooking was thirteen Turkish coppers, each holding about 450 pints. There was only one kitchen. There were no kettles, no saucepans; the only fuel was green wood. The tea was made in the coppers in which meat had just been boiled; water was short, the coppers were not cleaned, and the tea was undrinkable. The meat for each ward was issued to the orderly for the ward. When the orderly had the meat, he tied it up, put some distinguishing marks on it, and dropped it into the pot. Some of the articles used by the orderlies to distinguish their meat included red rags, buttons, old nails, reeking pairs of surgical scissors, and odd bits of uniform. The water did not generally boil; the fires smoked abominably. When the cook considered that sufficient time had been taken up in cooking, the orderlies threw buckets of water on the fires to put them out, and the contents of the coppers were distributed, the cook standing by to see that each man got his own joint. The joints which had been dropped in last were sometimes almost raw. The orderly then carried the meat into the ward and divided it up, usually on his bed, and never less than twenty minutes could elapse between taking it out of the pot and serving it. Not only were the dinners always cold, but the meat was issued with bone and gristle weighed in, and some men got portions which were all bone. Those who could eat meat usually tore it with their fingers—there were almost no forks, spoons, or knives. Men on a spoon diet got the water in which the meat had been cooked, as soup. There were no vegetables except, sometimes, dried peas.

The food was almost uneatable by men in rude health; as a diet for cholera and dysentery cases it produced agonies. "I have never seen suffering greater," wrote one observer.

The day after Miss Nightingale arrived she began to cook "extras." On the sixth of November, with the doctors' permission, she provided pails of hot arrowroot and port wine for the Balaclava survivors, and within a week the kitchen belonging to her quarters had become an extra diet kitchen, where food from her own stores was cooked. For five months this kitchen was the only means of supplying invalid food in the Barrack Hospital. She strictly observed official routine, nothing being supplied from the kitchen without a requisition signed by a doctor. No nurse was permitted to give a patient any nourishment without a doctor's written directions.

Cooking was all she had managed to accomplish when, on November 9, the situation completely changed. A flood of sick poured into Scutari on such a scale that a crisis of terrible urgency arose, and prejudices and resentments were for the moment forgotten.

It was the opening of the catastrophe. The destruction of the British Army had begun. These were the first of the stream of men suffering from dysentery, from scurvy, from starvation, and exposure who were to pour down on Scutari all through the terrible winter. Over in the Crimea on the heights above Sebastopol the army was marooned, as completely as if on a lighthouse. Thousands of men possessed only what they stood up in.

Seven miles below the heights lay Balaclava, the British base. There had been one good road but the Russians had gained possession of it. Moistened by the dews of autumn, and churned by the wheels of heavy guns, the rough track from Balaclava to the camp had become impassable.

The weather changed rapidly, icy winds blew—and the troops on the heights above Sebastopol had no fuel. Every bush, every stunted tree was consumed, and the men clawed roots out of the sodden earth to gain a little warmth. As it grew colder, they had to live without shelter, without clothing, drenched by incessant driving rain, to sleep in mud, to eat hard dried peas and raw salt meat. The percentage of sickness rose and rose, and the miserable victims began to pour down on Scutari. The authorities were overwhelmed. It was Miss Nightingale's opportunity—at last the doctors turned to her. Her nurses dropped their sorting of linen and began with desperate haste to seam up great bags and stuff them with straw. These were laid down not only in the wards but in the corridors, a line of stuffed sacks on each side with just room to pass between them.

Day after day the sick poured in until the enormous building was entirely filled. The wards were full; the corridors were lined with men lying on the bare boards because the supply of bags stuffed with straw had given out. Chaos reigned. The doctors were unable even to examine each man. Sometimes men were a fortnight in the Barrack Hospital without seeing a surgeon. Yet the doctors, especially the older men, worked like lions and were frequently on their feet for twenty-four hours at a time.

The filth became indescribable. The men in the corridors lay on unwashed rotten floors crawling with vermin. There were no pillows, no blankets; the men lay with their heads on their boots, wrapped in the blanket or greatcoat stiff with blood and filth which had been their sole covering perhaps for more than a week. There were no screens or operating tables. Amputations had to be performed in the wards in full sight of the patients. One of Miss Nightingale's first acts was to procure a screen from Constantinople so that men might be spared the sight of the suffering they themselves were doomed to undergo.

Winter began in earnest with storms of sleet and winds that cut like a knife as they howled across the bleak plateau. Dysentery, diarrhea, rheumatic fever increased by leaps and bounds. More and more shiploads of sick inundated Scutari. The men came down starved and in rags. They told the nurses to keep away because they were so filthy. "My own mother could not touch me," said one man to Sister Margaret Goodman. By the end of November the administration of the hospital had collapsed.

And then in the misery, the confusion, a light began to break. Gradually it dawned on harassed doctors and overworked officials that there was one person in Scutari who could take action—who had money and the authority to spend it—Miss Nightingale.

She had a very large sum at her disposal, derived from various sources and amounting to more than thirty thousand pounds sterling, of which 7,000 pounds had been collected by her personally, and Constantinople was one of the great markets of the world. During the first horrors of November, the gathering catastrophe of December, it became known that whatever was wanted, from a milk pudding to an operating table, the thing to do was to "go to Miss Nightingale." Gradually the doctors ceased to be suspicious and their jealousy disappeared.

One urgent work was the purchase of 200 hard scrubbing brushes and sacking for washing the floors. She insisted on the huge wooden tubs in the wards being emptied, standing quietly and obstinately by the side of each one, sometimes for an hour at a time, never scolding or raising her voice, until the orderlies gave way and the tub was emptied.

By the end of December Miss Nightingale was in fact purveying the hospital. During a period of two months she supplied, on requisition of medical officers, about 6,000 shirts, 2,000 socks, and 500 pairs of drawers. She supplied nightcaps, slippers, plates, tin cups, knives, forks, spoons in proportion. She procured trays, tables, forms, clocks, operating tables, scrubbers, towels, soap, and screens. She caused an entire regiment which had only tropical clothing to be refitted with warm clothing purchased in the markets of Constantinople.

Before Sebastopol conditions grew steadily worse. Men were in the trenches for thirty-six hours at a stretch, never dry, never warmed, never fed.

At the beginning of December, when the Barrack Hospital was filled to overflowing, a letter from Lord Raglan announced the arrival of a further 500 sick and wounded. It was impossible to cram any additional cases into the existing wards and corridors, and Miss Nightingale pressed to have put in order the wing of the hospital which had been damaged by fire before the British occupation; it consisted of two wards and a corridor and would accommodate nearly 1,000 extra cases. But the cost would be considerable, and no one in the hospital had the necessary authority to put the work in hand. Miss Nightingale took matters into her own hands. She engaged on her own responsibility 200 workmen, and paid for them. The wards were repaired and cleaned in time to receive the wounded.

Not only did she repair the wards; she equipped them. The Purveyor could provide nothing. One of the men described his sensation when he at last got off the filthy sick transport and was received by Miss Nightingale and her nurses with clean bedding and warm food—"We felt we were in heaven," he said.

The affair caused a sensation. It was the first important demonstration of what men at Scutari called the "Nightingale power." Respect for the "Nightingale power" was increased when it became known that her action had been officially approved by the War Department and the money she had spent refunded to her.

Miss Nightingale's position was strengthened by Queen Victoria. On December 6 the Queen wrote to Sidney Herbert:

"Would you tell Mrs. Herbert that I beg she would let me see frequently the accounts she receives from Miss Nightingale and Mrs. Bracebridge, as I hear *no details of the wounded* though I see so many from officers, etc., about the battlefield and naturally the former must interest *me* more than anyone. Let Mrs. Herbert also know that I wish Miss Nightingale and the ladies would tell these poor noble wounded and sick men that *no one* takes a warmer interest or feels *more* for their sufferings or admires their courage and heroism *more* than their Queen. Day and night she thinks of her beloved troops. So does the Prince. Beg Mrs. Herbert to communicate these my words to those ladies, as I know that *our* sympathy is valued by these noble fellows."

In January, 1855, the sufferings of the British Army before Sebastopol began to reach a fearful climax. Still no stores had reached the army. Huge quantities of warm clothing, of preserved foods, of medical comforts and surgical supplies had been sent out. Where did they all go? It was never discovered, but Miss Nightingale declared that stores were available all the time the men were suffering, never reaching them through the "regulations of the service."

In this emergency she became supreme. She was the rock to which everyone clung, even the purveyors. "Nursing," she wrote on January 4 to Sidney Herbert, "is the least of the functions into which I have been forced."

Her calmness, her resource, her power to take action raised her to the position of a goddess. The men adored her. "If she were at our head," they said, "we should be in Sebastopol next week." The doctors came to be absolutely dependent on her, and a regimental officer wrote home: "Miss Nightingale now queens it with absolute power."

In spite of the improvements in the Barrack Hospital, something was horribly wrong. The wards were cleaner, the lavatories unstopped, the food adequate, but still the mortality climbed. The disaster was about to enter its second phase. At the end of December an epidemic broke out, described variously as "Asiatic cholera" or "famine fever," similar to the cholera brought over by starving Irish immigrants after the Irish potato famine. By the middle of January the epidemic was serious—four surgeons died in three weeks, and three nurses. The officers on their rounds began to be afraid to go into the wards. They could do nothing for the unfortunates perishing within; they knocked on the door and an orderly shouted, "All right, sir," from inside.

In England fury succeeded fury. A great storm of rage, humiliation, and despair had been gathering through the terrible winter of 1854–55.

At the end of February Lord Panmure, the new Secretary at War, sent out a Sanitary Commission to investigate the sanitary state of the buildings used as hospitals and of the camps both at Scutari and in the Crimea. Miss Nightingale's name did not appear, but the urgency, the clarity, the forcefulness of the instructions are unmistakably hers. "It is important that you be deeply impressed with the necessity of not resting content with an order but that you see instantly, by yourselves or your agents, to the commencement of the work and to its superintendence day by day until it is finished." This Commission, said Miss Nightingale, "saved the British Army."

The Commissioners landed at Constantinople at the beginning of March and began work instantly. Their discoveries were hair-raising. They described the sanitary defects of the Barrack Hospital as "murderous." Beneath the magnificent structures were sewers of the worst possible construction. The water supply was contaminated and totally insufficient. The Commissioners had the channel opened through which the water flowed, and began to flush and cleanse the sewers, to lime-wash the walls. The effect was instant. At last the rate of mortality began to fall. In the Crimea spring came with a rush; the bleak plateau before Sebastopol was bathed in sunlight and carpeted with crocuses and hyacinths. The road to Balaclava became passable, the men's rations improved, and the survivors of the fearful winter lost their unnatural silence and began once more to curse and swear.

By the spring of 1855 Miss Nightingale was physically exhausted. She was a slight woman who had never been robust, who was accustomed to luxury, and was now living in almost unendurable hardship. When it rained, water poured through the roof of her quarters. The food was uneatable; the allowance of water was one pint a head a day.

When a flood of sick came in, she was on her feet for twenty-four hours at a stretch. She was known to pass eight hours on her knees dressing wounds. It was her rule never to let any man who came under her observation die alone. If he was conscious, she herself stayed beside him; if he was unconscious, she sometimes allowed Mrs. Bracebridge to take her place. She estimated that during that winter she witnessed 2,000 deathbeds. The worst cases she nursed herself. One of the nurses described accompanying her on her night rounds. "It seemed an endless walk. . . . As we slowly passed along the silence was profound; very seldom did a moan or cry from those deeply suffering fall on our ears. A dim light burned here and there. Miss Nightingale carried her lantern which she would set down before she bent over any of the patients. I much admired her manner to the men—it was so tender and kind."

Her influence was extraordinary. She could make the men stop drinking, write home to their wives, submit to pain. "She was wonderful," said a veteran, "at cheering up anyone who was a bit low." The surgeons were amazed at her ability to strengthen men doomed to an operation. "The magic of her power over the men was felt," writes Kinglake, "in the room—the dreaded, the bloodstained room—where operations took place. There perhaps the maimed soldier if not yet resigned to his fate, might be craving death rather than meet the knife of the surgeon, but when such a one looked and saw that the honored Lady in Chief was patiently standing beside him—and with lips closely set and hands folded—decreeing herself to go through the pain of witnessing pain, he used to fall into the mood of obeying her silent command and—finding strange support in her presence—bring himself to submit and endure."

The troops worshiped her. "What a comfort it was to see her pass even," wrote a soldier. "She would speak to one, and nod and smile to as many more; but she could not do it all, you know. We lay there by hundreds; but we could kiss her shadow as it fell and lay our heads on the pillow again content."

For her sake the troops gave up the bad language that has always been the privilege of the British private soldier. "Before she came," ran another letter, "there was cussing and swearing but after that it was as holy as a church."

When the war was over Miss Nightingale wrote: ". . . The tears come into my eyes as I think how, amidst scenes of loathesome disease and death, there rose above it all the innate dignity, gentleness, and chivalry of the men (for never surely was chivalry so strikingly exemplified) shining in the midst of what must be considered the lowest sinks of human misery, and preventing instinctively the use of one expression which could distress a gentlewoman."

She slept in the storeroom in a bed behind a screen. It was terribly cold, and she hated cold. There was no satisfactory stove in her quarters—one had been sent out from England, but it would not draw and she used it as a table and it was piled with papers. Her breath congealed on the air; the ink froze in the well; rats scampered in the walls and peered out from the wainscoting. She spared herself nothing.

Now that the Barrack Hospital was reasonably satisfactory, she determined to go to the Crimea. There were two large hospitals at Balaclava, the General Hospital, and a hospital of huts called the Castle Hospital on the heights above Balaclava harbor.

On May 2, 1855, Miss Nightingale sailed from Scutari for Balaclava in the *Robert Lowe*.

On May 5, six months after her arrival at Constantinople, the *Robert Lowe* anchored in Balaclava harbor. Balaclava was crammed to overflowing, and she was invited by the captain to make her quarters on board the ship.

She decided to visit the mortar battery outside Sebastopol. The astonishing sight of a lady in Balaclava accompanied by a crowd of gentlemen, many of them in glittering uniforms, produced "an extraordinary effect." The news spread like wildfire that the lady was Miss Nightingale, and the soldiers rushed from their tents and "cheered her to the echo with three times three." At the mortar battery Soyer requested her to ascend the rampart and seat herself on the center mortar, "to which she very gracefully acceded." He then "boldly explained, 'Gentlemen, behold this amiable lady sitting fearlessly upon the terrible instrument of war! Behold the heroic daughter of England, the soldiers' friend.'" Three cheers were given by all. Meanwhile, five or six of her escort had picked bouquets of the wild lilies and orchids which carpeted the plateau. She was requested to choose the one she liked best and responded by gathering them all in her arms.

The party then cantered home, Miss Nightingale looking strangely exhausted. It was, she said, the unaccustomed fresh air.

The next morning she began her inspection. It was a depressing task. The hospitals were dirty and extravagantly run, the nurses inefficient and undisciplined. She was received with hostility and, at the General Hospital, with insolence.

Miss Nightingale gathered herself together to do battle, but before anything could be accomplished she collapsed. She had admitted great weakness and fatigue, and the next day she fainted. The senior medical officer from the Balaclava General Hospital was hastily summoned. After he had called two other doctors into consultation, a statement was issued that Miss Nightingale was suffering from Crimean fever.

All Balaclava was in an uproar. It was decided that she must be removed from the ship. The harbor was being cleansed by the Sanitary Commission, and the men working to remove the ghastly debris found the stench so horrible that they constantly fainted and had to receive an official issue of brandy. Miss Nightingale must be taken to the pure air of the Castle Hospital on the heights. A solemn cortege transported her from the ship, four soldiers carrying her on a stretcher. By this time she was delirious and very ill. At Balaclava the troops seemed in mourning, and at Scutari the men, when they heard the news, "turned their faces to the wall and cried. All their trust was in her," a sergeant wrote home.

For more than two weeks, she hovered between life and death. In her delirium she was constantly writing. It was found impossible to keep her quiet unless she wrote, so she was given pen and paper. She thought her room was full of people demanding supplies and that an engine was inside her head. In the height of the fever all her hair was cut off.

At home the tidings were received with consternation, and

when it was known that she was recovering strangers passed
on the good news to each other in the streets.

A legend had been growing up in England, the result of
the survivors of the British Army coming home and telling
up and down the country the story of Miss Nightingale and
the Barrack Hospital. The legend was born and gained strength
in cottages, tenements, and courts. The rich might grow
romantic, and dukes, in the slang of the day, declared themselves "fanatico for the new Joan of Arc," but the legend of
Florence Nightingale belonged to the poor, the illiterate, the
helpless, whose sons and lovers she refused to treat as the scum
of the earth. "The people love you," wrote her sister Parthe,
"with a kind of passionate tenderness which goes to my heart."

The hacks of Seven Dials, where topical doggerel was produced for the masses, hymned her in innumerable songs. "The
Nightingale in the East," decorated with a woodcut of, apparently, a lady reposing in a tent bed, and to be sung to the
tune of the "Cottage and the Wind Mill," was still popular at
regimental reunions fifty years later. One of its eight stanzas
runs:

> Her heart it means good for no bounty she'll take,
> She'd lay down her life for the poor soldier's sake;
> She prays for the dying, she gives peace to the brave,
> She feels that the soldier has a soul to be saved,
> The wounded they love her as it has been seen,
> She's the soldier's preserver, they call her their Queen.
> May God give her strength, and her heart never fail,
> One of Heaven's best gifts is Miss Nightingale.

A Staffordshire figure labeled "Miss Nightingale" depicts
her not with the famous lamp, but carrying two cups on a
small tray and romantically dressed in a long, white, flowered

skirt, a blue bodice with a pink bow, and wearing red slippers. Her portrait was eagerly demanded, but the family did not dare supply it because she had an objection to having her portrait circulated. The likenesses of her were imaginary; one print shows her as a lady with a Spanish comb in her hair, dark and passionate; another depicts a golden-haired miss in a bower of roses. Strangers called at Embley and asked to be allowed to see her desk. Shipowners named their ships after her. A lifeboat was called the *Florence Nightingale*, one of the crew writing first to make sure the name was "got all correct."

The successive tidings of her illness, her recovery, and her determination to stay at her post until the end of the war raised public feeling to boiling point, and a public meeting was called "to give expression to a general feeling that the services of Miss Nightingale in the hospitals of the East demand the grateful recognition of the British people." The meeting was crowded to suffocation and wildly enthusiastic, and similar meetings were held throughout the country. The first intention was to present an article of gold or silver suitably inscribed, but so much money came in that it was decided to establish a Nightingale Fund, to enable Miss Nightingale to "establish and control an institute for the training, sustenance, and protection of nurses paid and unpaid."

After the formation of the fund Queen Victoria, to "mark her warm feelings of admiration in a way which should be agreeable," presented a brooch designed by the Prince Consort, a St. George's Cross in red enamel surmounted by a diamond crown; the cross bears the word "Crimea," and is encircled with the words "Blessed are the merciful." On the reverse is the inscription, "To Miss Florence Nightingale, as a mark of esteem and gratitude for her devotion towards the Queen's brave soldiers from Victoria R. 1855."

Her struggle was over, and the war was all but over, too. A peace conference was meeting in Paris, hostilities had ceased, and a formal declaration of peace was expected at any moment.

On April 29 peace was proclaimed to the Allied armies.

The nurses began to go home by detachments, and every nurse was to be provided for. No one was to be "thrown off like an old shoe." Those Miss Nightingale did not feel she could ask the Government to assist, she helped out of her private pocket.

At the end of June she returned to Scutari, where the camp was empty, the Inkerman Coffee House deserted, only a few convalescents lingering where once lines of dying men had lain on the bare floor.

On July 16, 1856, the last patient left the Barrack Hospital, and her task was ended.

Two figures emerged from the Crimea as heroic, the soldier and the nurse. In each case a transformation in public estimation took place, and in each case the transformation was due to Miss Nightingale. Never again was the British soldier to be ranked as a drunken brute, the scum of the earth. He was now a symbol of courage, loyalty, and endurance, not a disgrace but a source of pride. "She taught officers and officials to treat the soldiers as Christian men." Never again would the picture of a nurse be a tipsy, promiscuous harridan. Miss Nightingale had stamped the profession of nurse with her own image. She ended the Crimean War obsessed by a sense of failure. In fact, in the midst of the muddle and the filth, the agony and the defeats, she had brought about a revolution.

Dunant of the Red Cross

BY VICTOR ROBINSON

->>><<<-

Florence Nightingale was the greatest, but not the only, pioneer in the field of nursing during the nineteenth century. Another was Jean Henri Dunant, a Swiss businessman who accidentally witnessed the carnage which took place at one of the bloodiest battles of modern times, the battle of Solferino. As a result of his shattering experience, he had the inspiration for an organization which would succor the wounded in time of war, without regard to nationality or belief. From this dream has developed the world-wide system of the Red Cross. No longer is the work of the Red Cross limited to times of war. It stands ready to bring nursing and other aid to people anywhere who have been afflicted by great man-made or natural disasters. Every year it distributes millions of dollars' worth of medicines, food, and other supplies. And it all began with a vision of mercy in the mind of a single man.

THE DAWN OF THE TWENTY-FOURTH of June 1859 was beautiful in Italy, except that it was too hot. Men who should have been sleeping had been marching all night, and at daybreak they were tired and hungry. The dew yet glistened on the grass, and the awakening songs of the birds in the mulberry trees were drowned by the beating of drums and the blowing of bugles. At five-thirty in the morning peasants and cattle began to hide, for they do not like the peculiar music of musketry.

Men who had been brothers in the rain of bullets and the blinding smoke of cannon crashed each other's skulls, swung their swords at each other's necks, and sweated and screamed as they disemboweled each other with bayonets. The noonday sun was burning as the dying and the dead piled up in ravines and on the blood-covered hills. Human beings, changed into the wildest of beasts, rode their horses over their fallen fellow men until they fell in their turn. A black army of crows waited for the living to depart, and countless flies were buzzing about the wounded and the corpses. It was now intensely hot, but the cries for water were unheard or unheeded.

In this famous battle of Solferino between Franco-Sardinians and Austrians, among the three hundred thousand participants were generals, marshals, counts, barons, princes, a king, and a couple of emperors. Yet the most important personage at Solferino was none of these: Solferino is not recalled because of Francis Joseph, although he was then young and brave; nor is it remembered because of the tricky dictator, Louis Napoleon, who sat on a white horse, smoking cigarette after cigarette. Today the name of Solferino evokes the memory of one man, a man who had no function there, for he was a noncombatant and knew nothing about war or politics; he was a Swiss industrialist whose light linen suit contrasted with the impressive uniforms around him. More than once he was asked: "Who are you?" and "What do you want?" Such questions were not easy to answer, for the traveler from Geneva, with his fashionable whiskers and heavy gold watch and chain, having stumbled into the blood bath of Solferino, was no longer a gentleman with a comfortable soul; and he wanted what had never been on earth.

The wealthy banker from Geneva, the director of certain mills in Algiers, pampered in his childhood and self-indulgent in his manhood, was suddenly introduced to pain and suffering and death. Boys, graduated a few weeks from Saint Cyr, died from blood poisoning; veterans expired in the convulsions of tetanus. He saw men shrink from amputation, and later heard the same men begging for amputation, for their pain was intolerable. Three days and three nights the dead lay on the silent battlefield, more fortunate than those who perished in the hospital wards from gangrene.

The interloper hired a horse and cart, and made the rounds of the hospitals. On the way he saw that fields ripe for harvest were ruined, the grain trampled by the wheels of heavy cannon. He entered the operating rooms where he saw men die because there were no trained nurses who knew how to compress bleeding arteries; he heard men screaming as the doctors sawed muscle and bone because they did not have assistants to administer chloroform.

In one of the churches of Castiglione, called Chiesa Maggiore, five hundred soldiers are crowded together on the floor; outside one hundred more are suffering. His purse buys sponges, linens, pins, cigars, tobacco, camomile, mallow, sambuca, oranges, sugar, and lemons. He organizes a corps of volunteers to search for the wounded, to bring them to improvised hospitals, and to nurse them. The boys of the neighborhood run to the nearby springs with buckets; the women of Lombardy carry pitchers of clear water to the soldiers, assuaging their thirst and bathing their wounds; some of these amateur nurses are motherly old women, others are lovely young girls.

The Swiss stranger, who has purchased all the clothes and as much food as he can obtain, himself becomes a nurse, washing wounds, giving bouillon to patients, and wrapping them up. They do not know who he is, but because of his costume they call him the "Gentleman in White." Some English tourists enter the hospital-church out of curiosity, and soon wish to depart; without any authority except that of humanity, the Gentleman in White forces them to remain as helpers; other English visitors come of their own accord; an Italian priest, a merchant from Neuchâtel, and a journalist from Paris joined the volunteers. The Gentleman in White had arrived near the Chiesa Maggiore just as two enemy soldiers, too badly wounded to stand up, were being thrown down the steps of the church. "Stop!" he commanded. *"Tutti fratelli!"* Strange words to be spoken in hell, but the women of Castiglione were now repeating them: "All are brothers." Solferino inflicted upon the Gentleman in White a wound from which he never recovered: Jean Henri Dunant was reborn in the agony of Solferino.

With the passing of the years the number of wounded and killed at Solferino, which included three field marshals, nine generals, more than fifteen hundred officers, and forty thousand soldiers, was becoming merely a matter of military statistics: it would be called the most sanguinary struggle since Waterloo, the most murderous battle of the century, and thus be embalmed in the history books. Then a brochure appeared, which caused the blood shed at Solferino to flow afresh; one man remembered the thousand men he had attended with the aid of Italian peasant women; he remembered the eyes lighting with gratitude for a sip of water, the smile of thanks for a smoke. Governments still sent men into battle to bleed and die for their country, without providing for them the commonest necessities of life. No attempt was made even to distinguish hospitals from other buildings, and thus houses of mercy were shelled as if they were arsenals of war. This barbarism had survived beyond the mid-nineteenth century, and no voice had cried out against the outrage. The author of the brochure held no official position, but at times the printing press has magic power to shake the foundations of an ancient evil. The brochure was Dunant's *Un Souvenir de Solferino*.

The detailed accuracy of Dunant's book was impressive; his personal recollections disclosed his sensitive response to suffering; and his concluding suggestions revealed him as one of the major prophets of modern times. Dunant proposed the formation of an international organization before the beginning of hostilities; immunity of the medical and nursing staffs; rapid transportation of injured soldiers from battlefields to hospital; improvement of hospital service; neutralization of the wounded, and extension of the work of this organization to catastrophes, such as epidemics, floods, and fires in times of peace. Writing as a private individual in the secrecy of his study, Dunant at thirty-four produced a manuscript which had extraordinary results. In his native Geneva a commission was established to study the author's ideas.

This commission became the Comité International de la Croix-Rouge. These men were the organizers of the Red Cross, but Dunant alone was its originator. The international gathering at the Palais de l'Athénée in Geneva (1863) was followed by the Geneva Convention (1864), which adopted as its protective symbol a white flag bearing a red cross. Since that day all men of decency have held that international flag in honor, and the Geneva arm band has been a passport to every field of blood. The Red Cross was the new religion, a religion without superstition, a religion which included all creeds and sects of the brotherhood of pain.

Perhaps Dunant had been so absorbed in the furtherance of the Red Cross that he had neglected his private affairs. The grain mills in Algiers ceased to grind, and Dunant's best friends lost their investments. Dunant disappeared from his accustomed haunts; he who had walked with kings could not be found. From time to time inquiries reached Red Cross headquarters at Geneva. "Dunant? We know nothing about him."

In the hospice of Heiden in the canton of Appenzell lived a silent old man. He did not welcome visitors, and there were, indeed, few who thought of entering his cell. The deaconesses gave him food and kept his enemies away by locking the door. He was safe from the horror of the days when a pavement in Paris had been his bed, when his dinner had been a crust of dry bread which he furtively took out of his pocket. Strange shadows of memory fell upon that bare wall: decorations and diplomas, packed up in boxes . . . the approval of his plan by Louis Napoleon, who founded an empire by a bloody coup d'état and ended it by surrendering his broken sword on a dunghill . . . words of Victor Hugo, who had written so warmly to Dunant . . . the voice of the Queen of Prussia, See, I am wearing your arm band . . . the article by Charles Dickens on The Man in White . . . the lengthy interview with the Empress Eugénie . . . so many dinners with ambassadors and warriors and kings, all agreeing with Dunant . . . the Red Cross hailed in nation after nation . . . Dunant, the modern saint . . . Dunant, the thief who lost the savings of his friends . . . Dunant to whom monarchs gave banquets . . . Dunant who hid in the dark alleys of Paris, hungering for a loaf of bread.

It was in this condition that a Swiss journalist found the old man, and informed the world that Dunant was still alive, an inmate of a poorhouse. Red Cross headquarters was embarrassed at this resurrection of the founder, but again the trumpets of fame resounded with the name of Dunant.

The cell in the hospice of Heiden was flooded with testimonials of esteem: an inscribed portrait of Pope Leo XIII, a pension from the dowager empress of Russia, laudatory articles in newspapers and magazines, honorary membership in numerous societies, and gifts to pay off his debts. Then the door of the little cell opened, and when the old man in the black skullcap and long white beard looked up, he saw the woman who was to bring him back to sanity. It was Bertha von Suttner of

Prague, the Austrian field marshal's daughter, celebrated throughout Europe as the apostle of the brotherhood of nations; in her capacity of secretary to Alfred Nobel, the master of explosives, she was credited with interesting the discoverer of dynamite in the problems of peace.

When the Nobel Peace prize was awarded for the first time (1901), it went jointly to Dunant and Frédéric Passy. By an ironic twist of fate, the fortune built on nitroglycerin enriched two old men, one the originator of the Geneva Convention, the other the founder of the first peace society in France. The hand of Bertha von Suttner could be felt in this award.

The pauper Dunant had suddenly become the possessor of wealth, as in the days of his youth. But he had been away too long to think of returning to the world. He had never known an intimate friend, had never loved a woman, and no home of his own awaited his familar step; Dunant, like Nobel, had no family. He had buried himself in an almshouse, and there the world had found him and honored him. He donated his money to charity, and remained in the hospice of Heiden. There he passed away, at the age of eighty-two (October 31, 1910), as the leaves fell in the little Swiss village.

The work which he had long ceased to guide went on without him, though never beyond him, for he had envisioned its future. The Red Cross was the first effective international organization for human welfare in the world, though its originator was too impractical to live in the world. Dunant is the most anonymous of famous men, and countless thousands who have blessed the Red Cross have never heard the name of Dunant. It is a name which will increase in stature with the centuries: the gaudy decorations of kings and the parchments of emperors will be dross, outweighed by the Geneva armband. On the tablets of humanity will remain an unforgettable epitaph: The Little Gentleman in White, Jean Henry Dunant (1828-1910), the Founder of the Red Cross.

Mother Bickerdyke

BY MARY A. LIVERMORE

-»»«-

Only when brother fights against brother are the horrors of war present to their fullest extent, and that is one reason why our own Civil War has been described as one of the most terrible conflicts in history. When it began, no provisions had been made by either side for the care of the wounded. As in England during the Crimean War, they were left to feed themselves, to care for themselves, or, if that were impossible, to die alone. In the North, as in the South, devoted women, horrified by the torments which their husbands and sons were undergoing, sprang to the rescue. In every city and village they banded together to send food, medicines, and bandages to the battlefields and hospitals. Many of them journeyed to the areas of war to take an active part in nursing. Gradually order sprang from chaos, and nursing was placed on a more efficient basis. Among those who were foremost in the work were Mother Bickerdyke, who served with the armies of Grant and Sheridan, Mary A. Livermore of the famous Sanitary Commission which organized the work, and Dorothea Lynde Dix, who became the first United States superintendent of nurses. Clara Barton also was of this gallant band. After the war she induced the United States to join the International Red Cross organization and became its first head in this country.

In a group of extraordinary personalities, Mother

Bickerdyke was perhaps the most unusual. She made generals obey her command. For the sake of "her boys" she bowled over lesser officials like ninepins. Time and again she risked her life at the front, working herself to the point of exhaustion. Her fellow worker, Mary A. Livermore, wrote what is perhaps the finest account of nursing in the Civil War. It is from this account, entitled "My Story of the War," that the following vividly etched character study of Mother Bickerdyke is taken.

AMONG THE HUNDREDS OF WOMEN who devoted a part or the whole of the years of the war to the care of the sick and wounded of the army, "Mother Bickerdyke" stands preeminent. Others were as heroic and consecrated as she, as unwearied in labors, and as unselfish and self-sacrificing. But she was unique in method, extraordinary in executive ability, enthusiastic in devotion, and indomitable in will.

One day as that homely figure, clad in calico, wrapped in a shawl, and surmounted with a Shaker bonnet, emerged from the Sanitary Commission headquarters in Memphis laden with an assortment of supplies, every soldier saluted her as she passed. Those who were at leisure relieved her of her burden, and bore it to its destination. To the entire army of the West she was emphatically "*Mother* Bickerdyke."

Mary A. Bickerdyke was born in Knox County, Ohio, July 19, 1817. She married, when about twenty-five, a widower with four or five children, by whom she has been beloved as if she were their natural mother, and between whom and her own two sons she has never seemed to know any difference. The marriage was a happy one, although I suspect that the immense energy and tireless industry of the busy wife proved, sometimes, annoying to the easy-going husband. His death occurred about two years before the breaking out of the war.

She was living in Galesburg, Illinois, when the war of the rebellion broke out. Hardly had the troops reached Cairo, when, from the sudden change in their habits, their own imprudence, and the ignorance of their commanders on all sanitary points, sickness broke out among them. At the suggestion of the ladies of Galesburg, who had organized to do something for the country—they hardly knew what—Mrs. Bickerdyke went down among them.

There was at that time little order, system, or discipline anywhere. In company with Mary Safford she commenced an immediate systematic work in the camp and regimental hospitals at Cairo and Bird's Point. In the face of obstacles of every kind, she succeeded in working a great change for the better in the condition of the sick. The influence of her energetic, resolute, and systematic spirit was felt everywhere; and the loyal people of Cairo gladly aided her in her voluntary and unpaid labors. A room was hired for her, and a cooking stove set up for her especial use. She improvised a sick-diet kitchen, and carried thence to the sick in the hospitals the food she had prepared for them. The first assortment of delicacies for the sick sent to Cairo by the Chicago Sanitary Commission were given to her for distribution. Almost all the hospital supplies sent from the local societies of Chicago or Illinois, were, for a time, given to her trustworthy care.

After the battle at Belmont she was appointed matron of the large post hospital at Cairo, which was filled with the wounded. She found time, however, to work for, and to visit daily, every other hospital in the town. The surgeon who appointed her was skillful and competent, but he was not conscientious or trustworthy, and he had little sympathy with his patients. He had filled all the positions in the hospitals with surgeons and officers of his sort. In twenty-four hours Mother Bickerdyke and he were at swords' points. She denounced him to his face; and, when the garments and delicacies sent her for the use of the sick and wounded disappeared mysteriously, she charged their theft upon him and his subordinates.

He ordered her out of his hospital, and threatened to put her out if she did not hasten her departure. She replied that "she should stay as long as the men needed her—that if he put her out of one door she should come in at another; and if he barred all the doors against her, she should come in at the windows, and that the patients would help her in. When *anybody* left it would be he, and not she," she assured him, "as she had already lodged complaints against him at head-quarters." "Conscience makes cowards of us all," and he did not proceed to expel her, as he might have done, and probably would, if his cause had been just.

But though *she* was let alone, this was not the case with her supplies for the sick and wounded—they were stolen continually. She caught a wardmaster dressed in a shirt, slippers, and socks that had been sent her, and, seizing him by the collar, in his own ward, she disrobed him without ceremony before the patients. Leaving him nude save his pantaloons, she uttered this parting injunction: "Now, you rascal, let's see what you'll steal next!" To ascertain who were the thieves of the food she prepared, she resorted to a somewhat dangerous ruse. Purchasing a quantity of tartar emetic at a drugstore, she mixed it with some stewed peaches that she had openly cooked in the kitchen, telling Tom, the cook, that "she wanted to leave them on the kitchen table overnight to cool." Then she went to her own room to await results.

She did not wait long. Soon the sounds of suffering from the terribly sick thieves reached her ears, when, like a Nemesis, she stalked in among them. There they were, cooks, table waiters, stewards, wardmasters—all save some of the surgeons —suffering terribly from the emetic, but more from the apprehension that they were poisoned. "Peaches don't seem to agree with you, eh?" she said, looking on the pale, retching, groaning fellows with a sardonic smile. "Well, let me tell you that you will have a worse time than this if you keep on stealing! You may eat something seasoned with ratsbane one of these nights."

Her complaints of theft were so grievous that there was sent her from the Sanitary Commission in Chicago a huge refrigerator with a strong lock. She received it with great joy, and, putting into it the delicacies, sick diet, milk, and other hospital dainties of which she had especial charge, she locked it in presence of the cook, defying him and his companions. "You have stolen the last morsel from me that you ever will," she said, "for I intend always to carry the key of the refrigerator in my pocket." That very night the lock of the refrigerator was broken, and everything appetizing inside was stolen. The depredation was clearly traced to Tom. This was too much for Mother Bickerdyke. Putting on her Shaker bonnet, she hastened to the provost-marshal, where she told her story so effectively that he sent a guard to the hospital kitchen, arrested the thieving cook, and locked him in the guardhouse.

The story of Mother Bickerdyke's exploits in this hospital preceded her in the army. The rank and file learned that she was in an especial sense their friend, and dishonest and brutal surgeons and officials, of whom there were not a few in the early months of the war, understood, in advance, that she could neither be bought nor frightened. Throughout the war the prestige of her hospital life in Cairo clung to her.

After the battle of Donelson Mother Bickerdyke went from Cairo in the first hospital boat, and assisted in the removal of the wounded to Cairo, St. Louis, and Louisville, and in nursing those too badly wounded to be moved.

The hospital boats at that time were poorly equipped for

the sad work of transporting the wounded. But this thoughtful woman, who made five of the terrible trips from the battlefield of Donelson to the hospital, put on board the boat with which she was connected, before it started from Cairo, an abundance of necessaries. There was hardly a want expressed for which she could not furnish some sort of relief.

On the way to the battlefield she systematized matters perfectly. The beds were ready for the occupants, tea and coffee, soup and gruel, milk punch, and ice water were prepared in large quantities, under her supervision, and sometimes by her own hand. When the wounded were brought on board—mangled almost out of human shape; the frozen ground from which they had been cut adhering to them; chilled with the intense cold in which some had lain for twenty-four hours; faint with loss of blood, physical agony, and lack of nourishment; racked with a terrible five-mile ride over frozen roads, in ambulances, or common Tennessee farm wagons, without springs; burning with fever; raving in delirium, or in the faintness of death—Mother Bickerdyke's boat was in readiness for them.

"I never saw anybody like her," said a volunteer surgeon who came on the boat with her. "There was really nothing for us surgeons to do but dress wounds and administer medicines. She drew out clean shirts or drawers from some corner whenever they were needed. Nourishment was ready for every man as soon as he was brought on board. Everyone was sponged from blood and the frozen mire of the battlefield, as far as his condition allowed. His blood-stiffened and sometimes horribly filthy uniform was exchanged for soft and clean hospital garments. Incessant cries of "Mother! Mother! Mother!" rang through the boat, in every note of beseeching and anguish. And to every man she turned with a heavenly tenderness, as if he were indeed her son. At that time she held no position whatever, and was receiving no compensation for her services; not even the beggarly pittance of thirteen dollars per month allowed by the government to army nurses.

At last it was believed that all the wounded had been removed from the field, and the relief parties discontinued their work. Looking from his tent at midnight, an officer observed a faint light flitting hither and thither on the abandoned battlefield, and, after puzzling over it for some time, sent his servant to ascertain the cause. It was Mother Bickerdyke, with a lantern, still groping among the dead. Stooping down, and turning their cold faces toward her, she scrutinized them searchingly, uneasy lest some might be left to die uncared for. She could not rest while she thought any were overlooked who were yet living.

Up to this time no attempt had been made to save the clothing and bedding used by the wounded men on the transports and in the temporary hospitals. Saturated with blood and the discharges of healing wounds, and sometimes swarming with vermin, they had been collected and burned or buried. But this involved much waste; and as these articles were in constant need, Mother Bickerdyke conceived the idea of saving them. She sent to the Sanitary Commission at Chicago for washing machines, portable kettles, and mangles, and caused all this offensive clothing to be collected. She then obtained from the authorities a full detail of contrabands,* and superintended the laundering of all these hideously foul garments. Packed in boxes, they all came again into use at the next battle.

After the wounded of Donelson were cared for, Mrs. Bickerdyke left the hospitals, and went back into the army. There was great sickness among our troops at Savannah, Tennessee. She had already achieved such a reputation for devotion to the men, for executive ability, and versatility of talent,

* Released slaves.

that the spirits of the sick and wounded revived at the very sound of her voice and at the sight of her motherly face. While busy here, the battle of Shiloh occurred, nine miles distant by the river but only six in a direct line. There had been little provision made for the terrible needs of the battlefield in advance of the conflict. The battle occurred unexpectedly, and was a surprise to our men—who nearly suffered defeat —and again there was utter destitution and incredible suffering. Three days after the battle the boats of the Sanitary Commission arrived at the landing, laden with every species of relief—condensed food, stimulants, clothing, bedding, medicines, chloroform, surgical instruments, and carefully selected volunteer nurses and surgeons. They were on the ground some days in advance of the government boats.

Here Mother Bickerdyke was found, carrying system, order, and relief wherever she went. One of the surgeons went to the rear with a wounded man, and found her wrapped in the gray overcoat of a rebel officer, for she had disposed of her blanket shawl to some poor fellow who needed it. She was wearing a soft slouch hat, having lost her inevitable Shaker bonnet. Her kettles had been set up, the fire kindled underneath, and she was dispensing hot soup, tea, crackers, panado, whisky and water, and other refreshments, to the shivering, fainting, wounded men.

"Where did you get these articles?" the surgeon inquired; "and under whose authority are you at work?"

She paid no heed to his interrogations, and, indeed, did not hear them, so completely absorbed was she in her work of compassion. Watching her with admiration for her skill, administrative ability, and intelligence—for she not only fed the wounded men, but temporarily dressed their wounds in some cases—the surgeon approached her again.

"Madam, you seem to combine in yourself a sick-diet

kitchen and a medical staff. May I inquire under whose authority you are working?"

Without pausing in her work she answered him, "I have
received my authority from the Lord God Almighty; have
you anything that ranks higher than that?" The truth was,
she held no position whatever at that time. She was only a
"volunteer nurse," having received no appointment and being
attached to no corps of relief.

The Chicago boat took down more than one hundred boxes
of sanitary stores on which she was allowed to draw. But
they were only as a drop in the bucket among the 12,000
wounded, lying in extemporized hospitals in and around
Savannah. When every other resource failed, Mother Bickerdyke would take an ambulance, and one of her detailed soldiers
as driver, and go out foraging. She never returned empty-
handed. The contrabands were her friends and allies; and she
always came back with eggs, milk, butter, and fowls, which
were the main objects of her quest. These foraging expedi-
tions sometimes placed her in great peril, but she scorned any
thought of danger where the welfare of the boys was concerned.

The ladies of the city and country were continually sending
Mrs. Bickerdyke boxes of clothing for her own use. In her
life of hard work her clothes were soon worn out, and as she
never had any time to bestow on herself, she was greatly in
need of such kindnesses. Reserving for herself a few articles of
which she had imperative need, she would take the remainder
of the garments in her ambulance to the southern women in
the neighboring country and exchange them for honey, fruit,
milk, eggs, and butter, of which she never could have too
much.

Among the articles sent her at one time were two very
elegant long nightdresses, embroidered and trimmed with

ruffles and lace. They were the gift of very dear friends, and she had some scruples about bartering them away as she did other garments. Returning with the "plunder" she had received in exchange for her superfluous clothing, she crossed a railroad track on which stood a train of boxcars. Stopping the ambulance, she began to explore them, according to her usual custom. Inside of one were two wounded soldiers going home on furlough. Their unhealed wounds were undressed and full of vermin; they were weak for lack of food, were depressed and discouraged, and in all respects were in a very sorry plight.

"Humph!" said Mother Bickerdyke; "now I see what them furbelowed nightgowns were sent down here for. The Lord meant I should put 'em to a good use, after all."

The wounds of the poor fellows were washed and cleansed. Tearing off strips from the bottom of the nightdresses, she properly dressed and bandaged them. Socks, drawers, and handkerchiefs were found in the ambulance, but she was entirely destitute of shirts. A happy thought came to her.

"Here, boys," she said; "put on the upper half of these nightgowns; they're just the thing. My sakes, but this *is* lucky!"

But to this the men decidedly objected. "They would wear the dirty, tattered shirts, that had not been changed in two months, rather than go home in a woman's nightgown!"

"Oh, pshaw, boys, don't be fools!" persisted practical Mother Bickerdyke. "Night *gowns*, or night *shirts*, what's the odds? These will be softer to your wounds; and Heaven knows they're enough sight cleaner. Put 'em on, and wear 'em home. If anybody says anything, tell them you've jerked 'em from the secesh, and the folks will think a heap sight more of you for it."

The men were persuaded, and got into the garments. In passing through Chicago they halted for a brief rest at the

Soldiers' Home, where, when their wounds were dressed, their fancy shirts were discovered, marked in indelible ink with Mrs. Bickerdyke's name. We offered to exchange them for genuine hospital shirts, but the men had had such sport already that they clung to the abbreviated nightgowns, one of which is today preserved in a Wisconsin household as a sacred relic.

The battle of Corinth greatly increased the labors of Mother Bickerdyke. She had learned how to take care of men brought in from the battlefield, and was always prepared with soups, tea, coffee, milk punch, stimulants, rags, bandages, and whatever else might be needed. The rebel wounded fell into her hands, and, bitterly as our heroine hated the "secesh," all the bitterness died out of her heart when the wounded in gray uniforms were left to her tender mercies. She became a mother to them, as to the boys in blue. Her work was arduous beyond description. Had she been content to perform her work as a matter of routine, it would have been easy for her, but this would not suffice her great heart and conscientious nature. Her work was never done. If anything could be suggested to save a man who was dying, to soothe, or inspire, encourage, or strengthen a patient who was anxious or disheartened, her work was not done until this was accomplished. Nowhere in her department was there neglect or suffering, misrule or waste.

Orders had been given to bring the wounded lying in tents into her large hospital as fast as there was room for them. At last she was informed that the tents were all vacated. With her habit of seeing for herself if the work was done, she went from tent to tent, examining them. Turning from one, she thought she saw a movement under a heap of blankets in a corner. She raised the nauseous, fly-covered blanket, and there lay a man, still breathing, but hardly alive. He had been shot through both cheeks, a part of his tongue had been cut off, which was swollen to bursting in his mouth, and his left shoulder and leg were broken. How long he had been forgotten no one could tell, but the flies had rioted in his wounds, and he was in a most lamentable condition.

He was brought on a stretcher immediately to her hospital, where she devoted herself to his restoration, fighting grim death inch by inch, hour by hour, until she came off conqueror, and the man recovered. He is living today, and is proud to call Mother Bickerdyke his savior. It was something to witness the tempest that burst over the heads of the men who had been commissioned to remove the wounded and had passed by this poor fellow. Mother Bickerdyke was merciless on such an occasion, and flashed such lightnings of wrath on the offenders as to astonish them into speechlessness.

In November 1862 Mrs. Bickerdyke was compelled, for the first time, to take a furlough. She was thoroughly worn out, although she would not admit it, and was as indomitable in will, and as Herculean in energy, as at the first. She came direct to Chicago, and, as I had requested, to my house. I was not at home when she arrived, but returned that evening.

After tea, I accompanied my family to the wedding of a friend, which was solemnized in a church near by. Wearied as Mother Bickerdyke was, she insisted on making one of the company. She believed it would rest her to see the inside of a meetinghouse; it was a sight that had not blessed her eyes for eighteen months, she said. It was an intensely tedious ceremony, for the old clergyman who officiated at the marriage added to a very long prayer, a Scripture reading and a full half-hour's exhortation to good living, with directions for accomplishing it, which he counted off, firstly, secondly, thirdly, and so on. It was a sermon, in fact. After the marriage the newly wedded halted for a few moments in the church parlor, to take leave of their friends, as they were to proceed directly to the train, en route for the distant city of their future residence. Mother Bickerdyke was introduced, at her request, for she had learned that the young husband held the rank of major in one of the Illinois regiments.

"My dear," said our motherly heroine in a naïve way to the bride, "I have enjoyed your wedding very much; it has done me as much good as a prayer meeting. I am very much refreshed by it." [She had slept through the interminable service.] "I am sure you will make your husband a good wife, for you have got the face of a good girl; and I hope you and he will live together a good many years. If he gets wounded in battle, and falls into my hands, I will try to take good care of him for you."

"Why, Mother Bickerdyke! God bless you! I am glad to see you!" burst out the bridegroom with a mighty welcome. "You have already taken care of me. After the battle of Donelson I was brought up on one of the boats filled with wounded men, and you took care of me, as you did of the rest, like a mother. Don't you remember a lieutenant who had a Minie ball in his leg, and the doctors wanted to amputate the leg, and he fought against their doing it, and how you helped him keep it? I am the man. Here's the old leg, good as new. I have been promoted since." But she could not recall his case among the thousands more seriously wounded whom she had since carefully nursed. This one wedding, attended on the first evening of her arrival, was the only recreation of her furlough.

Rested and recuperated, and having placed her two sons at boarding school where she could feel easy about them, she reported to the medical director at Memphis, as she had been ordered, in January 1863. Immense hospitals were being organized in that city, which was also being made a base of military and medical supplies. She was first set to organizing the Adams Block Hospital, and, that completed, she was sent to Fort Pickering to reorganize the "Smallpox Hospital." There had been great neglect here and the loathsome place had been left uncared for until it was fouler and more noisome than an Augean stable. But Mother Bickerdyke was just the Hercules to cleanse it. She raised such a hurricane about the ears of the officials whose neglect had caused its terrible condition, as took the heads from some of them and sent back to their regiments several private soldiers who had been detailed as nurses.

In the meantime she organized anew her huge laundries, in which was performed all the washing of the Memphis hospitals, even when there were eight and ten thousand patients in them. General Grant had given her a pass anywhere within the lines of his department, into all camps and hospitals, past all pickets, with authority to draw on any quartermaster in his department for army wagons to transport sanitary or hospital stores. This pass, enlarged as his department extended, she held until the end of the war.

With the medical authorities she was for a time at variance. The medical director at Memphis was a young man belonging to the regular army—able, industrious, skillful, and punctilious. He wished Mrs. Bickerdyke to revolve in an orbit he marked out for her—to recognize *him* as the head, and never to go beyond him, or outside him, for assistance or authority.

Mrs. Bickerdyke cared little for what he said or thought, if he did not meddle with her, for she was no more in love with the medical director than he was with her. He inspected her hospital regularly, and never found fault with it for its perfect management defied criticism. Once, in passing through a ward, he espied some half-dozen eggs under a sick man's pillow. The man was recovering from a fever, and had a great craving for food that could not be allowed him in his weak condition. Especially, he coveted boiled eggs; and, as the poor fellow was very babyish, Mrs. Bickerdyke had petted him in her motherly way and tucked half-a-dozen hard-boiled eggs under his pillow, telling him he should have them to eat when he was well enough. The sick man found a vast deal of comfort in fondling the eggs with his hands. I have seen men in hospitals handling half-a-dozen potatoes under their pillows in the same way. The medical director espied the eggs, and ordered them to the kitchen, declaring "he would have no hen's nests under the pillows." The man was just weak enough to cry miserably over his loss and the nurse in charge hastened to report the story to Mother Bickerdyke.

If any unnecessary offense came to her boys, woe to him through whom it came. She would have "shown fight" to Secretary Stanton himself if he had been the offender. Catching up a large pail filled with eggs, she strode into the ward, her blue eyes blazing, her cheeks glowing. "Dr. ———, will you tell me what harm it does to humor a sick man in an innocent fancy? Let this boy have the eggs where he can see them. There, John, there's a whole pailful of eggs," pushing them under his bed; "and you may keep them there until they hatch, if you've a mind to." And she strode out again. The doctor chose not to hear, and the boy's eggs were not meddled with again.

A few days after, on her return from her regular visit to the Smallpox Hospital, she found that the blow which had been impending had fallen. The medical director had left a written order that all the contrabands detailed to her service should be sent to the contraband camp by nine o'clock the next morning, the hour for hospital inspection. It was night when she returned and received the order, and it was raining hard. Going to the door, she recalled the departing ambulance.

"Here, Andy," she said to the driver, "you and I must have

some supper, these mules must be fed, and then we must go to General Hurlburt's headquarters. I'll see if these men are going to be sent to the contraband camp. If Dr. —— is going to be ugly, he'll find two can play at that game, and a woman is better at it than a man." The Negroes stood around with doleful faces, like so many statues in ebony. They liked Mother Bickerdyke and the hospital, and they hated the camp with its forlornness.

"When's we gwine from dis yer hospittle?" they inquired.

"When I tell you to, and not before!" was her laconic answer. "Get yourself ready, Mary Livermore, to go with me!"

I protested against her taking this drive, for the streets had been torn up by the enemy before the city was surrendered, there was no gas, and no street lights, we had not the countersign, the rain poured in torrents, and the project was fraught with danger. She silenced me, "Oh, we'll leave you behind, if you're such a coward; but Andy and I'll go, safe or not safe!" Knowing that I had more prudence than she, I finally accompanied them.

Through the pouring rain, over broken and excavated streets, not a glimmer of light anywhere, save from the one lantern of the ambulance, halted at every few paces by the challenge of the closely set guards, for Memphis, though conquered, was still a rebellious city, Mother Bickerdyke and I toiled on to the headquarters of the post commander. By and by we met the officer of the night, making the grand rounds, and he gave us the countersign. Then we proceeded a little more comfortably.

It was hard work to get access to the commander, for he was in bed. But at last her importunity prevailed, and she was conducted to his presence. She told her story honestly, and with straightforwardness, and asked for written authority to keep her detailed contrabands until he, General Hurlburt, should revoke the order. It was granted; and back through the rain we rode, Mother Bickerdyke triumphant.

The next morning, at nine the medical director made his appearance at the Gayoso Hospital, according to appointment. The Negroes were all at their work in the kitchen, in the laundry, in the wards, everywhere, as if no order had been given for their dismissal. He came to the kitchen, where Mother Bickerdyke was making soup.

"Mrs. Bickerdkye, did you receive an order I left for you Saturday morning?"

"I did, sir!" continuing to season and taste her soup.

"An order for the dismissal of these black people to their camp?"

"Exactly, sir."

"I expected it to be obeyed!" in a positive tone of voice.

"I suppose so, sir!" very nonchalant in manner.

"And why has it not been?" in a louder tone, and with rising anger, menace in his eyes, and a flush of wrath on his cheek.

"Because, sir"—turning and facing him—"General Hurlburt has given me an order to keep 'em here until he dismisses them; and, as General Hurlburt happens to outrank you, he must be obeyed before you." And putting her hand in her pocket, she produced General Hurlburt's order.

There was a storm. The doctor was vulgarly angry, and raved in a manner that was very damaging to his dignity. He threatened all sorts of dreadful things, and wound up by telling Mother Bickerdyke that "he would not have her in Memphis"—that "he would send her home before she was a week older."

"But I sha'n't go, doctor!" she answered. "I've come down here to stay, and I mean to stay until this thing is played out.

And Doctor, I guess you hadn't better get into a row with me, for whenever anybody does one of us two always goes to the wall, and *'tain't never me!*"

The doctor had a keen sense of the ridiculous, and Mother Bickerdyke's novel method of pacification amused him when he got over his short-lived anger. He was really a very superior officer, but like many another clever man he was dominated by the inborn belief that all women were to play "second fiddle" to him. He had the good sense to appreciate blunt Mother Bickerdyke's excellences, and when mutual friends entered on the work of pacification they were successful.

A week after I was in her hospital about noon when the wardmaster of the fourth story came to the kitchen, to tell Mother Bickerdyke that the surgeon of that ward had not made his appearance, the special diet list for the ward had not yet been made out, and the men were suffering for their breakfasts.

"Haven't had their breakfasts! Why didn't you tell me of this sooner? Here, stop! The poor fellows must be fed immediately." And filling enormous tin pails and trays with coffee, soup, gruel, toast, and other like food, she sent half-a-dozen men ahead with them. Extending to me a six-gallon pail of hot soup, she bade me follow her, being freighted herself with a pail of similar size in each hand. I stood looking on at the distribution, when her clarion voice rang out to me in tones of authority, "Come, make yourself alive, Mary Livermore! Try to be useful! Help these men!" I never knew anyone who deliberately disregarded her orders—I had no thought but to obey—and so I sat down to feed a man who was too weak to help himself.

While we were all busy, the surgeon of the ward came in, looking as if he had just risen from sleep. Instantly there was a change in the tones of Mother Bickerdyke's voice and in the expression of her face. She was no longer a tender, pitying, sympathizing mother, but one of the Furies.

"You miserable, heartless scalawag!" she said, shaking her finger and head at him threateningly. "What do you mean by leaving these fainting, suffering men to go until noon with nothing to eat, and no attention? Not a word, sir!" as he undertook to make an explanation. "Off with your shoulder straps, and get out of this hospital! I'll have them off in three days, sir! This is your fourth spree in a month, and you shall go where you belong. Off with your shoulder straps, I tell you, for they've got to go." She was as good as her threat, for in less than a week she had made such charges against him that he was dismissed from the service, and that by the very medical director with whom she had had weeks' wrangling. The dismissed surgeon went to General Sherman to complain of the injustice done him. "He had been grossly belied, and foul charges had been made against him, which he could prove false," was his declaration. "Who was your accuser?" asked General Sherman. "Who made the charges?" "Why—why—I suppose," said the surgeon reluctantly, "it was that spiteful old woman, Mrs. Bickerdyke." "Oh, well, then," said Sherman, "if it was she, I can't help you. She has more power than I—she ranks me."

General Sherman was the beau ideal of Mother Bickerdyke. He was her great man and great soldier. She would always defend General Grant like a tigress if he were assailed; but it was clear to everyone that General Sherman was the special object of her idolatry. And today I think she would find it easy to give her life for Sherman, if the sacrifice were necessary. She would count it a small thing to die for him. She rates him higher than Grant, higher than Lincoln, and altogether superior as a soldier to Washington or Wellington; and woe to the luckless wight who would dare lower her ideal!

General Sherman, on his side, fully appreciated Mother Bickerdyke; and when he was curt and repellent to all agents, nurses, and employees of the Sanitary, Christian, and State commissions, she had the entree to his headquarters, and obtained any favor she chose to ask. There was something in her character akin to his own. Both were restless, impetuous, fiery, hard working, and indomitable. After the fall of Vicksburg Mother Bickerdyke became a special attaché of his corps, the Fifteenth. Ever after, during the war, she considered herself in a special sense under Sherman's direction; and the soldiers of the Fifteenth Corps have always claimed exclusive ownership of her.

When Sherman went to re-enforce Grant at Chattanooga, she came North, by Sherman's direction, and hastened to the same destination.

No pen can depict, and no tongue narrate the sufferings, hardships, and privations of our brave men in southern and eastern Tennessee during the months of November, December, and January, 1863 and 1864. Hunger and cold, famine and nakedness were their inseparable companions. Horses and mules starved also, ten thousand animals starving at Chattanooga. The reproachful, whinnying complaints of the famishing beasts wrung the hearts of the soldiers, even when they were slowly dying themselves from lack of food.

Mother Bickerdyke's field hospital was on the edge of a forest, five miles from Chattanooga. The weather was as arctic as in New England in the same season. Men were detailed to fell the trees and pile log heaps, which were kept continually burning, to warm the camps and hospitals. These log fires were her only means of cooking; nor could any other be hoped for until the railroad was completed. By these log fires Mother Bickerdyke, with her aids, contrabands, or convalescent soldiers, did all the cooking for her 2,000 patients. Here she made tea and coffee, soup and toast. Here she broiled beef and mutton without a gridiron. Here she baked bread by a process of her own invention, blistering her fingers while doing it, and burning her clothing. A dress which she wore at this time came into my hands, and was kept at the rooms of the Commission for some time as a curiosity. It was burned so full of holes that it would hardly hang together when held up. It looked as if grape and canister had played hide-and-seek through it.

The last day of the year 1863 was one of memorable coldness, as were the first few days of the year 1864. The rigor of the weather in Chicago at that time actually suspended all outdoor business and laid an embargo on travel in the streets. It was even severer weather in Mother Bickerdyke's location, for the icy winds swept down Lookout Mountain, where they were re-enforced by currents of air that tore through the valleys of Mission Ridge, creating a furious arctic hurricane that overturned the hospital tents in which the most badly wounded men were located. It hurled the partially recovered patients out into the pouring rain, that became glare ice as it touched the earth, breaking anew their healing bones and chilling their attenuated frames with the piercing mountain gale.

The rain fell in torrents in the mountains and poured down their sides so furiously and suddenly that it made a great flood in the valleys at their base. Before the intense cold could stiffen the headlong current into ice, it swept out into the swollen creeks several of the feeblest of the men under single hospital tents, and they were drowned. Night set in intensely cold, for which the badly fitted up hospitals were wholly unprepared.

All that night Mother Bickerdyke worked like a Titan to have her bloodless, feeble patients from being frozen to death.

There were several hundred in hospital tents—all wounded men—all bad cases. The fires were piled higher and higher with logs, new fires were kindled which came nearly to the tents, until they were surrounded by a cordon of immense pyres that roared and crackled in the stinging atmosphere. But before midnight the fuel gave out. To send men out into the forests to cut more in the darkness and awful coldness seemed barbarous. The surgeon in charge dared not order them out, and it is doubtful if the order could have been obeyed had it been given. "We must try and pull through until morning," he said, "for nothing can be done tonight." And he retired to his own quarters in a helpless mood of mind.

Mother Bickerdyke was equal to the emergency. With her usual disdain of red tape, she appealed to the Pioneer Corps to take their mules, axes, hooks, and chains, and tear down the breastworks near them, made of logs with earth thrown up against them. They were of no value, having served their purpose during the campaign. Nevertheless, an order for their demolition was necessary if they were to be destroyed. There was no officer of sufficiently high rank present to dare give this order; but after she had refreshed the shivering men with a cup or two of panado, composed of hot water, sugar, crackers, and whisky, they went to work at her suggestion, without orders from officers. They knew, as did she, that on the continuance of the huge fires through the night depended the lives of hundreds of their wounded comrades, for there was no bedding for the tents, only a blanket or two for each wounded, suffering man.

The men of the corps set to work tearing down the breastworks and hauling the logs to the fierce fires while Mother Bickerdyke ordered half-a-dozen barrels of meal to be broken open and mixed with warm water for their mules. Immense caldrons of hot drinks were made under her direction—hot coffee, panado, and other nourishing potables; and layers of hot bricks were put around every wounded and sick man of the entire 1,500 as he lay in his cot. From tent to tent she ran all the night in the icy gale, hot bricks in one hand and hot drinks in the other, cheering, warming, and encouraging the poor shivering fellows.

Suddenly there was a great cry of horror, and, looking in the direction whence it proceeded, she saw thirteen ambulances filled with wounded men who had been started for her hospital from Ringgold in the morning by order of the authorities. It had become necessary to break up the small outlying post hospitals and concentrate at Chattanooga. These had been delayed by the rain and the gale, and for hours had been traveling in the darkness and unparalleled coldness, both mules and drivers being nearly exhausted and frozen. On opening the ambulances, what a spectacle met Mother Bickerdyke's eyes! They were filled with wounded men nearly chilled to death. The hands of one were frozen like marble. The feet of another, the face of another, the bowels of a fourth, who afterward died. Every bandage had stiffened into ice. The kegs of water had become solid crystal, and the men, who were past complaining, almost past suffering, were dropping into the sleep that ends in death. The surgeons of the hospital were all at work through the night with Mrs. Bickerdyke, and came promptly to the relief of these poor men, hardly one of whom escaped amputation of frozen limbs from that night's fearful ride.

As the night was breaking into the cold gray day, the officer in command of the post was informed of Mother Bickerdyke's unauthorized exploits. He hastened down where the demolished breastworks were being rapidly devoured by the fierce flames. He took in the situation immediately, and evidently saw the necessity and wisdom of the course she had pursued. But it was his business to preserve order and maintain discipline, and so he made a show of arresting the irregular proceeding. By no mere order of his could this be done. Not until day dawn, when they could go safely into the woods to cut fuel, were the men disposed to abate their raid on the breastworks, which had served their purpose of defense against the enemy weeks before.

"Madam, consider yourself under arrest!" was the major's address to ubiquitous Mother Bickerdyke.

To which she replied, as she flew past him with hot bricks and hot drinks, "All right, Major! I'm arrested! Only don't meddle with me till the weather moderates for my men will freeze to death if you do!"

A story got in circulation that she was put in the guardhouse by the major, but this was not true. There was some little official hubbub over her night's exploits, but she defended herself to the officers who reproved her, with this indisputable statement, "It's lucky for you, old fellows, that I did what I did. For if I hadn't, hundreds of men in the hospital tents would have frozen to death. No one at the North would have blamed *me*, but there would have been such a hullabaloo about your heads for allowing it to happen that you would have lost them whether or no."

Now for the first time, and the only time, Mother Bickerdyke broke down. The hardships through which she had passed, her labors, her fastings, her anxieties, had been sufficient to kill a dozen women. She was greatly reduced by them, and as soon as her place could be supplied by another matron, she came North, a mere shadow of her former self.

The same efforts were made to honor her as on a previous visit; but, as before, she put aside all invitations. She had rendered great service to the Wisconsin regiments in the

western army; and the people of Milwaukee, who were just
then holding a fair for the relief of sick and wounded soldiers,
would not be denied the pleasure of a visit from her. I accompanied her, for she refused to go anywhere to be lionized
unless someone was with her "to bear the brunt of the nonsense," as she phrased it. She was overwhelmed with attentions.
The Milwaukee Chamber of Commerce had made an appro-
priation of twelve hundred dollars a month for hospital relief,
to be continued until the end of the war. And she was invited
to their handsome hall to receive from them a formal expression of gratitude for her care of Wisconsin soldiers. Ladies
were invited to occupy the gallery, which they packed to the
utmost. A very felicitous address was made her by the President of the Board of Trade, in behalf of the state of Wisconsin,
and she was eloquently thanked for her patriotic labors, and
informed of the recent pledge of the Board. A reply was
expected of her, which I feared she would decline to make,
but she answered briefly, simply, and with great power.

"I am much obliged to you gentlemen," she answered,
"for the kind things you have said. I haven't done much, no
more than I ought, neither have you. I am glad you are going
to give twelve hundred dollars a month for the poor fellows
in the hospitals, for it's no more than you ought to do, and
it isn't half as much as the soldiers in the hospitals have given
for you. Suppose, gentlemen, you had got to give tonight
one thousand dollars or your right leg, would it take long to
decide which to surrender? Two thousand dollars or your
right arm; five thousand dollars or both your eyes; all that
you are worth or your life?

"But I have got eighteen hundred boys in my hospital at
Chattanooga who have given one arm and one leg, and some
have given both, and yet they don't seem to think they have
done a great deal for their country. And the graveyard behind

the hospital, and the battlefield a little farther off, contain the bodies of thousands who have freely given their lives to save you and your homes and your country from ruin. Oh, gentlemen of Milwaukee, don't let *us* be telling of what *we* have given and what *we* have done! *We* have done nothing and given nothing, in comparison with *them*! And it's our duty to keep on giving and doing just as long as there's a soldier down South fighting or suffering for us."

It would not be easy to match the pathos and eloquence of this untutored speech.

As soon as she had regained health and strength, Mother Bickerdyke returned to her post. General Sherman was pouring supplies, provender, and ammunition into Chattanooga, for it was to be his base of supplies for the Atlanta campaign. He had issued an order absolutely forbidding agents of sanitary stores, or agents of any description, to go over the road from Nashville to Chattanooga. He alleged as the reason for this prohibition that he wished the entire ability of the railroad devoted to strictly active military operations. There was great distress in the hospitals below Nashville in consequence of this stringent order, and uneasiness and anxiety at the North, because of its seemingly needless inhumanity. Mother Bickerdyke found Nashville full of worried agents and of sanitary stores that were needed down the road and spoiling for lack of transportation. Her pass from General Grant would take her to Chattanooga despite General Sherman's prohibition. Before starting, her fertility of invention manifested itself in a characteristic act. Ambulances with mules in harness were being sent to various points against the day of need. No barrels were allowed in these ambulances, but all the bags they could hold could be crowded in. Getting such help as she could muster, they made bags, which were filled with dried apples, peaches, potatoes, and any other sanitary articles that could be sent in them as well as in barrels; and the ambulances went away packed with articles for the hospitals. Forty such left for Huntsville, Alabama, thirty for Bridgeport, and several for other points. Then Mother Bickerdyke, despite remonstrance and opposition, took the next train for Chattanooga, and made her unexpected debut at General Sherman's headquarters.

"Halloo! Why, how did you get down here?" asked one of the general's staff officers, as he saw her enter Sherman's headquarters.

"Came down in the cars, of course. There's no other way of getting down here that I know of," replied the matter-of-fact woman. "I want to see General Sherman."

"He is in there, writing," said the officer, pointing to an inner room; "but I guess he won't see you."

"Guess he *will!*" and she pushed into the apartment. "Good morning, General! I want to speak to you a moment. May I come in?"

"I should think you had got in!" answered the general, barely looking up, in great annoyance. "What's up now?"

"Why, General," said the earnest matron in a perfect torrent of words, "we can't stand this last order of yours nohow. You'll have to change it, as sure as you live. We can get along without any more nurses and agents, but the supplies we *must* have. The sick and wounded men need them, and you'll have to give permission to bring them down. The fact is, General, after a man is unable to carry a gun, and drops out of the lines, you don't trouble yourself about him, but turn him over to the hospitals, expecting the doctors and nurses to get him well and put back again into the service as soon as possible. But how are we going to make bricks without straw? Tell me that if you can."

"Well, I'm busy today, and cannot attend to you. I will

see you some other time." But though Sherman kept on writing, and did not look up, Mother Bickerdyke saw a smile lurking in the corner of his mouth, and knew she would carry her point. So she persisted.

"No, General! Don't send me away until you've fixed this thing as it ought to be fixed. You had me assigned to your corps, and told me that you expected me to look after the nursing of the men who needed it. But I should like to know how I can do this if I don't have anything to work with? Have some sense about it now, General!"

There was a hearty laugh at this, and a little badinage ensued, which Mother Bickerdyke ended in her brusque way with, "Well, I can't stand fooling here all day. Now, General, write an order for two cars a day to be sent down from the Sanitary Commission at Nashville, and I'll be satisfied."

The order was written, and for weeks all the sanitary stores sent from Nashville to Chattanooga, and the posts along that road, were sent directly or indirectly through this mediation of Mother Bickerdyke.

When General Sherman was prepared to move on his Atlanta campaign, Mother Bickerdyke with Mrs. Porter accompanied the army on its bloody but victorious march. They were constantly in the immediate rear of the fighting, and made extraordinary exertions to keep the department of special relief at its very highest point of efficiency.

I despair of giving any account of the work accomplished by Mrs. Bickerdyke and Mrs. Porter from April to November of 1864. What it is to "follow an army" when there is no fighting in progress can only be understood by those who have experienced it. What it was to follow Sherman's army in that Atlanta campaign, when it fought every foot of the way, over rugged mountains, through deep, narrow ravines, through thick, primitive woods, across headlong rivers—to follow with only the one aim of ministering to the exhausted, the suffering, the wounded, the dying—with only a blanket and a pillow for a bed—the roar of artillery, the clash of arms, the cries of distress, and the shout of battle continually resounding—to live night and day in the midst of these horrors, in constant attendance upon the mangled and anguished soldiers brought to them from the rear, or taken to their extemporized hospitals—this cannot be described.

While this book was in press I was called to Kansas, a state in which 180,000 soldiers are settled. While I was there, a Soldiers' Convention was held in Topeka, the capital city, which was very largely attended. Mother Bickerdyke came from San Francisco, the invited guest of the Convention, and, just as the veterans were entering on their deliberations, made her appearance in the rear of the house.

In an instant there was a joyful confusion in the neighborhood of the door, a rush, a subdued shout, a repressed cheer. The presiding officer called for order, and rapped vigorously with his gavel. But the hubbub increased and spread toward the center of the hall. Again the chairman sought to quell the disturbance, rapping forcibly and uttering his commands in an authoritative voice: "Gentlemen in the rear of the house must come to order and take their seats! It is impossible to transact business in this confusion!"

"Mother Bickerdyke is here!" shouted a chorus of voices in explanation, which announcement put an end to all thoughts of business and brought every man to his feet and sent a ringing cheer through the hall. All pressed toward the motherly woman, known by all soldiers in the West, many thousands of whom are indebted to her for care, nursing, tenderness, and help in the direst hours of their lives. Gray-haired and gray-bearded men took her in their arms and kissed her. Others wept over her. Men on crutches and men with empty coat sleeves stood outside the surging crowd with shining eyes, waiting their turn to greet their benefactress.

"Why, boys, how you behave!" was Mother Bickerdyke's characteristic exclamation, as, releasing herself from the smothering caresses and the strong, imprisoning arms, she wiped away tears of memory and gladness. This raised a shout of laughter. "Oh, Mother, your brown hair has grown white as snow," said one, "but I should know you by your speech if I met you in Africa."

"I should know her by the tender eyes and the kind mouth," said another. "I shall never forget how good they looked to me after the battle of Resaca, where I lost my foot and gave myself up to die, I was in such pain. I tell you, it seemed as if my own mother was doing for me, she was so gentle. She looked down upon me, and encouraged me, and nursed me, as if I were her son." And he wiped his wet eyes with the back of his hand.

Nurse Cavell

BY A. A. HOEHLING

→»«←

Sometimes, by the very nature of their work, nurses are placed in situations which require heroic actions having little to do with the profession itself. This has been especially true in time of war, and one of the greatest of such heroines, who sacrificed her life for her country, was Nurse Edith Cavell. Nurse Cavell had no idea of what lay in store for her when she left her native England to go to Belgium in 1907. She had studied nursing at the London Hospital and had worked in the London slums. As a superintendent of nurses in England, she understood the Nightingale methods of nursing thoroughly. A Brussels doctor who realized the low state of Belgian nursing called on her for aid and she responded. She came only to teach Belgian women how to care for the nation's sick, and she it was who established the profession of trained nursing in that country. Yet her greatest fame rests not on this achievement but on the events which took place at her nursing school in the Rue de la Culture in Brussels, after the Germans had invaded that unhappy country during World War I. With utter fearlessness she helped her countrymen to escape to England, and then admitted her crime, if crime it was. Here is her dramatic story.

PEOPLE IN BRUSSELS became poorer and poorer. Nurses looked about for side jobs, minding babies, giving French or English lessons, cooking, mending. But work was difficult to obtain, and those who sought it listened to the dreary refrain:

"*Pas d'argent . . . mais, merci. . . .*"

They were almost penniless in Belgium. As for French, or worse yet English, why should the conqueror have any interest in those tongues?

But people had to live and relax a little bit during the course of a day. That was the way it was at 149 Rue de la Culture. The soldiers in hiding played the piano and sang songs. In occupied Brussels the brash strains of "Tipperary" echoing from the windows of a *Belgian* nursing school were at least incongruous.

Directress Cavell took only passing notice. She was too occupied with a new and hazardous role. The job of smuggling Allied soldiers to the border was settling into routine, in many respects, with more and more citizens helping. The Girl Guides, for example, were now among the couriers of secret messages.

There were a number of carefully selected Brussels structures in addition to the school, where the men were harbored, since never more than eight were allowed in any one place at a time. Even eight were a lot, and the major concern was in keeping them quiet. They were boisterous, exuberant, and would rather be in the front lines than enduring this enforced inactivity, closeted like moles.

When it was time for the soldiers to leave, the "guides" (fearless men who knew Belgium blindfolded) took them away in groups of four or five, walking apart, Indian file. Late afternoon or night was the customary departure time.

Often these little broods of soldiers, dressed as workingmen in drab jackets and jaunty berets, started by tram for Haecht, a small town eighteen miles north of Brussels. To avoid guards at the end of the line, the men left the tram, one by one, on the outskirts of Haecht.

They carried forged identification papers. The German guards could not speak French, little knowing that most of the "workingmen" could not either, so there was scant interrogation.

The men were fed and housed in Haecht by other members of the organization, then continued on their way, generally to Turnhout, on the Dutch border about thirty-five miles to the northeast.

The crossing was perilous. Many lives were sacrificed in the chill of a Flanders night—the sudden blast from a concealed machine gun, the crackle of grounded electricity searing flesh.

In May a Pole arrived at the school in a sizable group of Allied soldiers. Taken ill, he had to be nursed back to health over a period of three weeks. Edith Cavell herself was in attendance. After he had gone, she found on the floor a torn note, in German. The soldier had scribbled cryptically that the house was a nice one and that he could not do anything "required" of him.

Was he a spy? Had kind treatment changed his mind? Now, Edith Cavell and her entire school must work with the realization that they might be known to the occupation forces.

As if to underscore the apprehension, "Verboten" proclamations appeared, warning against harboring English or French soldiers on pain of death. Some nurses said the notices "caused the blood to freeze in our young veins."

Then, one June evening, Miss Cavell was walking past the potato field. Her dog Jack was rolling on the grass, cavorting in the balmy weather. Up the adjoining Rue Darwin strode a tall, handsome man, well dressed, looking every inch a gentleman. He spoke in educated French to her, saying he was a *poilu*, seeking a hiding place for himself and his friend.

Jack, the dog, whined.

In a moment the man was joined by another man wearing a light gray summer coat. The Frenchman then introduced himself as George Gaston Quin and the other as an Englishman, identified ony as "Mr. X."

Edith Cavell did not question them as she gave Mr. Quin lodging with the other French soldiers and Mr. X with the English. The latter left for Holland the next day with a thirty-two-year-old, rosy-cheeked guide named Gilles. But Quin said he was sick, and remained at the school.

Quin's popularity was immediate at 149 Rue de la Culture. The presumed French soldier spoke well, quoted from literature, was amusing, and sympathetic with everyone's problems. His companion, the Englishman, however, was to cast a shadow over him.

Gilles returned from Antwerp to report that the mysterious Mr. X had suddenly disappeared from the group he had conducted to the border.

"I think he's a spy," Gilles announced.

A few days later, on June 20, a German officer entered the nursing school and asked to inspect the premises. This he did quickly but with sharp eyes. Not until he left did Edith Cavell notice that an English soldier's cap had been left prominently on the floor of the upstairs bath.

The following morning two men in civilian clothes arrived. They told her in half-broken English they wished to rent the premises after the school moved to its new quarters. They climbed up and down stairs and poked into almost every nook and corner of the old building. Finally they said good-day and left. But Sister Wilkins and a young nurse, Mania Waschausky, had noticed something.

Both men had on regulation German army shoes, and one

wore eyeglasses that discerning nurses recognized as of German manufacture.

The chemistry of Edith Cavell's personality became a source of fascination to those around her.

On the one hand, Edith Cavell hesitated to be severe with the girls. There was so much to endure: the lack of food, the wartime privations, the strain of knowing the Germans were watching.

On the other hand, she *must* make nurses of them all; she must endure and temper what seemed to an English matron the flippancy of French and Belgian girls. The Dutch were not much better. Would she be doing service to her profession if she relaxed discipline?

As her inward drive increased into an imponderable determination, her prim manner stiffened. She manifested a consuming obsession not to falter that often made her robotlike to the nurses.

On July 7 the nurses accepted nine English soldiers. They were put in the first-floor back room, the safest since it had a door leading to the garden.

They had been there but a few hours when two German officers arrived to talk to Edith Cavell. As they went into her office, Miss Wilkins led the Englishmen, some half-dressed, helter-skelter into the basement. From there, one by one, they fled into the garden and over a stone wall to a vacant house in the rear.

Other nurses were gathering up English and French magazines and stuffing them under bathtubs. Secret papers went into a water-closet storage tank. But one of the officers surprised the girls in the midst of their work.

"*Verboten!*" he reminded them. He was recognized as one of the men who had once discussed renting a room.

The directress' office had been turned almost literally upside down. Pictures, including family portraits, were torn from the walls, cups and saucers smashed in their cupboards, even floor boards pried loose.

Sister Wilkins implored her matron to ask permission to return to England, or go in hiding elsewhere in Belgium. She refused, pointing out, among other reasons, that two other English nurses remained at the Institute. Concerning her own safety she seemed "wholly apathetic."

However, Sister Wilkins was successful in persuading her to burn certain letters and documents.

The day's excitement over, one of the nurses glimpsed Edith Cavell in her room. She recalled:

". . . when we saw her, calmly seated there, by candlelight, so small and frail, so peacefully quiet in her great trials, we almost felt as if we could fall down and worship her."

The Germans sent an inspector to watch inside a front room, hoping patiently to obtain the clinching evidence. The nurses now had set up their own counterwatch in this beleaguered school. Dark, beautiful Mania Waschausky, who slept in the garret room overlooking the street, volunteered to play sentry all night.

The young probationer sat there in her long nightgown, her room candle extinguished, face pressed to the narrow leaded panes. The dusk of a July evening turned into night. The chimneys of Brussels etched a serrated outline against the skies. Mania Waschausky watched. The lives of many depended on her wakefulness.

At midnight Mania spied three Englishmen, who had fled over the stone wall earlier in the day, approaching the house. All they had to do was ring the bell. The German inspector would be on his feet in a hurry to arrest everyone in the hapless school.

Mania staved off history by rushing downstairs in her night-gown, pigtails flying, bare feet dulling the clatter her head-long flight would otherwise have made. Silently she opened the heavy front door where the soldiers were about to sound the bell.

She pointed to her feet. They understood and removed their shoes. She whispered:

"*Le Boche*," and pointed to the next room, where the *Boche* was at that instant dozing. His rank cigar smoldered on a saucer beside his stuffed chair. They understood, again.

Mania reported at once to Edith Cavell. She was beside her bed, praying. She was fully dressed, immaculate in spite of clothing and soap shortages. Her nurse's uniform had become a part of her.

This time the directress herself took the three soldiers out of the house, through the garden, across Brussels. At 6 A.M. she returned.

The door to the German inspector's room was open. He sat, puffing his cigar. Perhaps he knew.

The blow had fallen. Men and women were arrested in widely scattered sections of Belgium. Whenever a doorbell rang, day or night, the occupants of the house jumped in terror, and thought wildly of hiding.

On August 4 three men called at the school, saying they were English. Edith Cavell, explaining they were in the midst of moving, suggested that Louis Severin, a fifty-two-year-old chemist, might hide them temporarily.

Within the hour Severin was arrested.

In the early evening a German officer arrived at the Institute and spent two hours talking to Miss Cavell and Sister Wilkins. The other nurses were certain it was all over.

After he left, Edith Cavell appeared "as calm as usual." Yet the strain was telling on Sister Wilkins, who was "very, very upset," she admits to this day, but understandably "when you consider the terrible strain we were under for many months, not knowing at which moment we should be arrested."

All the nurses remained distraught, and Edith Cavell was hard put to console them. Before supper, a cold, cheerless ritual of carrots, thin soup, and bread that tasted like sawdust, she bowed her head as the nurses recited with her:

"Almighty God, who hast given us grace at this time with one accord to make our common supplications unto thee . . ."

Sometimes she was absent from meals. No one, however, disputed that her "serenity" was remarkable when she was seen.

At 3:30 P.M. on the following day three heavy men, not in uniform, entered the clinic.

"We want to look at furniture," one said to Sister Wilkins. Some discarded pieces were for sale. The question was a reasonable one.

Then, without warning, one of them leveled a large revolver —which appeared almost from nowhere—at her head and pushed her into a side room. The other two men clomped off in search of the directress.

Probationers who chanced into the same room were herded, one by one, shrieking, against the wall, and covered by the revolver: Jacqueline Van Til, Paula, Helen Wegels, Fernande Weil, Mania Waschausky, and two sisters, Maude and Claire Matthews.

"Don't move!" he commanded several times.

After a time, there was a light scuffle in the hall, as though someone were resisting. In the next instant Edith Cavell was pushed into the room.

"Don't be so sad, my children," she soothed. "Everything will be all right. I'll be back soon."

Her head was high as they led her through the front door and into a waiting automobile. Sister Wilkins was placed in another car, and then both machines drove off, leaving a swirling blue-gray cloud of exhaust in their wake. Jack, the dog, howled disconsolately.

Pauline, in a heartbroken, futile gesture, started to run down the street after the cars. She was brought back by a remaining uniformed guard.

In police headquarters in the Rue de Berlaimont the two women were placed in separate rooms for questioning. Elizabeth Wilkins stubbornly denied all accusations and suggestions of the secret police.

They tried to trick her into confessing.

"You might as well admit you were harboring enemy soldiers," Lieutenant Bergan advised, revealing that Quin had supplied a complete report.

Sister Wilkins confirmed nothing. She "did not" know them or anything about the presence of young men in the school. She frustrated their every effort, until they exhausted questions.

At 8 P.M., to her surprise, they released her. Jack barked and bounded up to be patted as Sister Wilkins returned to the clinic. The other nurses wept with joy as they crowded around her to ask, "What happened? When will the directress be back?"

Sister Wilkins, half sick from the experience, could not answer. She had not seen their madame at the Rue de Berlaimont. Involved herself in hiding the men, Miss Wilkins continued to marvel at her own release.

Spirits sank again as it became increasingly certain that Edith Cavell would not be returned for a long time. The chilling presence of the German guard was still very much with them. His permission must be asked every time they wanted to venture outside the building.

Edith Cavell was held incommunicado.

Only her nurses and probationers would risk wrath and possible punishment upon themselves by their very concern. As Miss Wilkins was aware, "no one in Brussels dared say very much or they were suspected."

Alone in her cell, Edith Cavell would not tell even the smallest untruth that might dismiss the firing squad.

What manner of woman, asked her nurses, was this daughter of a Norfolk vicar?

Sister Wilkins had easily talked her own way out of arrest; Sister Wilkins was just as English, just as hated by the Germans, just as guilty.

In September the fabric of "schrecklichkeit" was taking final shape. Its weaver was Lieutenant General von Sauberzweig, the city's new military governor. He was tall, powerfully built, a striking Prussian ex-cavalryman. An apostle of *Kriegsbrauch* (or military custom), he was trained to reject what did not conform to his own doctrines.

With him was Dr. Stoeber, his judge advocate, a career military lawyer. A "hanging judge," his mind had become as fixed as his master's, from years of balancing offense with punishment in the court-martial books. Physically, he was tall, commanding. He parted his dark hair in the middle and greased it flat.

"A horrible example," was his known credo.

Meanwhile, Edith Cavell busied herself in her small cell. Not bare as prisons go, it contained one high, barred window, one gas jet, a metal cot that she folded in the daytime into a table, a straight-backed chair, a wooden wall cupboard, a crucifix, and a washbasin. It was heated by hot-air vents; the floor was bricked.

She read the Bible, her prayer book, and the *Imitation of Christ*, written six centuries earlier by Thomas à Kempis, the German theologian. It had become one of the most widely translated books in the world and from it she obtained much comfort. Slowly she filled her prayer book with such notations:

It is no small prudence to keep silence in an evil time.

Into Thy hands I commend my spirit, for Thou hast redeemed me, O Lord, Thou God of truth.

So shalt Thou keep one and the same countenance always with thanksgiving, both in prosperity and in adversity, weighing all things with an equal balance.

She had signed a full statement. Her questioners told her that the others had confessed, and she apparently believed them.

A portion of her alleged confession follows:

". . . During the first part of the time I concealed in my house more especially Englishmen, sometimes for a fortnight or three weeks, as I was not sufficiently familiar with the means of transport nor with the roads they should follow in their secret journey across the frontier. When, later on, guides for the French and Belgians of military age were put at our disposal, I concealed in my house the people brought to me until a favorable opportunity arose for their departure. During this time the persons who were brought to me stayed with me from one day to a week."

As Henri Depage has recently told this writer, "she rendered her defense practically impossible for her barrister."

In her confession there was an undercurrent of proud resignation, almost the despair of abandonment, with no faith in those who might be able to help her.

"Two by two, surrounded by helmeted soldiers, we went to the entrance (of St. Gilles Prison) where motor busses were waiting. On the way the jailers stood at attention and saluted. All this suggested the firing squad, and we felt inclined to nervous laughter."

And so Georges Hostelet, engineer and scholar, began his report of Thursday, October 7, 1915.

It was a bright fall day. Leaves in the Parc de Bruxelles hung crisp and golden. In the air was the aroma of roasting chestnuts. In the flower markets the mums were offered in white, brown, and lavender bunches, *"Trois francs seulement!"*

But to the west the guns thundered as the French Second Army was hurled into the battle for Champagne. The smell of death hung like a miasma over the fields.

And death waited, too, over the terra-cotta roofing of the three-story stone Parliament House.

The four uniformed judges presented a formidable sight. All old *Landsturmers*, they wore Iron Crosses and other heavy decorations. To a man they were rendered the more severe by huge mustaches. Two wore monocles.

They had no power. Verdicts were predecided by the prosecutor, in this case Kriegsgerichstrat Dr. Stoeber, in turn answerable to von Sauberzweig.

Edith Cavell presented a strange, weary sight, dressed in a dark-blue dress and coat, wearing a high, dark cloth hat, with two feathers sticking up at a grotesque angle. She was "unimpressive." But although the Germans "respected a uniform," Miss Cavell preferred not to seek refuge in her own uniform, not wanting "to implicate the hospital or nursing."

Jacqueline Van Til is impressed with the significance of Madame's attire at the trial:

"Miss Cavell always wore her uniform. She was proud of that uniform. After all, she was a woman. That uniform may have sustained her. When she had to discard it, she may have suffered a psychological shock. It may have taken out of her the natural superiority she felt when wearing it. It may have caused her to weaken in her will to fight, or, on the other hand, it may have strengthened her feeling of martyrdom.

"When she stood before the German Court in the final act, a frail figure in prison drab, she must have looked forlorn . . . it may have instigated the Court to punish that once so proud Englishwoman."

Sadi Kirschen recalled his client:

"She was trusting, calm, speaker of the truth above all, a Quaker, speaking without fear, in a flat, fading voice, but with a kind of composure and inward calm which was its own force. . . ."

Edith Cavell had signed a further confession:

"I lay particular stress once more on the fact that of all the soldiers, English or French, lodged with me, two or three only were wounded, and in these cases the wounds were slight and already beginning to heal. I was aware that the identification certificates carried on their persons by the soldiers and eligibles whom I concealed were false, and ever since I was first associated with the affair, I knew that these false documents were supplied by the engineer Capiau. . . ."

The next day, October 8, Friday, was the climax of the court-martial. Stoeber was brisk as he introduced excerpts from the testimony of each defendant—not a great deal in any one case today, for he was only concerned with his "recommendations" for sentences.

Stoeber insisted that Miss Cavell's institute in Brussels was *the* center.

"All of this activity," he concluded, "is akin to high treason, and the law punishes it with the death sentence."

Then it came time for the lawyers to speak in behalf of

their clients, being discreet, as they did so, not to give offense to judges or prosecutor. The court was supreme.

One of the defendants, Hermann Capiau, denied that he had given Edith Cavell 1,000 francs, as she had stated in her confession. He said he had given her nothing.

She stepped forward at this point, calm and rigid, spectators reported. She admitted her mistake.

"Why did you lie?" snapped the court interpreter. His tone was "surly."

"My memories were confused. Afterward, I remembered it was not he," she said simply. Later, she commented to Capiau, "I believe I have gotten you in trouble. Pardon me."

She reiterated much of her confession. All questions were put to her in German, a tongue she had never mastered. The interpreter passed them on in French with embellishments.

She never once was reported to have trembled or faltered. She admitted all her activities as charged without hesitation, with a "conviction," as Kirschen reported, and "simplicity" that impressed even the judges. On the other hand, contrasted with her codefendants, fighting desperately for their lives, she appeared and acted like a woman in a dream world—certainly some "other world."

When asked why she helped the soldiers on their way to England, she replied that she thought the Germans would otherwise have shot them. She believed she was doing her duty in saving their lives; that in no way did she consider her offense to be associated with spying for the Kaiser's enemies.

One of the judges taunted her.

"You are foolish to aid English soldiers," he said. "The English are ungrateful."

"No, they are not ungrateful," Edith Cavell replied.

"And how do you know that?" Stoeber interjected.

Then she made the fatal mistake of admitting she had received letters from England thanking her. If she had said she had heard from them in Holland, a neutral country, it might have been less serious in implication. She also readily admitted sending "about two hunderd" men to the border.

Her lawyer, Sadi Kirschen, praised her as a woman whose whole life had been devoted to humanity. He recalled her work in the early part of the war, how she had ministered to the Germans without discrimination. He added that at first she had taken in only wounded English soldiers, entirely "natural" considering her own nationality. In other words, declared Kirschen, she was a most unfortunate victim of circumstances, and all because of her love for humanity, her dedication to nursing.

Kirschen had made his defense. But it was not enough. The interpreter was as unmoved as the judges. Finally he turned to Edith Cavell.

"What have you to say in your defense?"

"Nothing."

There was little for the judges to do but formalize Stoeber's recommendations. Yet they waited—Saturday, Sunday. The tension among the thirty-five defendants became unbearable and one man hanged himself in his prison cell. He was, ironically, among the few to be acquitted.

In mid-afternoon, Monday, October 11, the accused were taken from prison once more to the Parliament House, and assembled in the Salle des Deputés. It was a rainy, dismal day. The patter of drops against the windows of the busses was further dirge to the low spirits of the group.

Hostelet recalls the scene:

"The military prosecutor came in. With his high coloring, waxed mustache, elegant and brisk, he looked cheerful as ever. . . . He took a large sheet of paper from the portfolio carried by his faithful attendant. Everyone was silent, and instinctively we drew together.

"The prosecutor read the verdict in German as if he were reading a list of honors."

Stoeber read:

"The tribunal is of the opinion, partly on the strength of their own statements, and partly on the strength of the assertions of their fellow prisoners, that the following are the chief organizers:

> Prince de Croy (escaped)
> Philippe Baucq
> Louise Thuliez
> Edith Cavell
> Countess Jeanne de Belleville
> Louis Severin."

He pronounced the death penalty: "*Todestraffe!*"

It held for the condemned the very ring, the finality of death.

Hostelet walked over to Edith Cavell and tried to comfort her.

"Mademoiselle, make an appeal for mercy."

"It is useless," she replied. "I am English. And they want my life."

Capiau added his urgings; so did even a German guard, whom Capiau recalls saying in broken English, "Never say die!"

She merely repeated quietly,

"They wish me dead because I am English."

Darkness fell. The cold rain continued. It was Monday evening.

Puddles collected everywhere in the neglected streets of Brussels. Horses' hoofs splashed into them with a gurgling sound. German military lorries showered the sidewalks with mud and grime.

People kept in their homes, to miser the remaining warmth. Parlors were rearranged to conform to the coal scarcity and families sat in a semicircle of chairs close to the hearth. It seemed that winter had come early.

Nurses in the new Institut sought to keep warm like the rest of the population. A little group, finished with a meager supper at seven o'clock, were sitting in their schoolroom that still smelled with newness.

Looking out the window, one of them spied a familiar figure hurrying up the walk. Clutching his coat collar tight around his neck, his hat shapeless and wet, it was M. H. van Halteren, lawyer friend of the Institut and member of the board of directors.

The nurses greeted him excitedly at the front door. As they saw the expression of despair on his face they knew, without having to ask.

For a moment he stood there in silence, as droplets of water trickled from his hat brim, from his nose, from off his worn, stiff shoes onto the bare floor boards. The clinic's smell of disinfectant swelled out of all proportion to dominate the moment with an aseptic foreboding.

He cleared his throat, then whispered.

"Poor child—poor nurses."

"When?" Paula asked.

He looked away, and started to unbutton his coat.

"Tomorrow morning—at five o'clock. Possibly as early as two," he said finally.

"*C'est impossible!*" gasped one of the nurses.

Miss Wilkins threw on her cape and, accompanied by another nurse, Miss Smith, set out for the prison, determined to appeal directly to the Germans.

The two women reached St. Gilles where Marin, the sympathetic warden, reported the prisoners had been "paraded," but no one had apprised him of the sentences.

Meanwhile, four nurses and probationers at the Institut, including Jacqueline Van Til and her friend Paula, could bear the suspense no longer. They, too, set out for St. Gilles.

Marin repeated what he had told Miss Wilkins. He could neither confirm nor deny the report, nor allow them to see Miss Cavell. There were German wardens guarding her cell.

"*C'est dommage, mais, impossible . . .*"

He added that he might possibly be able to convey their good-bys to her. He also believed a chaplain was en route— the Reverend H. S. T. Gahan, freed recently from concentration camp at the request of the United States Legation.

And even as they put the gray stone walls of St. Gilles in back of them, Mr. Gahan was being admitted to their matron's cell. Moments before a messenger had delivered a curt note to him:

"One who has not long to live wishes to see you. Come at once to my lodging for direction and the necessary permit."

It was signed by Paul le Seur, one of the German military chaplains.

The German guards stepped aside as a jailer turned the key in Edith Cavell's cell door. Mr. Gahan walked in.

She had been resting on her metal cot.

As he entered, she stood up, drawing a dressing gown about her, and gave him "a pleasant greeting." Her motions were deliberate, composed, with no indication that she might be distraught.

But he was shocked at her wasted quality. Ten weeks' imprisonment had cost her precious weight.

"To my astonishment and relief," Mr. Gahan later reported, "I found my friend perfectly calm and resigned. But this could not lessen the tenderness and intensity of feeling of either party during an interview of almost an hour."

She sat upon the cot, while the minister sat on the straight-backed chair. It was almost as though she had gone over in her mind what she would say during this visit. She cleared her throat.

"I have no fear nor shrinking," she said quietly. "I have seen death so often it is not strange or fearful to me. I expected it would end thus. I thank God for this ten weeks' quiet before the end . . . life has always been hurried and full of difficulty. This time of rest has been a great mercy."

To Gahan it seemed "like a solemn fasting, free of all earthly and ordinary distractions or diversions of any kind . . . no visitors, perfect quiet, perfect solitude with God. It was of His mercy and goodness to prepare for the end."

She appeared resigned to her fate, even as she had indicated to Hostelet in Parliament House's corridor just a few hours before. Self-preservation was no longer of great consequence.

"They have all been very kind to me here," she continued to Mr. Gahan, staring at the bare wall in front of her. "But this I would say standing as I do in view of God and eternity: I realize that patriotism is not enough. I must have no hatred or bitterness toward anyone."

Mr. Gahan then drew his worn leather prayer book from his pocket. He knelt and Edith Cavell knelt beside him.

In the prison's silence, broken only by the periodic shuffle of heavy-shoed guards, the two celebrated the Communion service:

"Our Father who art in Heaven, hallowed be Thy name. . . ."

They spoke the words slowly, flatly, pausing occasionally. Mr. Gahan looked away when he had finished. The walls stared back at him. The hour had passed and he knew he must leave. He drew his coat on, as she gave him final messages for her family, her nurses, and friends.

"Perhaps I had better go now, as you must rest," Mr. Gahan said.

He recalls that she "quietly acquiesced" and added,

"Yes, I have to be up at 5 A.M."

"Good-by," he spoke.

"We shall meet again," Edith Cavell replied softly, flatly.

The nurses started homeward.

Tuesday was just beginning. The rain had slowed to a drizzle, but everything was damp. It was as though the earth had recoiled in mourning. There was the feeling of finality in the cold air to everything that was right and familiar.

Hurrying along, they were not even certain the dawn would come this morning. They could not anticipate the everyday cycle returning, ever. It seemed beyond the scope of probability that the morning lights would wink on again in the pensions and houses of Brussels and smoke curl up from chimneys in testimony to warmth, food, and security.

Brussels' buildings sprawled before them like the headstones in a long-abandoned cemetery.

The nurses went to bed. But they could not sleep. In their cold, new-smelling rooms they lay awake and stared at the ceiling. It all seemed so futile—their work, their hopes, this modern institute, with its fifty rooms for nurses and thirty for patients, that they all had helped build. Without their matron, it meant nothing to them. It was a shell.

As nurses, even the young ones were familiar with death. But that a person they loved could be snatched from out of their daily experience was almost inconceivable. Now the young nurses suddenly understood the expressions on the faces of those who waited outside operating rooms.

Someone was going to die in an hour or two, perhaps in minutes. And they could do nothing.

They lay awake and listened, and only the imperceptible sighing of a building as it expanded and contracted, expanded and contracted, in the night air came back in answer to their wonderment.

And in St. Gilles Edith Cavell was left alone after Mr. Gahan's visit. She continued to read her Bible, her prayer book, and Thomas à Kempis' *Imitation of Christ*, and make notations in them. Exact and disciplined even in contemplation of death, Edith Cavell still had a few more things to tend to.

By 3 or 4 A.M. the nurses could endure their tossing no longer. A small group, including Elizabeth Wilkins and Jacqueline Van Til, put on their hats and capes and walked through the darkness to the prison. Ugly and menacing as it was, it seemed the last earthly association with their matron. They could not keep away from it.

The rain had stopped, and the sidewalks were drying. Their shoes, however, still sodden, made a dull, flabby sound as the girls hurried along.

Now the city was barely beginning to stir—a light peeping from a window, a wisp of smoke, a telltale whiff of soft coal, a sound of coughing, a baby's cry, a man pedaling on his bicycle.

The sky was clearing of clouds and stars were poking out. The city *was* returning to life, and another morning *was* commencing on this strange old earth, Jacqueline admitted.

A dog barked from an alleyway as they neared St. Gilles, then subsided; rooks cawed overhead, fresh from a night's belfry roost; a motorcycle pop-popped an avenue away, to be answered by the shrilling of a locomotive's whistle—troop trains to the front, to stem the Allied offensive.

Then they reached the prison. Their feet hurt and their eyes burned from anxiety and lack of sleep. One of them rang the bell.

"It struck our ears with a dismal sound," said Jacqueline, "that made our souls shiver with horror. When Mr. Marin, the superintendent, opened to us, we halted before the entrance and exclaimed with voices choked with emotion:

" 'Oh, give her to us! God help us!'

"The poor kindhearted Mr. Marin had tears in his eyes. He tried to console us by saying that Madame was very brave. He learned this much from one of the German wardens, who was, it seemed, more truthful than the others.

"The superintendent told us that if we waited a while we might possibly catch a glimpse of our beloved mistress when the automobile would come out of the prison to take her to the Tir National, or rifle range, where she was to be executed. . . ."

They waited, once more, this time with no hope of an eleventh-hour reprieve. Now they knew that they had lost their matron.

Shortly after 4:30 A.M. the German Lutheran army chaplain, Paul Le Seur, was awakened by guards who served him black coffee. He dressed. He had been apprised the night before of the duty ahead, but what could he do? He says today, from his home in Potsdam, he voiced his horror to Stoeber, but what more could he, a soldier himself, do?

Edith Cavell was neat in a plain black dress, her blue nurse's cloak, and black hat when they knocked on her cell door just before 5 A.M. Her hair was freshly combed.

She had made her cot and folded it back. The cell was as tidy as her old room at 149 Rue de la Culture before the beginning of classes, surgical operations, the endless inspections of the wards, endless disciplinings to make nurses out of schoolgirls.

"Are you ready?" a matron asked.

Edith Cavell nodded in seeming composure. Offered tea, she declined. By the side of the Reverend Paul Le Seur, a guard in front of her carrying a rifle, and another behind her, she started down the stone corridor. Her chin was high, her steps firm. A warden remarked later, *"Ein Fraülein sehr mutig,"* a very courageous lady.

A few prisoners saw her, "pale and erect," as she moved silently past the eye slits in their cell doors. They could not really be sure, afterward, if it were but an apparition—it seemed so unreal.

The nurses' vigil was finally rewarded.

"At five o'clock in the morning," young Jacqueline continued, "on October the 12th, of memorable date, two hideous cars issued grimly from the prison entrance. Anxiously and expectantly we gazed at them.

"In which one of these horrid vehicles was Madame?

"In which one was she?

"It seemed to me that I caught sight of her blue uniform. Was it merely imagination or was it really she?

"Who knows?"

Elizabeth Wilkins was certain it was Directress, seated in the first car "straight, next to the guard in front." She believed Edith Cavell recognized her.

"That was all we saw.

"The stillness of the city houses seemed to come to our aid. We could only cry out with one voice:

" 'Madame! Madame!'

". . . as the horrid death cars rapidly vanished from our tearful eyes."

The gray military sedans stopped in the Place des Carabiniers, in front of the Tir National. Dawn had almost arrived.

There was some delay. Perhaps Colonel Bulke, in charge of the firing squad, was reflecting on the enormity of what was about to happen, not to mention Dr. Stoeber, who had summoned his courage to be among the nearly two hundred and fifty witnesses present.

Edith Cavell paused in the cold corridors of the shooting gallery long enough to study recent notations in her prayer book:

Court-martialed 7th Oct. 1915.
Condemned to death 8th Oct. in the Salle des Députés at 10:30 A.M. with 7 others.

Then make one final entry, meticulous as always:

Died at 7 A.M. on Oct. 12, 1915.
    With love to My Mother
      E. Cavell.

Before she was led out to the range and the posts she requested several large pins. Her wish was granted, and she pinned her long skirt tightly around her ankles. She did not wish her dress to flare up after she had been shot.

(The guards at the Tir National narrated this later to Mr. Marin, the jailer.)

Chaplain Le Seur recalls "some gentle words of faith" she murmured to him as they walked out to the post, bathed in the clear, chilly light of day, the execution squad facing them. She was tied to the post, blindfolded. He said good-by as he walked several paces to the side, praying fervently all the while since he was convinced then, as he is now, that Miss Cavell "had sinned."

Father Leyendecker had just taken his adieus of Philippe Baucq, tied to a post about fifteen feet away from the English nurse.

She died, not prettily, as in grand opera, but in lonely horror, bathed in blood, at 7 A.M.

The Solace: Mercy Ship

BY ELLSWORTH NEWCOMB

->>)《《‹-

There is little resemblance between the haphazard
nursing of the Crimean and Civil wars and the carefully planned organizations, replete with every con-
ceivable type of nursing and medical equipment,
which now take care of our country's sick and
wounded. In World War II and the Korean war,
there were hospital ships and hospital planes. There
were front-line stations and evacuation hospitals and
great base hospitals at which miracles of cure were
daily occurences. Only the bravery of the nurses
and the doctors bore any resemblance to those of
a bygone day. Many nurses sacrificed their lives.
Many received medals for heroism. The adventures
which follow, by Ellsworth Newcomb and Mary
Jean Kempner, show us war nursing as it has been
practiced in our own time. The equipment and the
nurses stand ready, should the need arise again. It
is the hope of all of us that it will not arise.

THERE WAS NOT A SOUL on the ship, from the admiral down
to the youngest bluejacket, whose heart did not beat faster
on that August day in 1941 when the orders were read which
made the U.S.S. *Solace* part of the fleet. It was a solemn moment, for a new floating hospital—the first since World War I
—had joined the Navy.

Officers and men in crisp white stood straight and proud as
the American flag soared skyward to the gallant strains of

"The Star-Spangled Banner." No one seemed to breathe as the blue-and-white commissioning pennant was raised; no one moved as the captain assumed command.

"I accept this ship."

Speaking the traditional words, the captain's voice was grave and firm. Even in peacetime his was a heavy responsibility. For although there was not so much as a toy gun aboard the *Solace*, the big white ship was a fighting ship. From this day on she would be fighting to save men's lives. Wherever the fleet sailed the *Solace* would serve. And if war should come, the task of the hospital ship and her personnel would be immeasurably greater. Yet there was not one person aboard but was proud to sail under the banner of mercy.

Standing with the twelve young women of her staff, Chief Nurse Grace Lally silently echoed the captain's words: "I accept this ship."

Behind her glasses her Irish eyes blurred with thankful tears. Whatever lay ahead, the *Solace* with its magnificent modern equipment, its skilled doctors, nurses, and corpsmen, would be able to meet it. Lieutenant Lally was glad to be aboard. In all her twenty years of service with the Navy she had never been happier. To have a worth-while job to do and the tools to do it with—what more could anyone ask?

His brief speech ended, the captain gave the order to set the watch. It was as if the giant pulse of the ship began to beat. The U.S.S. *Solace* had come to life. The largest, most modern hospital ship in the world was now a member of Uncle Sam's fleet. Like every mercy ship, it was armed only with the green band and bright red crosses prescribed by the Geneva Convention. In 1864 that great humanitarian organization had established the International Red Cross to which all civilized countries belong and, among other functions, this organization

insures the neutralization of those agencies whose objectives
are the relief of war wounded.

The sky above the Brooklyn Navy Yard was cloudless, with
not so much as a tiny white puff to hint that in the space of a
few months this proud white ship would be black with the
oil of shattered battleships; that her decks would be crowded
with wounded and dying; and that the new commissioning
pennant whose seven stars shone so bravely would be slit and
tattered by gunfire.

But before they were to know that dark chapter there were
many busy days ahead for all aboard the seagoing hospital.

In her office and in her quarters, which along with those of
the other nurses were aft on the main deck, Lieutenant Lally
pursued what she called the "open-door" policy in regard to
emergencies. That meant that the twelve lieutenants and en-
signs who constituted her nursing staff could bring important
problems to her at any hour of the day or night. Routine business, however, was confined to the office where Miss Lally
was on duty every day from eight to five.

Before the *Solace* sailed to join the fleet there were plenty
of both kinds of calls. Sending a four hundred and thirty-two-
bed hospital to sea was no easy task. The big ship, a former
luxury liner, had six hospital wards, each with its own pantry;
two main operating rooms, three auxiliary operating rooms,
three main medical storerooms, an X-ray department, an eye,
ear, nose, and throat operating room, a urological operating
room, a physiotherapeutic department, a pharmacy, and a clini-
cal laboratory. Huge refrigerators had to be stocked with
countless doses of serums and antitoxins. Thousands of units of
blood plasma had to be stored as well as a fortune in narcotics
and two thousand dollars' worth of gold for use in the dental
department. All this had to be organized by the hospital staff,

consisting of a general medical supervisor with the rank of captain, seventeen other doctors, two dentists, thirteen nurses, three pharmacists, and about one hundred and fifty crew members with hospital ratings.

For days on end the big white ship, still berthed at the Brooklyn Navy Yard, hummed with activity. Under Miss Lally's expert direction her corps of nurses took inventory of shining new instruments and busily prepared dressings, field sheets, and sponges. As the chief nurse got acquainted with her girls (some of whom were newcomers or "boots," as the Navy calls recruits), she assigned them to their various jobs of running the wards, operating rooms, and diet kitchens and of supervising the hospital corpsmen, who under the Navy system do all the fetch-and-carry nursing.

"Give people a good standard to live up to, then trust them," was Lieutenant Lally's wise philosophy.

In the flower-decked, chintz-hung nurses' quarters, which the officers called the "holy of holies" since they went there only by invitation and in groups, Miss Lally had many informal talks with her twelve women in white.

"Never talk shop when you are off duty," she told them. "You'll go stale if you do."

And, "No matter what differences of opinion you have, settle them in your quarters, and come out smiling."

The young nurses were proud to serve under the woman who, with twenty years of service, held the Navy Nurse Corps' record for sea duty, and who was one of only four women in the corps entitled to wear the China ribbon. This distinction commemorated Lieutenant Lally's baptism of fire at the time of the Japanese invasion of China in 1938, when she had helped to evacuate American women and children. Although the twinkle might fade from her blue eyes when she looked up from the needlepoint work which was her hobby, to scotch some bit of unworthy scuttlebutt (Navy rumor), the girls knew that their chief was thoroughly human and fair. Like the lilt in her voice, the advice which she gave them when they went off duty was characteristic:

"Go where you like." She smiled. "Do what you like. Act as ladies act and make the N.N.C. proud of you. And have fun!"

But a day came when the nurses no longer exchanged starched white for their blue off-duty uniforms with the brass buttons matching the anchor on their white visorless hats. Though the spicy autumn breeze and the sight of the jagged New York skyline beckoned them shoreward, there was no more leave. The *Solace* was about to sail. It was a breathless moment—happy, exciting, and at the same time sad, for the twelve Navy nurses were taking their leave of all that was familiar. However, as the chalky wake lengthened between ship and shore, they listened to the throb of the engines and felt a new pride in the service of which each of them was an integral part.

It was a quiet cruise, that first trip on the *Solace*, as she swung halfway around the world to drop anchor in Pearl Harbor. On the way out the nurses enjoyed the novelty of sleeping on the horseshoe-shaped deck surrounding their quarters; of playing games and watching movies at sea. Off duty, too, they practiced the Morse code and tried to learn something about the constellations of the various latitudes. Those who, till now, had been landlubbers, enriched their vocabularies with Navy lingo such as "deck" for floor, "swab" for broom, "sick bay" for hospital, and dozens of other seagoing terms.

In early December the nurses were joyfully extolling the luck which had sent them to the Pacific paradise that was the

Hawaiian Islands. Nothing could have been more peaceful, more perfect. There were tennis and dancing at the Officers' Club, swimming and surfboarding at famous Waikiki. And where on earth was there a more entrancing place to do your Christmas shopping than in Honolulu, where the shops were stocked with the treasures of half-a-dozen nations?

Twenty times a day Miss Lally was asked to admire an assortment of straw mats, rice bowls, slippers, and scarves before they were mailed to the States. Meanwhile, the chief nurse was making her own plans. It was a cherished Navy tradition that every ship, wherever she might be, must have a Christmas tree atop her mast on the day of days. Miss Lally was determined that the *Solace* should have an extra-fine one to celebrate her first Christmas as a mercy ship. She would see about it right away.

Christmas! The day of carols and rejoicing, the day of peace. Already it seemed near, yet there were many brave men there in the lovely harbor who would not be alive when it dawned.

Miss Lally was up earlier, as usual, on Sunday, December 7. The light, rosy and tender, gave the harbor a pearl-like appearance that made its name beautifully appropriate. Against the sky the great ships were proud and dark and, as if there were no limit to Nature's largesse, a vivid rainbow arched in breathtaking splendor above one gray warship. As they waited for colors the nurses gathered to enjoy the scene.

What followed happened so suddenly it numbed the senses.

All at once the sky was filled with swooping yellow planes —planes so close that leering enemy faces were clearly visible.

"The Japs!" someone shouted before all sound was drowned by the crash of bombs, the staccato of machine-gun fire, and the mighty answering thunder of ships' guns.

At the end of the pipeline that separated her from the *Solace*, the *Arizona* burst into flame. Wherever the yellow wings flashed in their murderous dives, a fountain of twisted wreckage spewed up into the smoke-darkened sky. Then the sea itself was on fire. Explosion after explosion rent the air, leaving ruin and horror as a ghastly signature. Except for the *Solace*, which still remained untouched, the entire fleet seemed to be shattered, sinking.

For one stricken moment Miss Lally watched, her mind reeling. Then, "You're the chief nurse," she told herself. "You can't be afraid. You can't let the girls down. You can't let the Navy down!"

The threat of panic left her as she set about helping to transform an entire ship into one vast emergency ward ready for the grim task of receiving the first American casualties of World War II. In the space of a few minutes everyone aboard the *Solace* was functioning as part of an efficient team. The officers' lounge, where people had been assembling for Mass when the raid began, was turned into an additional ward with sixty-seven double-decker bunks quickly set up. The crew's recreation rooms, the outer decks, every available inch of space, was pressed into service. Plasma bottles, supplies of drugs, and great stacks of bandages were rushed to strategic points. The entire ship's crew became volunteer stretcher-bearers as burned, mangled, and oil-soaked men were brought aboard. Some were carried on stalwart shoulders. Some walked. Some came over the side in Stokes stretchers—those shallow wire baskets shaped to fit a man's body which prevent him from being joggled as he is taken up a ship's ladder or hoisted from a boat.

The nurses toiled alongside the doctors and corpsmen while their once-trim uniforms grew sodden with oil and blood. They cut shoes and uniforms away from ghastly wounds. They bathed and bandaged and sped pitiful victims toward operating rooms which were taxed to capacity during the long nightmare that would not end for many days to come. They watched beside the dying; they eased the shock of those who, having seen their friends blown to bits, did not seem even to try to rally.

While the desperate rescue work continued, the mercy staff did not pause to look up when, time after time, loud-speakers blared a warning that more planes were overhead.

That night—a night punctuated by the chatter of machine guns and antiaircraft—the *Solace* seemed terribly alone in the stricken harbor. In the black-out her battle lights cast an unearthly blue glow on men with blackened faces and charred hair. Beyond, in the darkness, sister ships lay wounded and helpless. Even the mercy ship, for all her gleeming white paint, her red crosses, and her guardian green stripe, had not been wholly spared, for the last rags of her proud commissioning pennant had been torn away and were now lost amidst the twisted wreckage strewing the oil-black sea.

Long afterward Lieutenant Lally was asked how she and her nurses ever got through the terrible experience.

"If God is with you," she replied, "your training, discipline, and innate character somehow carry you through to the way that always opens up before you."

The way did open and the business of healing went forward. But in the space of a few minutes Japanese infamy had changed the face of the world. With the bursting of that first stick of enemy bombs, life aboard the *Solace* was altered almost beyond recognition.

Now that the United States was at war the big ship, fouled with the oil of sunken battleships, kept steam up at all times. Decks were wet down, stateroom doors were kept open to avoid jamming in case of a hit. Alerts became commonplace, with the loud-speaker urging, "Up all hands. Up all hands." The nurses' quarters, built to accommodate thirteen, were now crowded with nurses sent by the Red Cross to augment the ship's own staff.

In the wards Miss Lally moved tirelessly from bunk to bunk comforting and cheering the wounded. She never ceased to marvel that many of them managed a grin even though it was half obscured by bandages. One boy, however, could only hang onto her hand and sob. Half his face had been burned away. Thankful that he could not see her own tears, the chief nurse told him of the miracles of skin grafting.

"Listen, son," she said. "When we get through with you, you'll be as good as new. Better, maybe." Patiently, then, she sat beside him and slowly fed him soup through a tube.

Miss Lally encouraged her boys to talk of their homes and families. She found ways to make them laugh. "Fun," she told her girls, "is the best antidote against bitterness, weariness, and even fear."

As often as she could the nurse gratified the whims of these gallant, stricken men. There was, for instance, the lad who loved angel cake.

"We always had it at home on Sunday," he told her wistfully.

Somehow Miss Lally managed to get him his cake even though she had to "invent" a pan to bake it in, with the help of a paper cup from the dental clinic.

And of course all the nurses duly admired the weird assortment of bullets and pieces of shrapnel which the patients had brought aboard *inside* them and which, as they recovered, they proudly displayed as souvenirs!

Soon some of the less seriously wounded were able to go out on deck and watch the suction machines drawing the oil off the water. For weeks that oil slick had been a hazard, since a single careless spark would have been sufficient to set the entire harbor ablaze. The men leaning over the rail, some cheerful, some apathetic, were the lucky ones. Below decks were the terrible burns, the multiple fractures, those who had lost arms, legs, even sight.

Thinking of them, Miss Lally wondered how she could face Christmas—the holiday which only a short while ago had promised such joy.

It was while she was wondering that along with others of the medical personnel she was sent on one of the Navy's grim, routine tours of the wrecked harbor in an effort to find the bodies of victims of the Japanese attack. The party, on its pitiful mission, boarded the blackened skeleton of a ship and went from gun position to gun position. At each one they found only helmets and buttons—pathetic small monuments to the courage of men who had died faithful to their tasks. Finally one of the doctors with Miss Lally stooped beside a wrecked weapon. When he stood up he put a twisted bit of metal into the nurse's hand. It was a chaplain's shoulder cross. They turned back then, but Miss Lally fingered the cross reverently. Once again a symbol of man's faith had remained to triumph over destruction.

The men and women of the *Solace* should have their Christmas, thought Miss Lally. They would celebrate, anew, that eternal victory.

And so it was that on Christmas morning presents sent out by the Red Cross were distributed—one for each wounded man on the mercy ship. Some of the fingers, untying bright ribbons, fumbled weakly, and sometimes a smiling nurse did the unwrapping. But the floating hospital echoed with greetings and there was laughter and hope in full measure. Aloft, on the mast—true to Navy tradition—a little tree was silhouetted against the blue Hawaiian sky.

In the spring the *Solace* began her long series of voyages to pick up wounded from many of the Pacific islands. And once again life aboard ship underwent a change. During the long nights at sea, instead of being blacked out as she had been while in the harbor, the floating hospital traveled with blazing lights, her red crosses fully illuminated as prescribed by the Geneva Convention. While under way the nurses wore life jackets at all times. They got so that they could dress with lightning speed. Miss Lally's own record for getting into uniform was a minute and a half.

Until they neared their destination, the girls did not know where they were going. Curiously they would watch a strange island come into view. Surely, they thought, war had not touched this emerald dot with its rioting blossoms and painted hills. But as the *Solace* slipped between submarine nets and neared shore, they could see gun emplacements, jeeps, Quonset huts, and the ever-present fuel oil fouling the harbor.

At each island where the mercy ship called, a shore medical officer came aboard with a list of wounded, so that the staff would know how many cases of malaria, fractures, gunshot wounds, burns, and mental illness they must be prepared for. By the time she was anchored the *Solace* was surrounded by boxlike, light-armored Higgins boats and barges laden with ill men.

Up on deck a young nurse moved close to Miss Lally.

"This is always the worst moment," she said softly.

The chief laid a sympathetic hand on her slim shoulder.

"I know." She nodded. "I never get used to the first look at those stretchers. But if they can smile I guess we can and, look, they *are* smiling."

It took hours to get five hundred ill men settled aboard ship, and if the task was not completed by sunset, the submarine nets closed. Then the *Solace* had to stay in the harbor overnight with the threat of bombs and the heat adding to the tension.

It was always a thankful moment when the anchor came up

and the white ship headed back toward her base. As the sea widened around them and the war zone vanished like an evil dream, the men began to take their first slow steps toward recovery.

Sometimes there were periods of almost unbearable strain. Once the port from which the *Solace* had just evacuated wounded was bombed immediately after she had left it. On another occasion only the swift action of the captain in backing away from the place where he had intended to land saved his ship from deadly enemy bombs.

After one battle there were fifty-two patients in casts and one hundred who had undergone serious operations. The hospital ship was in dangerous waters, alone, as she always was at sea—her destination a long voyage away. Overhead, planes were dropping bombs and torpedoes. What if they should fail to see the Red Cross markings? The faces of many of the nurses were as white as their winged caps.

In the mind of each was the unspoken question: "What if we have to abandon ship with this helpless load?"

The ship's family—always a closely-knit one—drew even closer together during those perilous hours. The doctors themselves helped nurse the critically ill during the night watches and the crew volunteered to serve during their hard-earned off-duty hours. Through it all Miss Lally moved about her tasks, her courage setting that high standard she so sincerely believed in, her Irish wit bringing smiles to anxious faces.

It was over at last. The *Solace* had made port. On the dock where the ambulances waited a band played "The Star-Spangled Banner." Suddenly Miss Lally remembered the day —it must have been a lifetime ago—when the ship had been commissioned. Then the new seagoing hospital and many of the nurses, too, had been untried. Yet Grace Lally had had faith that they would meet whatever came. She knew now how well her faith was justified. She was proud of her girls.

She was still glad to be aboard.

For her fine performance during the tragedy of Pearl Harbor, the *Solace* and her entire personnel earned the rare distinction of being commended by the commander in chief of the Fleet. During the first twenty months of the war 7,500 casualties were treated aboard the U.S.S. *Solace*. Only sixteen were lost.

Flying Ambulance from Okinawa

BY MARY JEAN KEMPNER

→»«←

"IT DOESN'T HURT MUCH but would you hold it . . . please hold it." From a litter on the middle tier of the Navy evacuation plane a pair of dazed blue eyes in a very white face were looking anxiously up at me. Two days before the boy's left arm had been amputated just below the shoulder, sheathed—guillotined was the word used on his chart. *It* was the stump, sheathed in stockinette, wrapped in blood-patched bandages. I crouched beside the litter and slipped my hands around the stump.

The plane was flying past the southern end of Okinawa where seventy-eight bitter days of fighting were drawn to a close. Crouching there beside a one-armed boy called Jim I could see ground activities from the plane's window—the flash of our fleet's guns still pounding the shore, our fighter planes strafing the enemy, the smoke of the battle down among the vicious hillocks and ridges that Jim and the rest of the men on the plane had fought so hard to secure.

I had had little time to spend in Okinawa where I landed on Yontan airfield which boasts with Chamber of Commerce placards "Welcome to Okinawa where every night is like the Fourth of July." I was there to see what happened to men after they were wounded; but in doing that, I saw other things as well. I drove past soft rice paddies, beautifully terraced fields, ruined villages with only an occasional tile roof still supported by stone walls. These are the roads over which casualties must travel on the way back from the front.

I watched the casualties being brought in to the evacuation hospital on Okinawa. It was noon, and following some distorted, senseless pattern of war, the bulk of the wounded at Okinawa inevitably came in either at noon or four in the afternoon. Upon arrival they were carefully screened to determine which, if any, could be evacuated by air the same day.

Once a patient is diagnosed as fit for evacuation, he is taken from the hospital to the plane by ambulance. Litter cases are lifted from ambulance to plane directly, while ambulatory cases wait in a nearby Quonset till takeoff time. The air commander or senior pilot and the flight nurse are briefed by the doctors on the condition of their patients, whether or not they can stand high altitude. Then, as rapidly as possible, the patients are loaded aboard—evac planes spend little time on Yontan airstrip; it isn't healthy.

We had lost all sight of land and still I crouched beside the one-armed boy called Jim. The corpsman, who with the flight nurse cares for the patients aboard, was making rounds. "Feeling O. K.?" he asked as he stopped beside Jim's litter. The boy nodded; he didn't want to complain and the corpsman, sensing it, went to the nurse for permission to give Jim a sedative; one look at the boy spelled pain. After a moment the corpsman returned with codeine; the medication plus the effect of seven-thousand-feet altitude soon brought tired eyelids over the blue eyes. I freed my hands from the amputated arm, or what was left of it, and the corpsman helped me to my feet. My knees were stiff. I had been crouching for a long time and even a bucket seat seemed comfortable. Sitting on one beside me was the flight nurse making out information tags—like the ones on Railway Express packages—which she fastened on each patient.

There were thirty-one patients aboard, eight of them ambulatory, the rest on litters. The corpsman was going from one to the other, wrapping a khaki blanket around the shoulders of a man in a MacArthur seat, handing out magazines and chewing gum, straightening pillows, giving aspirin or a drink of water, and talking to the men. Most of them had never flown before and were apprehensive of this first flight over fifteen hundred miles of water, knowing themselves to be helpless in case of a ditching. Without ever mentioning it the corpsman managed to dispel these unspoken fears. (Because in the Navy a nurse's job is largely administrative, it is the corpsmen who do the bulk of the actual nursing work. This particular corpsman happened to be a music student of twenty-one. Dark-haired, with deep-set eyes and deft, sure hands, he had been studying at the Boston Conservatory before the war, plans on going to Juilliard after the shooting is over. But right now he is a Navy corpsman, one of the boys you never hear about unless you talk to men who have been in battle.)

The faces of the men aboard the plane were expressionless, the deadly glaze of war still clung heavily, as heavily as the stink of it. Above Jim's litter lay a boy whose chart read "multiple wounds." The pulse in his throat was beating wildly, but he lay there saying nothing. He didn't speak of his pain; they don't, these battered boys. They lock it inside them, like the loneliness that goes with it. But the corpsman understood, and in a few minutes he had the nurse's permission to give codeine. (Morphine is rarely used in flight, because of the altitude.)

Most of the casualties were scheduled for penicillin and the flight nurse was preparing needles and mixing sterile water in the little bottles of yellow powdered mould. Although at the beginning of the trip the men sat or lay rigid, as though afraid to move, now the fact that at last they were getting out of battle had had a chance to percolate. Their bodies, reacting to this growing sense of relief, sank into deep creases of fatigue. Listlessly they looked at their magazines, puffed at cigarettes, and before long went to sleep.

With his patients resting, the corspman now started opening cans of soup which he began heating on a white-enameled electric stove in the rear of the plane. The flight nurse unpacked some chicken sandwiches. There was fruit juice, too, all in such quantity one felt it must be foolish waste. Sick men couldn't possibly eat all that. But they did. When they were wakened they were told that the trip was half over; they could look down on a sea of little golden clouds patching the blue water, the skyline pink and puffy, a typical air view of a Pacific sunset.

Finally the full impact of what had taken place struck them. They were out of it. Out of the hell and the noise. The filth and the fear. The mud, the dust, the fatigue. The burn case, two litters down, knew there would be months of skin grafting ahead, of surgery and hospitalization. What the devil, the war was over. The stench, sweet, nauseating, and inescapable that rose up and hit you when you went near the boy whose whole left side was in a cast told part of his story: of the months-to-be lying in traction, waiting for the day when he could learn to walk again. Sure, he knew about that, but he also knew there would be no more foxholes or Jap mortars. And Jim had lost an arm; but he was alive, through with fighting, through with death. These were the old-young men of war; they had met the enemy, had fought him. Now they were getting out, free of the enemy, free of war.

All the wounded on the plane had finished their sandwiches, drunk their soup, and come back for seconds. All except the boy with the multiple wounds who lay just over Jim. He ate only part of a sandwich. He lay still and silent, his brow wet, his face white, and that pulse pounding at his throat. The corpsman called the flight nurse, quickly they clamped an oxygen mask on his face and called me to hold it in place rather than alarm him by strapping it on. While I handled the oxygen, they turned to prepare blood plasma; the patient gave every sign of sinking into shock; his pulse had risen to 131. After the plasma bottle was secured to the roof of the plane, a tourniquet was applied to the boy's arm, the needle made ready. The boy signaled me to remove the mask, then softly said: "The last time they tried to give me plasma it took them two hours to get the needle in." No one spoke. We didn't have two hours. I put my hand on his forehead, the flight nurse picked up the needle, tried for a vein in his arm, and failed. Again and again the tourniquet was applied, the needles sunk in, the tourniquet loosened but the needle would slide out; the boy lost so much blood his veins had collapsed.

While the nurse and corpsman were looking at his legs and ankles, hoping to find one vein which would open to the life-giving fluid, I went forward to tell the plane commander what had happened. He immediately ordered us down from seven thousand feet to fifteen hundred, then followed me aft. The corpsmen and the nurse were still working, they were trying a finer needle, but it wouldn't stay in. Alarm had filtered through the plane. The patients asked as we made our way past them, "Will he be all right?" Fortunately, our "Yes, of course," sounding more convincing to them than it did to us. There was only one alternative—force fluids, keep giving oxygen, and get to Guam as quickly as possible. There was an extra gas supply for just such emergencies. The plane commander reported we could shear an hour off our estimated time of arrival.

It seemed forever, although the time it took was only an hour and a half; we stood beside the boy's litter or wandered about the plane talking to the other patients, talking out of the top of our minds, about home and movie stars. Thinking all the time, "Will we get there in time, will we make it? We must, we must." The sick boy didn't talk or ask any questions, except with his eyes. He lay very still. Only the frantic pulse beat harder and harder as though racing the plane's engine. The air commander came back to check up, told us we were just fifteen minutes out. Guam looked very beautiful to all of us. At last the wheels hit the runway, we taxied quickly to the evacuation center and two doctors were aboard as fast as the plane doors opened. There was also a mobile elevator that rose to the level of the plane, carrying the ambulatory patients down to its deck. One by one the litter cases were carried off.

Before he left, I promised Jim to come to see him in the hospital. The doctors had been unable to do anything for the desperately sick boy on the plane and now they were moving him into the center. Although he was actually not yet in shock, his pulse was 180; the doctors were ready to fling everything in the book at him, whole blood, the slimmest needles, bright lights to search out the strongest vein. On the fourth try the needle went in and stayed; the reaction was immediate, like a miracle, the color coming back, the pulse quieting down.

Color came back to our faces, too; it had been a close shave. Only then did I look around for the other patients. They had already gone and the hospitals were calling in to confirm their arrival. Fifteen hundred miles, seven and a half flying hours from a battlefield to a base hospital via the war's greatest lifesaver, the flying ambulance.

They Were the Bravest

BY WILLIAM J. LEDERER

➤➤≪≪

No longer are women nurses permitted by our military leaders to go on or near the battlefield, although many of them, like the nurses aboard the *Solace*, have accidentally come within range of gunfire. Instead of the Nightingales and Clara Bartons of a bygone day, the armed forces train their own male nurses to treat and rescue the wounded during the heat of battle. "Medics," they have been labeled. "Call me Doc," they plead. They are the bravest, says William J. Lederer, and their grateful buddies agree.

IN ORDER TO GET THE FULL STORY I NEEDED, I decided that I should talk with the badly wounded men, those still on the critical list. To find these men I went to what was called the "dirty surgical ward" of the Navy's hospital ship, U.S.S. *Haven*. The *Haven* was receiving casualties straight from the front lines.

Dirty surgical was a dismal place. Here were the new amputees; here were the guys with a pound of shrapnel in their guts; here were the unfortunates whose smashed faces needed plastic surgery.

The majority of the wounded soldiers and marines lay quietly in their bunks. A few read; a few laboriously wrote letters; but most of them stared blankly at the overhead or watched the smoke curl up from their cigarettes.

Walking up to a corporal who had a head injury, I said

cheerfully, "Hi, feller, I have a tape recorder here. What about you speaking a message for the folks at home? You can say hello to your parents, your wife, or friends. We'll either have it broadcast in your home town or we'll mail the record directly to your family."

He answered by shaking his head.

"You don't want to?"

He turned his face into the pillow.

The nurse tiptoed to me and whispered, "They're very depressed. Don't push any of them on the broadcast. Maybe you can make a recording of the whole ward—sort of a group thing. Can you? It might pep them up if they all get into the act at the same time."

I went to the middle of the ward and said, with as much zip as I could, "Look, fellers, we're running a contest. I need your help. We want to find out who is the bravest man in Korea. If only one medal were handed out, who should get it? A couple of the guys told me that the hospital corpsmen should get a crack at it. Well, now, let me ask you something . . . you've all been up where it's tough. Did you see any hospital corpsmen actually in the front lines? Not just hear about them being there. I mean, did you actually see any?"

No one answered right off, so I repeated the question.

"Any of you guys meet up with corpsmen at the front?"

Then, bam! It was as if an atom bomb had hit the place. The ward energized. If six movie starlets had walked through there they couldn't have stirred up more commotion. Men propped themselves up on their elbows, swung around, and sat up. One patient got out his crutches and limped in my direction. Everyone started talking at the same time.

A Marine private shouted, "Darn right I've seen corpsmen at the front. If I hadn't, I'd still be out there in a muddy foxhole. Who do you think brought me in?"

All hands in the ward were trying to horn in with stories of their own, but our Marine outshouted them all. "When we got to the first-aid station I says, 'Doc, I sure want to thank you for saving my life. What's your name and outfit?' He says, 'Don't bother me now, there's another guy wounded on the other side of the hill.' And he starts out again, with blood dripping from his pants leg. How do you like that?"

A flier said, "Nobody better say anything against medics when I'm around. My plane crashed near the Red lines. It was beginning to burn, and I couldn't move and started praying 'cause I knew I was a goner. I heard someone hacking at the plane, and a few seconds later a medic jumped through the flames and pulled me out. His face and arms were flash-burned and he didn't have much eyebrows or hair left.

"I thanked him for wading through the fire to save me. He growled, 'Whatcha expect me to do, flyboy, let you fry?' After examining me he ordered me to the first-aid station. I told him he was in worse shape than me and ought to get his burns looked after.

"'That's my business,' he snapped. 'Now get back to the first-aid station. I got work to do.' Giving me a shove, he walked the other way into the dark. That night he got killed."

A second Marine: "We lost thirty men in my outfit. Five of them were corpsmen. I guess the Reds know how important Doc is and try to pick him off first."

A soldier: "There's nobody like those medics! Don't take my word for it. Just go out with the Ninth or Thirty-fourth, or ask any GI you meet on the road." He patted his wound. "The Reds gave me mine around Fungyan. Well, you know how they bayonet all the wounded—just to make sure. There I was in no-man's land, bleeding like crazy. Guns popping from every place. All of a sudden a medic dashes out like he's running down a football field. He grabs two of us and drags us back right from under the Commies' noses.

"He sure was brave. That night when he was fixing our bandages we said we'd like to do something for him. You know what he wanted? He just asked us to call him 'Doc' instead of 'pill roller.'

"I'd say," he went on, "if only one medal were to be given out, give it to a hospital corpsman."

Just about everyone in the ward agreed.

One of the wounded Marines said, "You know, it's eerie. Sometimes I think these docs are too brave."

A couple of bunks away a white-faced sailor stirred. He hadn't said a word since I entered. It was obvious he suffered from loss of blood, and shock. As I remember it, he tried to prop himself up, but couldn't make it, and fell back on his pillow. Pointing a skinny arm at the Marine who had just spoken, the sailor said hoarsely, "Say, feller, you, over there with the bandage on your head . . ."

"Me?"

"Yeh. You said you think sometimes the corpsmen are too brave. Maybe you got something. Maybe the way we rush around like crazy looks like we're putting on a show, but maybe there's a reason . . ."

The Marine jerked his head around, "The way *you* rush around? Are you a doc?"

"Yes."

The Marine pointed his crutch at the medical card on the foot of the sailor's bunk. "Hey, commander," he said, "read what it says about him."

I read the card aloud, "Sznowski, Joseph L., hospitalman, first class. Shrapnel in abdomen. Scheduled for operating room eleven hundred on twenty August."

The Marine on crutches hobbled over and put his cigarette

in the wounded corpsman's mouth. "Today's the twentieth. They ought to be coming for you soon, kid."

"Yeh," said Doc, looking at the Marine's watch, "they'll be here any minute. Thanks. Say, you know maybe we do risk our skins too much. I think maybe we're trying to prove ourselves. In peacetime a lot of guys think we're sissies . . ."

A nurse came in and told Doc they'd operate on him next and that she'd come back for him in a few minutes.

"Oh," she said, pausing on her way through the door. "The executive officer just told me you've been recommended for the Navy Cross."

We all crowded around Doc to congratulate him.

"Gee, a Navy Cross!" he said, dragging on his cigarette.

A soldier pointed at me. "Doc, you heard what the commander said earlier, that if there was only one medal to be given in this war it would go to one of you guys."

The nurse wheeled in a stretcher. "We're going to make you healthy, Doc."

As he was lifted onto the table, blood seeped through the bandage.

"You know," he said, "I don't even know what a Navy Cross looks like."

"Hey!" shouted the Marine on crutches. "Wait a minute!" Stumping back to his bunk as fast as he could, he grabbed a small leather case from under his pillow. Rushing out to the door, he placed the opened leather case in Doc's hand.

"Kid," he said, "here's one you might like to hold on to while you're in the operating room."

The nurse wheeled Doc out into the corridor.

Pledges of Military Nurses

→»«←

No soldier in battle exhibited more patriotism than the nurses of our armed services. Their vows were noble and they fulfilled them to the utmost. Here are the pledges of the Army, Cadet, and Flight Nursing Corps, all inspiring documents of service.

PLEDGE OF THE ARMY NURSE. As an Army nurse, I accept the responsibilities of an officer in the Army Nurse Corps. I shall give faithful care to the men who fight for the freedom of this country and to the women who stand behind them. I shall bring to the American soldier, wherever he may be, the best of my knowledge and professional skill. I shall approach him cheerfully at all times under any conditions I may find. I shall endeavor to maintain the highest nursing standards possible in the performance of my duties. I shall appear fearless in the presence of danger and quiet the fears of others to the best of my ability. My only criticism shall be constructive. The reputation and good name of the Army Nurse Corps and of the nursing profession shall be uppermost in my thoughts, second only to the care of my patients. I shall endeavor to be a credit to my country and to the uniform I wear.

PLEDGE OF THE CADET NURSE. I am solemnly aware of the obligations I assume toward my country and toward my chosen profession. I will follow faithfully the teachings of my instructors and the guidance of the physicians with whom I work. I will hold my body strong, by mind alert, and my heart steadfast. I will be kind, tolerant, and understanding. Above all, I will dedicate myself now and forever to the triumph of life over death. As a Cadet Nurse, I pledge to my country my service in essential nursing for the duration of the war.

PLEDGE OF THE FLIGHT NURSE. I will summon every resource to prevent the triumph of death over life. I will stand guard over the medicines and equipment entrusted to my care and ensure their proper use. I will be untiring in the performance of my duties, and I will remember that upon my disposition and spirit will in large measure depend the morale of my patients. I will be faithful to my training and to the wisdom handed down to me by those who have gone before me. I have taken a nurse's oath reverent in man's mind because of the spirit and work of its creator, Florence Nightingale. She, I remember, was called the lady with the lamp. It is now my privilege to lift this lamp of hope and faith and courage in my profession to heights not known by her in her time. Together with the help of flight surgeons and surgical technicians I can set the very skies ablaze with life and promise for the sick, injured, and wounded who are my sacred charges. This I will do. I will not falter. In war or in peace.